BIBLICAL REVELATION

The History of Salvation

BIBLICAL REVELATION

The History of Salvation

by J. SALGUERO, O.P.

Translated by

SISTER JUDITH SUPRYS, F.M.A.

CHRISTIAN CULTURE PRESS
ARLINGTON • VIRGINIA

For the English Translation:

    Nihil Obstat: REV. MSGR. EUGENE KEVANE, Ph.D.
                 Censor Deputatus

    Imprimatur: MOST REV. THOMAS J. WELSH, D.D.

March 19, 1976

Arlington, Virginia

Library of Congress catalog card number: 76–100100
Copyright © by Institute for Christian Culture, Inc.—1976
Printed in the United States of America

Foreword

I consider it a very important fact that the Notre Dame Institute for Advanced Studies, Middleburg, Virginia, has desired to translate into English this book which treats of Revelation and the History of Salvation in a simple and clear manner. I think it will offer helpful service to students of the Religious Sciences and especially to those who are dedicated to catechetics. As a matter of fact, whoever achieves a good understanding of biblical Revelation and God's way of proceeding in the History of Salvation, will have covered a great stretch of the way in the study of Catechetics. The notion of biblical Revelation is so rich that one clarifies many other obscure theological concepts by penetrating deeply into its meaning.

It is of supreme importance to follow the progressive evolution of Revelation from within the Bible. This helps greatly in understanding God's way of making use of men, of historical events, and of the necessities and problems peculiar to each epoch, in order to do his work of opening new perspectives. Along these lines prophets and theologians go forward, discovering new aspects of the Unique Truth that is God. The Eternal Father did not wish to reveal all things to us all at once; rather, He allowed human events to do His work as they proceed, directing the attention of theologians to new problems. Thus God reveals His Divine Attributes more perfectly each passing day.

Furthermore, by following the progressive evolution of Revelation one becomes aware of the tension which exists within the

Bible itself. Biblical Revelation moves constantly from the imperfect to the more perfect. Seen in this way, there is no need for wonderment that many imperfect things, both doctrinal and human, are to be found in the Old Testament as related to the New Testament. The Old Testament represents an imperfect stage, even if a necessary one, in the Revelation which tends continually forward toward the perfection brought by Christ. The New Testament illumines the entire Old Testament; in fact, the latter obtains meaning for a Christian only insofar as it is seen to be an admittedly imperfect preparation for the New Testament perfection brought about by Christ.

In this way the wonderful plan of salvation comes into view which God has projected for the welfare of mankind.

Father José Salguero, O.P.

Contents

FOREWORD .... v–vi

INTRODUCTION 1

CHAPTER I: Divine Revelation
Considered in its Biblical Aspect 2

CHAPTER II: Divine Revelation in
the Old Testament 12

CHAPTER III: Revelation in Judaism at
the Time of the New Testament 114

CHAPTER IV: Divine Revelation in
the New Testament 117

CHAPTER V: Revelation in the Church and
in Contemporary Catholic Theology 172

INDEX 197

BIBLICAL REVELATION

The History of Salvation

Introduction

The Bible offers to us the Message of Salvation that God wishes to send to men by means of the sacred authors. In order to put into greater light the plan of God for our salvation and the revelation that He makes of it in Sacred Scripture, we will direct our attention to the entire Bible, trying to present the divine plan and show how it unfolds little by little. The Bible presents us with not only a series of facts and happenings in Salvation History, but also and above all the intention of its invisible Author Who intervenes in it continually. The Old Testament recounts, step after step, the march of the Chosen People towards a destination which is well known to us: Jesus Christ. And this destination casts His light, like a beacon, on all that has happened.

This study is intended to guide us in discovering in the Bible a supremely active God, Who maintains the liveliest of dialogues with men. Indeed, God acts and speaks to us through a chain of witnesses who live in each age and who connect all men into a close unity. God, through marvelous promises, nourishes and sustains the hope of His faithful ones; and through His presence in the midst of His Chosen People, He responds to the most intimate aspirations of the human soul athirst for God.

The Bible shows us how God little by little and with the wisest of pedagogy has revealed Himself to the men of the Old and the New Covenant.

In this work we propose to stress the wonderful goodness of God and the immense delicacy of His love in wanting to give Himself to men in order to render them participants in His Divine Nature.

CHAPTER 1

Divine Revelation Considered in Its Biblical Aspect

PRELIMINARY GENERAL NOTIONS

1. What Is Revelation.

Revelation can be *defined* as: a free, divine act by which God manifests Himself to us in different ways, in order to guide the human race to its supernatural end, the vision of the divine essence.

Revelation is the principal and first fact of the mystery of Christianity. Indeed, Revelation is the "primary and fundamental reality" of Christianity. Nevertheless, Catholic theology has not always sufficiently considered this theme in its biblical aspect. However, in our days, Catholic theology is studying ever more the mystery of the "Word of God": in Sacred Scripture, in Tradition, in preaching, in the liturgy. The expression "Verbum Dei" (Word of God) is used to designate almost all of the mysteries of the history of salvation and all the realities of Christianity. Nevertheless, the expression "Word of God" is applied in the first place and of itself to Revelation, i.e., to the first interaction of God with humanity, with which God intended to manifest His salvific counsel."

The "word of God" is contained in Sacred Scripture and in the Apostolic Tradition; later on it was transmitted through the tradition of the Church. The preaching of the Church transmits this word; the liturgy celebrates and actualizes this word, but everything derives from the original Word, i.e., the Word of God given to mankind.

Therefore, it is of the maximum importance to know the true

concept of *Revelation* as it is presented to us in Sacred Scripture: This is in perfect harmony with the ecumenical preoccupation of our times. In fact, as an example, for Protestants, Sacred Scripture constitutes the only point of preoccupation. However, the theology of the word of God in these times occupies a most important place not only for Protestants, but also for Catholics. The word of God lends itself in an extraordinary manner as a most excellent means to true ecumenism.

The traditional definition was "revelatio est locutio Dei attestans" (Revelation is the Word of God Who affirms). Therefore the scholastic concept of Revelation was above all intellectualistic, because it was a *discourse* of God to men. God was like the teacher who spoke, taught and imposed laws. For this reason theology, preaching, catechesis tended to be rather abstract and theoretical.

Today, instead, Catholic theology studies Revelation more in its concrete, vital and personal aspect—that is, in Scripture itself, in Tradition, in preaching and in the liturgy. This new approach is found in Vatican II, which defines Revelation as an *interpersonal relationship* of the three Divine Persons with some chosen men (intermediaries between God and mankind) and that of these men with the rest of mankind. This relationship is not only a manifestation; it is also a communion, a union and communication. We read in the documents of Vatican II: "Through this revelation, therefore, the invisible God out of the abundance of His love speaks to men as friends and lives among them, so that He may invite and take them into fellowship with Himself" (*Dei Verbum,* n. 2).

This shows us that instead of using the abstract Scholastic concept, the Council makes use of a *dynamic, living, historic* concept of Revelation. In fact, one is not dealing with the communication of "notions," of "truths," but rather with intimate communion and encounter with God (*Dei Verbum,* n.2).

Sacred Scripture presents us this encounter between God and man under the image of a colloquy, dialogue, between friends (*Dei Verbum,* n. 2). To indicate the intimacy of this colloquy and of

3

this meeting, both the Old and the New Testament use the image of conjugal love (Os 2, 14ss; Ez 16, 1 ss, Cant).

Revelation therefore is an action, a divine word generating a friendly colloquy between God and men (*Dei Verbum,* n. 2). It is a word or colloquy begun already in the Old Testament by means of the action of the Prophets (*Ibid.,* n. 3); it is a word fulfilled in Christ (*Ibid.,* n. 4); it is a word to which man, conscious of his vocation, responds (*Ibid.,* n. 5); it is, finally, a word justified by the sovereign goodness of God and by the profound indigence of creatures (*Ibid.,* n. 6).

2. Revelation Is a Colloquy Between God and Men.

"Through this revelation," says Vatican II, "the invisible God out of the abundance of His love speaks to men as friends and lives among them" (*Dei Verbum,* n. 2). It is therefore a colloquy, a friendly dialogue. The protagonists of this colloquy or marvelous encounter are:

God: "In His goodness and wisdom, God chose to reveal Himself . . ." (*Dei Verbum,* n. 2).

Christ: Word made flesh, fulfills and completes Revelation with His presence, with His words and His works, especially with His death and resurrection, and with His sending of the Holy Spirit (*Dei Verbum,* n. 4).

Men: Men, by means of Christ, in the Holy Spirit, have access to the Father and are made participants in the divine nature (*Dei Verbum,* n. 2).

God is therefore the first agent of Revelation. He is such through pure condescension ("He chose") without any kind of force being imposed upon Him. Besides being subject-agent, God is also the object of Revelation. That which God reveals is in fact His Deity; he reveals Himself in a personal form.

At the opposite pole is man in his condition as creature. Revelation guides him toward salvation, it gives him access to the Father and it introduces him into the intimacy of the family of God.

But all of this would be unimaginable without the existence of

4

a bridge, which could span the abyss which separates men from their Creator. The bridge is *Jesus Christ*. One cannot therefore conceive a complete Revelation which is not Christian. The reason is that Christ is the only mediator between the two poles.[1]

Therefore the description of the concept of Revelation given us by Vatican II is marvelous: a colloquy between God and man, founded on the person of Christ; an intimate exchange of love and authentic friendship which shares the immense treasures of the friend, i.e., of Christ.

3. How God Has Revealed Himself.

Traditional theology ordinarily considered the deposit of Revelation from the point of view of the truth, regarded as eternal, immutable and somewhat extraneous to the rhythm of history. This is true, but at the same time we must not forget that God, moved by an ineffable condescension towards man, translates His action into human categories. The historicity of His Revelation is therefore reflected necessarily in the whole of the revelatory process.

All revealed truths are related to the mystery of the Incarnation. Now, the Incarnation signifies the insertion of the Word into human history with all of its consequences. Two of these are Christian Revelation as the history of salvation and the history of Christ as Revelation in the strict sense. *Christ* reveals Himself *by means* of *His person, His deeds* and *His words*.

Vatican II tells us, in fact, that not only the words but also the historical deeds and words have an inner unity: the deeds wrought by God in the history of salvation manifest and confirm the teaching and realities signified by the words, while the words proclaim the deeds and clarify the mystery contained in them" (*Dei Verbum*, n. 2).

In intimate unity between themselves, words and deeds are therefore directed to manifest the complete story of the love of God the Father. Some deeds of God are, for example, the Exodus,

---

[1] A. Javierre, "La divina rivelazione" in *La Cost. dogmatica sulla divina Rivelazione,* Torino, Ed. Elle di Ci, 1967, p. 182ss.

the conquest of Palestine, the Babylonian exile, the Restoration, etc. The whole history of the Chosen People constitutes, in a certain sense, a prophetic event.

4. The Acceptance of Revelation.

Revelation is the divine word which speaks to us in different ways. But the divine word cannot be without correspondence. The adequate response of man is called faith. Faith establishes a personal contact with God the Revealer, because Revelation is none other than a loving colloquy stimulated by the benevolence of God. It is God Who calls man by means of Revelation and requires a response.

The Constitution *Dei Verbum* presents faith as *oboeditio*. The reply of faith is in fact religious submission, permeated by love as it corresponds to the word of a friend. The word *oboeditio* evokes the attitude of Abraham, the man of the word. Abraham was the type (figure) of the authentic believer because his attitude traced a splendid path of robust faith and of unconditional availability to the word of Yahweh (Rom 4, 18).

5. The Transmission of Divine Revelation.

The introduction to the second chapter of the Constitution *Dei Verbum* attributes the transmission of Revelation to a gratuitous disposition of God (n. 7). Since Revelation coincides with the actualization of salvation, its transmission embraces the whole complex of events and divine teachings ordained to save the world. Revelation, before being fixed in written form, lived in the dynamic, oral tradition of the people of Israel and in the primitive Christian Church. Therefore, Sacred Scripture comes from Tradition; and hence Scripture cannot be in contradiction with the living and oral preaching from which it derives. But neither does Sacred Scripture substitute for Tradition entirely. It is one thing, for example, to narrate the institution and the celebration of the Eucharist. It is another thing to celebrate it and participate in it. The transmission of the apostolic preaching outside of Scripture, as well as everything that is the object of it, is known as Tradition. Tradition is the Revelation made to the Apostles by Christ and by the Holy Spirit. The Apostles expressed it and applied it in their teaching, in the organization and life of the Church, in the interpretation of Scripture, and in the celebration of worship. In these various forms they transmitted it to their successors, so that it might thus continue uninterruptedly for the entire duration of the Church.

Tradition embraces the whole of Christian reality. It transmits not only divinely revealed doctrine but also its concrete application, not only that which the Church believes but also that which she is and does according to the exigencies of her Faith. Tradition, like Sacred Scripture must establish the principle of continuity and of identity between the Apostolic Church and the Later Church. Tradition is the living transmission of all apostolic preaching and activity. It therefore remains open and subject to continual development. Progress is consequently a constitutive element of Tradition. But this progress can take place only in absolute fidelity to the apostolic message. Tradition therefore cannot undergo an external increase of truths which could alter its content. There can be nothing in Tradition which does not derive from the Apostles. Hence, one is dealing with a development which is born from within. This progress of Revelation is achieved through the intellectual study of the truths and things transmitted, through the spiritual experience of these shared by the whole community; and through authentic preaching proper to the successors of the Apostles.

6. The Relationship Between Sacred Tradition and
   Sacred Scripture (*Dei Verbum*).

In the transmission of Revelation, Tradition and Scripture are both necessary, and therefore neither one nor the other is sufficient by itself. Between them exists a rapport of mutual interdependence. Both have the same origin from God and the same end, i.e., to transmit Revelation. This transmission, however, happens in different ways. Scripture is indeed the Word of God both in its content and in its verbal enunciation. Tradition, instead, although divine in its content, is not such in its human enunciations. There can be nothing in Tradition which does not agree with Scripture, just as there can be nothing in Scripture which does not agree with Tradition. The Second Vatican Council considers both strictly connected and communicating to the point of forming in some way one single object. At the same time, however, the Council rejects the Protestant principle of "Scripture only," and also the principle of the Counter-reformation's "Tradition only." The Council affirms simply that the Church, in order to enter into the certainty of the whole Revealed Deposit, has recourse to Scripture and to Tradition, both together. Says Vatican II: ". . . it is not from Sacred Scripture alone that the Church draws her certainty about everything which has been revealed. Therefore both Sacred Tradition and Sacred Scripture are to be accepted and venerated with the same sense of devotion and reverence," ". . . there exists a close connection and communication between Sacred Tradition and Sacred Scripture. For both of them, flowing from the same divine wellspring, in a certain way merge into a unity and tend toward the same end" (*Dei Verbum*, n. 9).

Sacred Tradition and Sacred Scripture constitute the only sacred deposit of the Word of God entrusted to the Church. The office of interpreting authentically this Word of God, written or transmitted, is entrusted only to the living Magisterium of the Church. This Magisterium, however, is not superior to the Word of God, but serves it, teaching only what has been handed down. Vatican II states: "It is clear, therefore, that Sacred Tradition, Sacred Scripture, and the teaching authority of the Church, in accord with God's most wise design, are so linked and joined together that one cannot stand without the others, and that all together and each in its own way under the action of the one Holy Spirit contribute effectively to the salvation of souls" (*Dei Verbum*, n. 10).

7. The Divine Word and the Peoples of the Near East.

a. *The Babylonians.* According to primitive peoples, the word assumed a certain mysterious character; in fact it exerted a certain constricting power over man.

From the Sumeric Age until the time of the Seleucids some texts and documents give a certain real power to the revealed word.

This power is clearly manifested in the magical literature. The rites and formulas for casting spells, once uttered, are efficacious. Even the confession of sins frees man from slavery of these sins.

The efficacy of the word grows if the name of a person or thing is pronounced, because the name constitutes the inseparable substitute and expresses a certain essential property of being.

For these reasons, names, prayers, curses, are put down in writing so that their power and efficacy may be perpetuated.

From this appears the realistic, material and dynamic character the ancients attributed to the spoken word.

In Babylonian hymns, the divine word is represented as something of an impetuous, beneficial or evil force. The dynamic reality of the divine word appears under poetic images in many texts, particularly in the annals of the Kings. The divine word is called great, sublime, elevated, terrible, lofty, just, magnificent, powerful, firm, true, sad, like the "mountains," unchangeable "as the heavens." The word of the gods can neither be changed nor upset, nor revoked; and it reaches its scope in an infallible way. It remains occult, mysterious, inaccessible, distant. The Sumeric-Accadic namedays demonstrate the great importance of the word of the gods.

The Sumerians consider the divine word as the creating and ordering force of the universe. The Accadians attribute to the divine word the power of creating, conserving and regenerating physical and moral things.

In the poem *Enuma Elis* (III, 120–122) the creative power of the word of Marduk is clearly expressed. Furthermore, personified

9

abstractions: *Mesaru, Kettu, Uznu, Hasisu, Dimêtu,* etc. are found in Mesopotamian religious literature. Nevertheless, it can still be affirmed that the tendency to hypostatize the divine word is quite weak; and almost always, deals with a poetic hypostasis.

The gods' normal way of speaking is through the kings, the priests, the prophets; the prophetic dream is frequently used as a means of communicating the divine word.

From the allusions regarding Mesopotamian literature it can be concluded that in Sumeric-Accadic literature the divine word constitutes a certain cosmic and creative power. Once the word has been uttered, the work comes about as if it were a physical, living and destructive entity. The intelligible content of the word can be divinized inasmuch as it is a divine property, it already acts as a subsisting spiritual reality.

b. *The Egyptians.* In Egypt, too, there existed a belief in the efficacious power of the spoken, or even the merely written word. This appears clearly in the funeral rite. The very enumeration of the oblations made to the dead already, of itself, produces in the deceased joy and happiness. In the same way just saying the name of something or someone exerts on that same [object or] person a certain constrictive force. In the theology of the god Amon, the divinity's action on the universe is conceived as operating through the power of his name. Even creation comes about through the utterance of the name. The ritual of the god Amon says expressly that Amon created himself through the utterance of his name even before he was issued forth from primordial Nun. For the Egyptians nothing can be if it has not first been named. They consider all of creation as the effect of the utterance of a divine word. The cosmogony of Edfu says that Horus created matter with his word: "Deus dixit: fiat . . . facta est. . . ." However, not only the voice and the word of the gods but also the voice of the kings (as in Mesopotamia) are efficacious and create. The reason for this is that the king is considered the son of the gods.

Even among the Egyptians personifications of the concept of

10

the *word* and of the *voice* are found. Thus from the time of the Ancient Empire, *Hou* and *Sia* appear as beings that can have relationships with the divinities.

At the beginning Sia represents the *heart,* and Hou the *word.* Later, they are personified; in fact they are conceived as emanations of Ptah (Aton, Ra). Therefore, they begin as being considered different entities and they end as divinities. However, even if it does seem that they are given a real divinization, Sia and Hou always remain second-rank gods.

In this we can already see the doctrine that the Greek and Hellenistic culture will develop later through their doctrine of the *Sophia* and the *Logos.*

In conclusion it can be said that the Egyptians have a concept of the divine word which was very similar to that of the Babylonians and that of the Jews. In fact, they consider it something creative, dynamic and personified.

CHAPTER II

Divine Revelation in the Old Testament[1]

PRELIMINARY IDEAS

1. Philological and Conceptual Notions.

In the Hebrew language of the Old Testament there are different terms which indicate and express the word of God indirectly: *qol* + "voice", *saphah* = "sermon", *miswah* = "precept", *torah* + "doctrine, law", *pitgam* = "decree", *massa* = "oracle", etc.

However, there are also terms which express the idea of the word directly—thus the Aramaic term *millah* and the terms derived from the Hebrew root *'amar* = "to say, to speak". However, since *millah* is Aramaic and its use is very limited, we will leave the study of it aside. The same thing holds for the words derived from *'amar*, since they are poetic and used in a later time.

For these reasons our study will be limited to the term *dabar*, which constitutes the normal and more universal expression used to convey the idea of word and of revelation.

In the Hebrew language, in fact, *dabar* means "word" but also "thing" or "event" (1 Kings 2,41). *Dabar* therefore expresses very well the revelation that occurs through words and events. The

---

[1] Cf. C. Charlier, *La Lectura cristiana de la Biblia,* (Barcelona, Ed. Liturgica Española, 1956); P. Grelot, *Le sens chrétien de l'A.T.* (Tournai, Desclée, 1962); L. Malevez, "Les dimensions de l'Histoire du Salut" in *Nouvelle Revue Théologique* 36 (1964) 561–579; O. Cullmann, *Le salut dans l'histoire* (Neuchâtel, Delachaux, 1966); versione ital: *Il mistero della redenzione nella storia* (Bologna, Il Mulino, 1966); P. de Surgy, *Le grandi tappe del mistero della salvezza* (Torino 1966); J. S. Croatto, *Historia de la Salvación* (Buenos Aires, Ed. Paulinas 1970).

word of God is in a certain way the incarnation of the salvific Will of God, i.e., it coincides with the natural and historic events that God Himself directs and arranges in favor of His Chosen People. *Revelation* is the divine manifestation through words, but this divine word is transmitted to us by historical events and by the interpretation of the prophets who explain their salvific meaning to us. In fact, the word of Sacred Scripture is not only a "sound of the voice"; it also implies a *dianoetic* and *dynamic* concept. The word is "dianoetic" in as much as it is directed to the intelligence; and "dynamic" in as much as it presupposes a certain objective efficacy.

The word of God is also a force, an active virtue, a power which accomplishes what it signifies.

In the Old Testament other expressions are also found—like *niglah,* from the verb *nagal* = "to reveal", which in its niphal form is best translated *to reveal one's self.* However, God not only reveals Himself; He also *appears,* He *unveils* Himself, He *makes Himself known.* All of these expressions signify that God reveals what was previously unknown (cf. Deut 29,28).

Nevertheless, these expressions, especially the visual ones, cannot be taken in their strict sense. In fact, most of the time one is not dealing with a vision in the ordinary sense, but rather with "vision" in a semitic sense, i.e., with a certain *encounter,* a certain *contact* with the divine. Therefore in the interpretation of the visual expressions the metaphorical use of these expressions must be considered with prudence, since the expression *the Lord appeared* is used many times in the Old Testament to indicate a manifestation or a communication of some message or of some promise (Gen 12,7; 17,1; 26,2; 1 Sam 3,1 ss).

In the Old Testament expression of Revelation, listening is of greater importance than seeing. The word of God echoes in the ear, in the mind, in the spirit, and in the heart of the prophets. If then there is also a vision in the prophetic communication, often or almost always the word is added for its interpretation (Is 6,8; Ez 2,1; Jer 1, 11–14; Zec 1, 9).

Often it is only the word which is heard. There is, for example, the literary expression: "The word of Yahweh came . . . saying" (2 Kgs 7,4; 3 Kgs 6,11; 13,20; Jer 1, 4, 11; Ez 3,16). Various prophetic books begin with the expression: "The word of Yahweh which came to . . ." (Osee 1, 1; Mich 1, 1; Joel 1,1; Soph 1, 1; Mal 1, 1). This expression is equivalent to the other literary expression: "The word that Isaias *saw*" (Is 2,1) and also "The *vision* of Isaiah, Amos, Nahum, Habacuc . . . which he saw concerning . . ." (Is 1, 1; Amos 1, 1; Nah 1, 1, Obd 1, 1, Hab 1,1).

In the Old Testament, although the technical term for the idea of revelation does not exist, the expression "word of Yahweh" is frequently used and sufficiently indicative to designate the divine communication. Even in the theophanies of the Old Testament, what is more important is not the fact of the vision of the divinity but rather the *hearing* of the divine word. Therefore all of Sinaitic revelation is founded on the spoken word of God. Even in prophetic revelation, when the prophet has a vision, the essential is not the vision, but rather the words he hears. In the Old Testament, "The word of God" says Jacob, "directs and inspires all of history which begins with the word of God creating all things and ends with the Word made Flesh."[2]

The religion of the Old Testament is characterized by the affirmation of the intervention of God in human history. And this intervention of God is dependent on His free choice.

The intervention of God is conceived as the *encounter* of one person with another; in fact, it deals with the encounter of someone who speaks with another who listens and gives a reply. God speaks with men, like a master with his servants. He calls them, and man, listening to God, replies with faith and obedience.

The subject and the fact of this divine communication is called *Revelation*. This divine revelation manifests itself to us as a certain power and divine virtuality that speaks, announces, explains to us and presents to us the plan of the Will of God. The word of

[2] *Théologie de l'A.T.* Paris, 1955, p. 104.

14

Yahweh is an objective energy that "comes" (Jud 13, 12. 17), that "is fulfilled" (3 Kgs 2,27). This energy, subsistent in itself, is sent by God into this world as an agent of a sublime efficacy: ". . . so shall my word be, which shall go forth from my mouth: it shall not return to me void, but it shall do whatsoever I please and shall prosper in the things for which I sent it" (Is 55, 11). It is a creative word: "God *said:* and so it was . . ." (Gen 1, 1ss). It is a word that directs all of history. Therefore, to study the history of the word of God is to study the history of revelation (Is 44, 26–28).

2. The Unity of the History of Salvation.

The concept of revelation, which is realized in history and through salvation history itself, should not be considered a univocal concept which is fulfilled in different periods. It should be considered instead in a univocal way. Revelation constitutes a *unified* and *unique* process, whose true essence does not always present itself in the same way in every period but which does manifest itself at the end and culmination of this event, i.e., in Jesus Christ. The history of revelation is a unique, total story; it is *one* event that is fulfilled throughout time.[3]

Therefore the preceding phases of the history of salvation are to be considered as the phases of the same, unique history, which reach their scope and end in Christ. For these reasons the Old Testament must never be separated from the New Testament otherwise the one history of salvation would be divided into different histories of salvation independent of each other. This would be opposed to the Christian concept of a unified history of salvation. To consider the individual phases of this history as coming from the one and true God, and at the same time, to consider them as successive salvific actions of God without any intrinsic and objective relationship, would also be a contradiction of the Christian concept of salvation history. The salvific Christian era must be considered as definitive and eschatological while all other

---

[3] Cf. A. Darlap, in *Mysterium Salutis,* vol. I, Brescia 1967, p. 139ss.

preceding times must be considered as moments and phases of one and the same history of salvation, which, directed by God Himself in its internal dynamism, leads to the event of Jesus Christ. They are therefore preparatory phases of one and the same history of salvation, which reaches its true essence and its true scope in Christ.[4]

Revelation and the history of salvation, from the beginning to us today should be considered uniquely formed, sustained and guided by the Divine Will, with the different phases revealing God's salvific plan to us. These different phases cannot be separated one from the other as if the individual phases in themselves formed a particular and determined essence which is repeated in each of the others. The history of salvation is *unique* and one *only* throughout all the different periods.

One is not dealing with a multiple repetition in time of the same thing or of the same subject; but with a single history of salvation having different phases. The different periods that occur cancel each other and they surpass themselves in their final stage. For us, Jesus Christ is the beginning and the end of the history of salvation, i.e., the *final cause* of the whole history of salvation. In Jesus Christ the history of salvation has its beginning and its end. Christ, in fact, is *telos* and *arche*. The incarnation of the Son of God constitutes the real and irrevocable fulfillment of the promise of salvation that God made to mankind. In Jesus Christ the history of salvation reaches its intrinsic and full perfection.

3.   The Concept of Time in the History of Salvation.

Revelation is of a temporal dimension, not a spatial one. In fact, it indicates *yesterday-today-tomorrow*.[5] In the Old Testament there exists the following determination of time: every event happens *here and now*, but that which happens is actually the promise of the future. The present always includes a future, and this future is greater, more extensive and truer than the actual fact. Therefore

[4] Cfr. A. Darlap, *op. cit.,* p. 140s.
[5] Cf. O. Cullmann, *Cristo e il tempo,* Bologna, 1965.

every moment in the history of salvation and each single event have in themselves a certain meaning, but at the same time they are related to a future event.

An essential and decisive property of the Old Testament is its looking towards the future, towards that which is to come, i.e., towards the coming Messiah. Even today, for orthodox Judaism the future constitutes a decisive determination in time.

On the contrary, in the New Testament the property and the determination of time considered decisive and essential is *today, the actual,* the *present* in *Jesus Christ.* In fact, time finds its *center* in Christ. And this center can be the origin of that which is to come. Nevertheless, that which is future, that which is to come, will never be able to excel the center, Christ.

The Revelation of the New Testament consists in the announcement, in the message according to which the event of the cross with the related Resurrection of Christ constitutes the supreme and decisive moment in the whole of the history of salvation, even though this history continues. According to the concept of revelation proper to the New Testament the fullness of time will be at the end of time. The desires of Christians are directed towards the future, towards the coming of Christ in the Parousia. Therefore in the New Testament the promise still exists. But this promise has a form different from that of the Old Testament; it has another meaning, another relationship.

Thus there is no contradiction in saying that fulfillment has been reached in Christ, but that the end has not yet been reached. In fact, the coming of Christ implies a certain presence and a certain expectation: *already* and *not yet.* In Christ the present is the future already begun and the future is the present which goes toward an end. No event, neither before nor after Christ, has the central importance of the event of Christ. Time acquires its own order and its own rightful position when it begins from Christ. The fulfillment of revelation in the sense of *today* is expressed in the New Testament very clearly and forcefully. The hagiographer affirms that whatever happens in Christ, happens

17

"once for always" ($ἄπαξ$ – *semel*/once/that is transformed into $ἐφάπαξ$ = *semel in perpetuum*/once forever/: Rom 6, 10). The present, the *now* (nunc) of Christ is fulfilled in such a way that all past time refers to it and no future time surpasses it, since all the time which is still in the future will always be the future of *this present time*.

4. Revelation Has Taken Place in a Progressive Way.

Revelation, and in particular biblical revelation, aims at leading man out of sin and ignorance to the fullness of truth and salvation.

Nevertheless, divine truth is not discovered all of a sudden; neither does the personal encounter of man with God happen immediately; with a sudden and magical transformation. This would be something inhuman. When He speaks to men, who are weak and sinful and who find themselves in darkness, the Spirit of God adapts Himself to their way of speaking and thinking and uses suitable for transmitting His Will and His Revelation.

The Fathers of the Church speak very appropriately of "condescension" inasmuch as God uses patience and admirable "pedagogy" in instructing man. In this sense the Second Vatican Council speaks. "In Sacred Scripture, therefore, while the truth and holiness of God always remain intact, the marvelous 'condescension' of eternal wisdom is clearly shown; that we may learn the gentle kindness of God, which words cannot express, and how far He has gone in adapting His language with thoughtful concern for our weak human nature.' For the words of God, expressed in human language have been made like human discourse, just as of old the Word of the eternal Father, when He took to Himself the weak flesh of humanity, became like other men."[6]

And in another place the same Vatican Council continues: "The principal purpose to which the plan of the Old Covenant was directed was to prepare for the coming both of Christ, the universal Redeemer, and of the messianic kingdom, to announce this

[6] Cost. Dogm. *Dei Verbum* sulla divina Rivelazione, cap. III, n. 13.

coming by prophecy, and to indicate its meaning through various types. Now the books of the Old Testament, in accordance with the state of mankind before the time of salvation, established by Christ, reveal to all men the knowledge of God and of man and the ways in which God, just and merciful, deals with men. These books, though they also contain some things which are incomplete and temporary, nevertheless show us true divine pedagogy."[7]

As Sacred Scripture shows us, with infinite repetitions of the story of salvation and innumerable expressions untiringly repeated, God adapts Himself to the capacity and to the mentality of men, manifests to them the secrets of His love, and patiently corrects them. He does not show them all of His truth all at once, as they would never be able to grasp it and understand it. But He invites them, He draws them to Himself, and He subjects them to the experience of human life. So it is that through various moments that seem separated among themselves (but which are unified by His Wisdom in a wonderful way), He guides men until the day of the coming of Christ, in which revelation is fulfilled. Thus is explained the great and marvelous diversity of Sacred Scripture, in which the single narrations form a progressive revelation. In this way, the whole of Revelation is reached in Christ, in Whom the entire complex of Revelation is contemplated.

The Second Vatican Council teaches expressly that the books of the Old Testament ". . . contain some things which are incomplete and temporary . . .", but ". . . nevertheless show us true divine pedagogy."[8] Furthermore the Second Vatican Council gives us this golden rule of exegesis: ". . . no less serious attention must be given to the content and unity of the whole of Scripture, if the meaning of the sacred texts is to be correctly brought to light. The living tradition of the whole Church must be taken into account along with the harmony which exists between the elements of the faith."[9]

What the Second Vatican Council states refers to a larger con-

---

[7] *Ibid.* cap. IV, n. 15.

[8] Cost. dogma. *Dei Verbum* cap. IV, n. 15.

[9] *Ibid.* cap. III, 12.

text. Therefore, what it says in one place about Sacred Scripture is repeated in other places but in different ways. God leads men to the perception of His mystery through different and successive explorations, and He teaches them through the guidance of the Holy Spirit to reach an ever deeper understanding of revealed truth.[10]

The Apostolic Tradition, which is kept alive in the Tradition of the Church, evolves continually and expresses in progressively better ways the definitive encounter of the incarnate God with men, i.e., the definitive Revelation made by Christ. Vatican II says: "This tradition which comes from the apostles develops in the Church with the help of the Holy Spirit. For there is a growth in the understanding of the realities and the words which have been handed down. This happens through the contemplation and study made by believers, who treasure these things in their hearts, through the intimate understanding of spiritual things they experience, and through the preaching of those who have received through episcopal succession the sure gift of truth."[11]

In the course of the centuries, the Church meditates and reflects upon the deposit of revelation and expresses in new ways adapted to the different times, places, and cultures. In fact, the Church is the holy people that transmits the word and composes the Sacred Scripture. She has been instituted by Christ to preserve the faith and present it to men. The Church can do this because she possesses the Holy Spirit, Who has inspired Revelation.[12]

II. Revelation in the History of Salvation:
The Most Important Stages

1. The First Stage of Divine Revelation.[13]

Authors frequently consider the vocation of Abraham and his

[10] Cf. *Ibid.* cap. VI, n. 23.

[11] *Ibid.* cap. II, n. 8.

[12] Ibid, cap. II, n. 8. Cf. P. Benoit, *Inspiration et révélation:* in *Concilium,* n. 10, 1965, 13–32.

[13] Ch. Hauret, *Origini dell'Universo e dell'uomo secondo la Bibbia* (Gen 1–3),

election as father of the Chosen People (Gen 12) as the beginning of the history of salvation. Nevertheless, the Bible begins with a series of chapters in which the origins of the world and of mankind are narrated. These eleven chapters (Gen 1–11) also belong to the history of salvation. They are like different answers given by the same man on questions concerning his existence, his condition, his future. Who has created the universe? Where do evil, suffering, sin, death come from?

The first chapters of Genesis respond to all of these questions, revealing the truths that constitute the foundation of the plan of salvation. Without these chapters it would be very difficult to understand correctly the salvific history of Israel and of mankind. Therefore, they are a necessary foundation for all of salvation history. It is for this reason that, in the Bible and in ecclesiastical tradition, the history of salvation does not begin with the election of Abraham but with the creation of the world. In fact, creation is a historical action of God in time; it is the beginning of time, the necessary supposition in the study of salvation history.[14]

This is the reason that leads us to consider the first chapters of Genesis as the first stage in the history of salvation.

The people of Israel lived their reply before they put to themselves the question of the origin of the world and of man. They had lived it in their own history as a people. Israel, like all Semitic peoples interested in their origins, discovered, upon reflection, that the beginning of her history as a people was due to the word of

---

Torino 1953; L. Arnaldich, *El Origen del mundo y del hombre según la Biblia* (Madrid, Ed. Rialp, 1958); S. Bartina, *L'uomo e la sua origine* (Roma, 1958); J. De Fraine, *La Bible et l'origine de l'homme* (Bruges 1961); H. Renckens, *Preistoria e storia della salvezza* (Alba 1962); A. Diez Macho, El origen del hombre según la Biblia in *Est. Bib* 21 (1962) 213–272; A. M. Dubarle, Le péché originel dans l'Ecriture, *Lectio Divina* (Paris, Ed. du Cerf, 1967); P. Grelot, *Réflexions sur le problème du péché originel* (Paris, Casterman, 1968); J. Salguero, *Pecado original y Poligenismo* (Guadalajara-España, Ed. OPE, 1971).

[14] Cf. J. Daniélou, *Essai sur le mystère de l'histoire*, Paris 1953, p. 34; J. M. Gonzales Ruiz, *El cristianismo no es un humanismo*, Barcelona, ed. Peninsula, 1968, p. 45.

Yahweh, her God, Who called Abraham to leave his land and his home (Gen 12, 1ss). The later history of Israel was a continual experience of this word and of the power of Yahweh Who delivered them out of Egypt, Who gave them the Promised Land, and Who saved them in all difficult moments. Everything in Israel was the work of the word, the power and the love of Yahweh (Deut 7,8).

Later, when the theologians and the prophets began to reflect on the origin of the other peoples and of the world, they concluded that these too were the work of Yahweh. At the origin of all things, they saw an absolute beginning, an intervention of God, Who with His word and power gave life to all beings. In Israel this answer is called *creation*. But this answer, or this clear idea on the creation of all things, Israel arrived at only in a later time when the faith of the Chosen People discovered that Yahweh was the God of the universe and of all peoples.

1. *Revelation by Means of Creation and the Self-Communication of God.*

Once man is created, God reveals Himself to him by means of created things and by means of divine self-communication. Thus begins primitive *transcendental* Revelation. We do not know how such primitive Revelation was transmitted by the first men, but inasmuch as it is the salvific will of God and divine self-communication it is received by every man as a member of the human race. In this sense, one can speak of a certain transmission of primitive transcendental Revelation.

If there truly does exist a certain historical tradition of primitive Revelation expressed in human words, it certainly has not been transmitted by written narrative expositions, but rather by a living and transcendental preservation of the experience of God and of man the sinner. It is, in fact, "natural" revelation because God, beginning from the creation of the world, lets Himself be seen by the intelligence through His works (Rom 1, 18–23).

In man himself is given the revelation of the Will of God, of

22

His law written in man's heart as attested by his conscience and by the interior judgments he feels. One is dealing therefore with a manifestation, a revelation of the Will of God, which can be recognized by the conscience present in man, which guides him and obliges him (Rom 2, 14ss). One can speak here of a revelation since the natural law written in the heart of men has God for author. One is dealing, therefore, with something arranged by God. Conscience gives testimony to this: that God is the author of this constitution of man which manifests itself as a command and as a judgment in the voice of conscience.

But although men have known God by means of creation, they have not wanted to recognize Him. On the contrary they have tried to live founding themselves upon themselves. The knowledge of God exacts and implies obedience, availability. Man's sin consists precisely in refusing this attitude. A consequence of this conduct is that men, living immersed in created works and investigating them, are led astray by their appearance and beauty (Wis 13, 6s). Men have not corresponded at all to the revelation of God manifested in creation, and have fallen into error, becoming guilty. But this error and failure have different degrees of gravity. The Bible suggests however that latent in this error is the search, the desire to find the true God, the truth. In fact God has revealed Himself even to peoples of polytheistic religion.

Man with his intelligence can ascend through creatures, to their first cause. In fact from visible creatures the human intellect concludes that there is a greater and more perfect power which produces them, and that all things depend on this power for their existence. Such power is necessary and therefore eternal. Furthermore, through creatures, man can understand even the eternal majesty of God, since He is not only the Principle of all things, but also their supreme Lord, Who rules all things, and the Last End, for Whom all things exist and to Whom all things tend. Man also understands God's eternal Wisdom, through which He arranges all things in an exact way and guides them to their pre-established

23

end; His eternal goodness, through which He continually does us good; His eternal justice, and all His other divine attributes. St. Paul teaches us all of this in his letter to the Romans 1, 19ss. And following St. Paul, the First Vatican Council affirms: "The Church believes and teaches that God, beginning and end of all things, can be known by the light of human reason through created things; the invisible things can be understood by means of creatures . . ." (Denz 1785).

2. *The Effect of Natural Revelation on Man*

Biblical testimony concerning the *natural* revelation of God made to men considers its effect under almost dramatic aspect. This dramatic character can be understood well from the classical text of the letter to the Romans 1, 18–23. This passage of St. Paul draws its inspiration perhaps from the book of Wisdom 13, 1–5. There is also another passage of St. Paul in the same letter to the Romans 2, 14ss, where the Apostle speaks of the Revelation of the Will of God and of His law in man. According to this text the revelation of God, i.e., the manifestation of His Will, is found in the law innate in the heart of men. It deals with the revelation of the Creator in the creature, with the revelation of a just and holy Will that the conscience of man can know. The conscience of man testifies to the existence of God. For man this conscience is a command which obliges him, for in his conscience he feels the exigency of the Divine Will.

In the first act of the drama of natural revelation the *principal actor is God Himself*. God, hidden and invisible, becomes visible from the beginning of the world through His creatures. These creatures, however, must not be confused with God; they are the effect of the First Cause. Being effects, they reveal the Cause, their Creator. In fact, when man reflects that he has been created and where he thinks about the origin of the world, he then begins to know God. All that can be known of God naturally is communicated to men through experience and reflection without any

24

particular revelation. The revelation of God in creatures and in man constitutes something which is experienced, is seen.[15]

The second act of natural revelation is presented by man. God has given His revelation to men, but they have not wished to respond. The letter to the Romans (1–2), where the sin of infidelity of both the Jews and the pagans is described, speaks to us of men's infidelity to God. They ". . . in wickedness hold back the truth of God" and do not wish to recognize God (Rom 1,18ss). For these reasons they do not wish to give God glory and thanks. And this has led them to change ". . . the glory of the incorruptible God for an image made like to corruptible man and to birds and four-footed beasts and creeping things" (Rom 1,23).

However, we also find a positive aspect of natural revelation in Sacred Scripture. Thus the book of Wisdom 13,6ss recognizes that man, even if he does often err, nevertheless seeks God and hopes to find Him. This positive aspect is also found in the discourse of St. Paul at the Aereopagus (Acts 17): in fact, the Apostle declares that the Athenians are extremely religious, for they worship the *Unknown God*. In this sermon Paul exalts the positive elements of the religion of the Greeks.

The third act of the drama has its origin in God Himself. God presents Himself to men, angry at their infidelity. The wrath of God is shown in His abandoning man as a slave to his passions and perversions. This state of man is not *natural;* it is truly a state of perversion. This perversion consists principally in the exchange of the Creator for creatures, in the exchange of God for idols. This fundamental perversion leads man to the perversion of his own nature in its physical, sexual, juridical and social sectors (Rom 1, 25–30.32).[16]

3. *The Revelation of God in the First Chapter of Genesis.*

Above all, it is necessary to caution the reader that the sacred

[15] Cf. H. Fries, in *Mysterium Salutis I,* 252–254; A. Feuillet, in *Lumière et Vie,* 1954, 207.

[16] Cf. H. Fries in *Mysterium Salutis,* I, p. 258.

author has described the events in Gen 1–3 in the way those of his time believed and knew. God in fact always adapts Himself most wisely to the mentality of the sacred authors and of the Israelites for whom the narration of events is ordained. A scientific explanation of the creation of the world and of things should not be looked for in these chapters, for that which the hagiographer intends to put forth is the fundamental truths of religion: i.e., God has created the world and all the universe, and has intervened in a most special way in the creation of man and woman, etc. The arm of the sacred author is of a totally religious character.

It is also of great importance to clearly distinguish the sacred writer's form of expression, i.e., the literary genre in which he presents the religious truths and doctrine he intends to transmit. In fact one can narrate a true fact in an artful manner. In this sense, the narration of the first chapters of Genesis on the origin of mankind is not to be understood as a "story", transmitted from the beginning from generation to generation and describing the happenings of primitive history. It is rather an *etiology* (= study of the causes of things), which draws from present experience to arrive at the determination of the cause (which in reality can be the historical cause of this present experience). These first chapters of Genesis present us that which Israel, basing herself on her own specific, historic and concrete experience with God, thinks of the origin of the world. Born from living experience, from theological reflection and from divine illumination, these chapters constitute a narration of what was at the beginning, of what would be at the beginning if we could now find ourselves in that state.

Therefore, although the presentation of the origin of mankind offered us by the first three chapters of Genesis is fundamentally true and historic, it has nevertheless been constructed with imaginative and descriptive materials taken from the times in which the sacred author lived. However, it is not an arbitrary narration, because even under a mythological form a transcendent truth of primitive Revelation can be found.

This history of the origins (Gen 1–3) was written relatively

26

late, in the period of the Kings, during which the prophets and the Israelite theologians were battling against the myths and mythologies (principally Babylonian) of the time. It constitutes a "glance of Israel over the past." One is dealing therefore (in Gen 1–3, and also in Gen 4–11) with a literary, cultural, and prophetic document, elaborated from different traditions and testifying what Israel, basing herself on her own experience, thought of the origin of the world. Genesis 1–11 is therefore a *prophecy* toward the past. These first chapters of Genesis testify that men can perceive and understand, hear and see God in the works of creation. This means that from creation there exists a revelation of God to men.

In Genesis we have a double narration of creation, i.e., that of the Priestly tradition (Gen 1,1–2, 4a) and that of the Yahwistic tradition (Gen 2, 4b–25). But both narrations are quite different in regard to ideas and in regard to literary form. The Yahwistic narration (J) of creation is older than the Priestly narration (P).[17]

---

[17] The Yahwistic tradition is the oldest of all. It narrates the history of salvation from paradise and the sin of Adam and Eve to Moses or, rather, to the taking possession of the lands of Chanaan. It was outlined about the year 750 B.C. in the kingdom of Judah. It presents the accomplishments of the patriarchs in Hebron, Beersabea, etc., and also puts Judah before his brothers. The Yahwistic traditions uses natural causes of events, and its way of speaking of God is anthropomorphic.

The Elohistic tradition (E) starts from the northern kingdom of Israel, in fact, it narrates the deeds of the Patriarchs in Bethel, Sichem, etc. In this tradition not Judah, but Ruben, Joseph and Ephraim are presented. It narrates of the vocation of Abraham up until the occupation of the lands of Canaan. The Elohist uses the name of Elohim; the theophany occupies a great place in his narration and "reflection"; he attributes great importance to the action of God and His universal causality.

The Priestly tradition (P) is the most recent of all. It was composed during the Babylonian exile by the prophet Ezechiel and by his school (c. 500 B.C.). It presents us the history and the laws of worship (Lev., Ex. and Num., Gen. 1, 1–2.4a). It treats of the Ark of the Covenant, the sacrifices, the priests, the Levites, etc. The style and the general outline are full and abounding in words and doctrine. Theological "reflection" and "nomism" prevail. The idea of God is very transcendent.

The Deuteronomic tradition (D) comprises more or less Deuteronomy. This book was composed at the time of the King Manasses (c. 685–643 B.C.) and

In the first narration (Gen 1,1–2.4a), the sacred author inculcates the theological significance of the deeds. First of all God is considered as the *one God* and the *Creator,* different from the world and anterior to it. In comparing this narration with the Assyro-Babylonian narration of creation, one observes a strict *monotheism:* God does not proceed from chaos the way the Babylonian gods do; the sun, the moon, the stars are not gods. The one God has created the world *wisely* and *all-powerfully;* He has made it without fatigue: "God said . . . and so it was." The special intervention of God in the formation of the first man and the first woman is also taught, as well as the dignity of man over all the other creatures, for he was created to the image and likeness of God. The Lord created them man and woman. All creation issued forth from the hands of God and it was good.

In the second narration of creation (Gen 2, 4b–25) and in the narration of paradise (Gen 3), the sacred author is aware of a constitution of man which transcends the confines of a creaturely reality and of the revelation founded on it. Man is made worthy of a particular and gratuitous self-manifestation of God and he participates in the intimate closeness, friendship and love of God. This state, which is described by the image of the terrestrial paradise, belongs to the revelation of the origins, and in its turn should be understood as an etiology; i.e., as the glance of Israel and mankind over their past.

The key for understanding this is the experience of fault, suffering, evil, death. Where do all of these evils come from? God created everything good. The image of paradise, in fact, presents the world to us without shadows and suffering, the world of the closeness of God, of union with Him. This paradisiacal world was destined for man as a given state of his unwounded nature. The

at the time of the King Josiah (c. 622 B.C.) by the priests that intended to reform cult, to abolish privileges and to declare the temple of Jerusalem as the only legitimate one. After the Babylonian Exile or a little before, the compiler joined D with JE. Furthermore, JE was treated again in different parts according to the Deuteronomic sense. This same thing was also done later to the other existing books (Josue, Kings).

28

actual world instead appears as the loss of paradise. This loss is brought about by an action of man, i.e., by his decision against the creaturality of his own given being; or, as the Bible says, by his rebellion, his refusal to obey, his lack of faith, his presumption of "wanting to be like God", by wanting to put himself in God's place, by wanting to possess what belongs to God alone (Gen 3,5). That paradise has been lost means that man has fallen into a culpably lacerated creaturality.[18]

According to Gen 2,7, man was created from the dust of the earth, from the ordinary *adamah*. Only *afterwards,* through a special privilege of God, was he transferred to the terrestrial paradise (Gen 2,8.15). It is commonly admitted that man was created in the state of original justice. But the sacred author describes man according to his natural constitution in order to express later, through the transferral into the Garden of Paradise, the supernatural privilege gratuitously granted by God. Man, therefore, by nature was a finite, limited, mortal being like all other creatures. By a special privilege, God elevated him to a state which was not his by nature, to a supernatural state, represented by the image of paradise. However, man did not wish to remain in this marvelous state. He rebelled against God his benefactor, and thus lost the preternatural gifts God had given him. He returned to his primitive state as a creature, with the grave consequence that he now bore a sin, making him God's enemy.

The second narration (Gen 2,4b–25) presents man from a pessimistic aspect. Sorrow, death, and various sufferings come from sin, from the rebellion of man against God. The truths taught by the sacred author are the creation of man, sin, the consequences of sin, and the promise of redemption. Man was created by God and is superior to the animals (Gen 2,7.19s). Woman also was created by God and is similar to man and superior to the animals (Gen 2,18.20). Marriage is instituted by God Himself (Gen 2,21–24). The devil is represented in the form of a serpent, because this

18 H. Fries, in *Mysterium Salutis,* I, 262s.

animal was venerated in the oriental cult of fecundity. The fault committed is considered grave; a fault of pride and disobedience. The consequences of this sin are various: the first is the loss of the friendship of God (Adam and Eve are cast out of the Garden of Paradise—Gen 3,23–24). Other consequences are death (3, 19), the loss of integrity and the awakening of concupiscence (3,7), suffering (3,16). In the midst of these miseries, however, shines the light of hope: God promises man salvation and final victory over the devil (3,15). This first promise of salvation is called the Proto-evangelium. The demonstration of its fulfillment will be seen in the historical development of the other stages of Revelation in Israel and in the Christian Church. In a drastic manner, Genesis 4,11 presents us with figures grown darker through the growth of sin in the world. However, just men such as Abel, Enoch and Noah are not lacking. The covenant of God with Noah (Gen 6,7) shows us man's possibility of knowing God through creation, of considering creation and his own life as gifts of God, and of showing his own gratitude to God in the form of religion.

4. *Monogenism or Polygenism?*

The study of Gen 2–3 shows us that the sacred author considers Adam and Eve as concrete individuals, rather than as a collectivity. But this is not sufficient to resolve the problem definitively, since the hagiographer never even thought of polygenism. We cannot exact from the hagiographer the solution to a question of which he never thought. Today, instead, the paleontologic science poses the question: was mankind produced by one couple only or by various couples? The reply of paleontology today seems to tend towards polygenism.[19]

From the time of the encyclical, *Humani Generis* (August 12, 1950), the Catholic Church has permitted Catholics to hold the evolutionistic theory of the origin of mankind; but in regard to polygenism the encyclical affirms that "up to this time it does not

[19] J. Salguero, *Pecado original y Poligenismo,* 1971, p. 191ss.

appear how polygenism can be reconciled with the dogma of Original Sin" (E.B. 617; Cf. NRTh 1951, 337ss).

2. Revelation as a Promise.[20]

The Revelation which begins with Abraham is indicated with the expression *Revelation of the Promise* (E. Brunner). God manifests Himself in a very special manner to this man; and this man Abraham responds to the divine promise with faith and obedience. Furthermore, this promise presupposes a history, i.e., the history of Old Testament salvation. The one God, Yahweh, with His historical action has willed to enter into a particular relationship with the people of Israel. Although Yahweh has chosen the Hebrew people in the person of Abraham, this does not mean that up to this time He has not saved those men who have been searching for him. Quite the contrary. The Bible itself presents God as Savior even before the time of Abraham. His choice of Israel is not made with the aim of blessing just Israel, but with the intention of manifesting Himself in a new way in order to transmit a more concrete and efficacious Message of Salvation.

All of Revelation concerns Christ Who is the center of the history of salvation (Gal 4,4; Eph 1,10). The election of Abraham begins the time of "preparation" for the coming of Christ. God communicates Himself by means of historic deeds and as the Word of Life which will have its culmination in the Incarnation and in the revelation of the Johannine "Logos".

In the dialogue established with men, God wished to begin His

[20] H. Cazelles, "Patriarches" in *DBS,* 7 (Paris 1961) coll. 81–141; A. Parrot, *"Abraham et son temps* (Neuchâtel, 1962); F. M. Cross, Yahweh and the God of the Patriarchs" in *Harvard Theological Review* (1962) 225–259; A. Rolla, *La Bibbia di fronte alle ultime scoperte* (Roma 1961) n. 104ss; A. Gonzalez, *Abraham, padre de los creyentes* (Madrid, Taurus, 1953); R. De Vaux, "Les patriarches hébreux et l'histoire" in *Revue Biblique* 72 (1965) 5–28; H. Gaubert, *Abrahán el amigo de Dios* (Barcelona, Estela, 1966); L. Rubio Moran, *El misterio de Cristo en la historia de la salvación* (Salamanca, 1968) p. 103–120; A. Robert-A. Feuillet, *Introduction á la Bible* vol. I, Ancieu Testament (Tournai, Desclée 1957).

conversation with the Hebrews in a special way. He did not choose the more civilized and developed Sumerians or Assyro-Babylonians or Egyptians; all of these were too much anchored in polytheism—a grave danger for the transmission of the true Revelation. The clan of the Hebrew Patriarchs instead was much more adapted, for it was more isolated from the influences of polytheistic civilization, more attached to the God of the tribe or family and less bound to a culture or a definite country. They were semi-nomads who, as such, received a special name. In Accadic, the language of Mesopotamia, they were called *habiru;* in Egyptian, *'apiru;* in Ugaritic, dialect of the Syrian coast, *'apirim,* and in the Hebrew language: *'ibherim* (= Hebrews). Therefore the name "Hebrew" does not refer originally to an ethnic group but to a social group: the semi-nomads.

The story of the Patriarchs narrates the intervention of God in the life of a small ethnic group which will become God's providential means of handing His Revelation down to posterity. It describes to us the origin and the development of a new bond between God and a group of human beings. This bond is the objective starting point of the posterior covenant between Yahweh and Israel. The covenant is a historic fact which also demands an equally historic starting point. The one God, Yahweh, wants to enter into a particular relationship with the people of Israel through His historic action, and this is what happens in the covenant.

The history of salvation and of Old Testament revelation constitutes a history of limited, special, "zone" salvation; indeed it is directed towards the people of Israel. But then, because of the covenant of the one God with Israel, this event is considered by the prophets and the Hebrew theologians in all its profundity: they conclude that this pact has a universal scope. This is proven later by the prophetic promise found in the Old Testament of the future conversion of the pagans. Therefore the ultimate scope of the particular revelation made to Israel is universal.[21]

The history of Old Testament revelation is a history of salva-

[21] Cf. H. Fries, in *Mysterium Salutis,* I, p. 210.

tion *open to future time,* and hence it is not to be considered definitive. The Old Testament, in fact, is the prologue to Christ, the preparation to receive Christ. It is the guide that leads to Christ. For this reason, all the Old Testament structures of the history of salvation can be surpassed in the future, i.e., in Christ.

The religious history of the Old Testament is important to us only inasmuch as it leads us to Christ and always refers to Christ. Without such a connection with Christ, the Old Testament religious history would indicate the special historical rapport of another people (Israel) with God, certainly not with us. Hence the history of the Old Testament is of value to us inasmuch as it is the immediate pre-history of Christ, and thus can be considered our own history of revelation.

The New Testament does not constitute just a homogeneous stage of general salvation history and of the special, zonal salvation history of Israel. It is the end and the fullness of it because of its eschatological character. The new and eternal covenant in Jesus Christ is the fullness and the end of all salvation history because it is no longer ambiguous and open to the future; it has already been decided by God Himself. And inasmuch as Christianity is considered the fullness of all salvation history, it can and must expose its message to all the peoples of the world in a challenging way.

1. *The History of the Patriarchs*

The history of the Patriarchs constitutes a tradition which survived in the group of the twelve tribes of Israel and which is founded on a certain historic manifestation of God to the Israelites, which later had great importance as an element of the faith of Israel.

The particular revelation made by God to the Hebrews begins with Abraham around the second millennium before Christ. The greater part of the historians consider Abraham a historic personage who lived in the 19th century (c. 1850) B.C. Others instead prefer 1700 B.C. because the customs, the proper names, and the emigrations coincide with the "Ammorite" epoch (18th century B.C.). Abraham was a semi-nomad of Ur of the Chaldees, or rather, of Haran (Gen 12,4).

The narrations on Abraham form a collection of popular stories that were conveyed orally for many centuries. They contain real and historical deeds, at least in substance, although they are mixed at times with imaginative and fabulous descriptions.

The essence of the patriarchal traditions embraces two fundamental themes: the *election* and the *promise* (Gen 12,1–9, 15, 1–20).

a. *Abraham* is called by God Himself to become the father of the Chosen People (Gen 12,1ss). Abraham therefore will constitute the nucleus of a people destined by God for a great spiritual mission. Therefore he inaugurates the new "holy" people, i.e., the isolated, separated people destined for the service of Yahweh. The Sinaitic Covenant will realize fully this profound idea.

The *vocation* and *election* of Abraham offer us various notable characteristics. First of all, it is an election which God initiates and it is totally gratuitous. But at the same time it exacts from man an attitude of faith and hope (Gen 12,1). It is also a compelling call: he must leave his homeland and his family, and go to an unknown land. His own voice enters perfectly into the divine plan and is intimately bound to it; therefore his sacrifice will not be useless: "I will make a great nation of you. . . . In you shall all the nations of the earth be blessed" (Gen 12,2ss). The election of a single man concerns the salvation of all men. Abraham replies to the Lord's call with obedience (Gen 12,4). And this reply constitutes the *faith* of Abraham, who is for us "our father in the faith" (Heb 11,8). The existence of the Chosen People (Israel) is bound in some manner to his reply.

Hence the history of salvation in the Old Testament begins like the history of salvation in the New Testament—with an act of faith (the faith of the Madonna).

The *promise* made to Abraham and, through him, to all the people of Israel is oriented towards the future, and presupposes a salvific plan. Hence it constitutes the basis of hope. This is a characteristic exigency of the pedagogy of God in the Bible, for when God promises a gift, He hopes that man with effort and trust in Him will reach it. This is the reason why God's plan is so anchored into human history.

Revelation is progressive, and it is realized little by little in the religious experience of the People of God. From the time of Abraham there exists a tension between the promise and its realization. This is a process proper to the history of salvation. When a part of the promise made to Abraham is fulfilled, another tension arises and then a third and so on. . . . The greatest tension is inaugurated with Christ, i.e., that tension which places the Church between the Ascension and the Parousia. Every successive tension brings us closer to the Parousia.

God made Abraham a promise in two parts: 1). "I will make a great nation of you" (Gen 12,2), although Abraham has no children and humanly speaking is incapable of having them because he is too old (Gen 17,17ss. 2). He is also promised the possession of the land of Chanaan: "To your posterity I will give this land . . ." (Gen 15,18). To this divine promise, Abraham again responds with *faith* (Gen 15,6). Then God concludes a *covenant* with Abraham by means of a sacrifice, in which the two parties contracting the agreement have to pass between sacrificed animals (Gen 15,17). God commits Himself solemnly to the fulfillment of the Alliance, passing between the immolated victims under the form of fire (Gen 15,7–10.17s). In this way, the divine transcendence remains secure, since God manifests Himself under the image of fire.

b. *How God Deals with Abraham.* The way in which God has guided Abraham is totally unusual: Abraham leaves his homeland for an unknown country in order to obey God. God promises him a great number of offspring, even though he is already too old and has no children. When he does have a son, Ismael, by Agar, God tells him that Ismael will not be the heir. The son of the promise is Isaac, who will be born of Sara, who is sterile (Gen

17,21). When Isaac is a boy, God demands from Abraham the sacrifice of his son (Gen 22).

In the narration of the sacrifice of Isaac, the sacred author teaches us two things: God and the Israelites are not pleased with the frequent Chanaanite sacrifices of babies or adults. Furthermore God wants obedience through faith. Abraham is the greatest example of this total and unconditional faith and of this heroic obedience. Indeed he always looks toward the future.

Ordinarily God does not proceed according to the rules of human wisdom. He chooses whomever He wills with the greatest freedom: first Abraham, then Isaac, not Ismael, then Jacob, not Esau (Gen 25,23).

The faith that urged Abraham to painful renunciation at the same time won for him great goods and gifts. First of all the faith of Abraham had as an effect "justification" (Gen 15,6), which made him a "friend" of God (Is 41,8). For this reason Gen 18,17. 23–33 presents him as the confidant of God. Then the renunciation of his fatherland and of his family to follow the voice of the Lord, converts him into "the father of a great nation"; God will besides give his descendants the land of Chanaan in possession. Therefore, Abraham, the great "friend" of God (*El-Khalil,* the Arabs say) should be for us the example *par excellence* of faith and obedience.

c. *Isaac, Jacob and Joseph.* These Patriarchs continue along the same spiritual path as Abraham. The cycle of Isaac (Gen 25,19–28.9) shows us how God remains faithful to His word to Abraham, *blessing* his son in the Promised *Land* (Gen 26,1–14). The cycle of Jacob describes for us the risk-filled life of this Patriarch (Gen 28,10–35.29). In Jacob, we see manifested the free plans of God, Who chooses whom He will, preferring the younger son to the older (Gen 26,24.27.27ss; 28,1–4.12–15; 32,25–33; Rom 9,12s). In comparison with the story of Abraham, the story of Jacob is less spiritual. In it are found some disedifying manifestations of human nature (Jacob's lie, his way of acting with Laban; the conduct of his wives, etc.: Gen 27, 6–41; 30–33). However, the narrations connected with the sanctuaries of Bethel and Phanuel (Gen 28,10ss; 32, 22ss) are more religious and entirely concerned with God and His direct action on Jacob as father of the people of Israel.

The story or cycle of Joseph (Gen 37–50) serves as a bridge between the cycle of the Patriarchs and the experience of the Exodus. It has a direction which is different from that of the traditions of Abraham, Isaac, and Jacob. These are centered around Palestinian sanctuaries. Recent studies have shown that the cycle of Joseph has a "sapiential" or didactic-narrative character and belongs almost entirely to the J and E traditions. In its actual location the story of Joseph represents a stage of salvation history, as is shown by the theophany of Gen 46,1–5. It expresses faith in the salvific presence of God Who has always accompanied His people Israel. In fact, in the story of Joseph God directs everything for the good of his people (Gen 45,5ss; 50,20). Even though God acts in a mysterious way, His hand is always ready to protect the Patriarchs of the people of Israel (Gen 50,24).

d. *The Revelation of God Made to the Patriarchs.* The story of the Patriarchs is made up of elements coming from different regions and places in Palestine. The traditions that have some connection with Jacob come principally from the sacred places of central Palestine: Bethel, Sichem, and Phanuel. Instead the traditions that are connected with Abraham and Isaac have their origins in southern Palestine, especially in Beersheba and Mambre.

The God Who intervenes in the history of the Patriarchs is Yahweh. However, historically speaking, this constitutes an evident anachronism, since God revealed Himself as *Yahweh* for the first time to Moses (Ex 6,2ss = P). The Israelites before Moses gave worship to the "God of their fathers." Such worship certainly had affinity with later Yahwehism, but it did have to be very different. The Yahwistic (J) and Elohistic (E) traditions know almost nothing of this patriarchal worship.

God reveals Himself in patriarchal history as God Who is good, merciful, just, omnipotent, and faithful. The word of God is what moves all salvation history from the vocation of Abraham to the victory of Josue over the Chanaanites. The life of the Patriarchs always tends toward the fulfillment of the promise of the land of Chanaan, towards the future time. The Priestly tradition (P) adds something to the story of the Patriarchs: it considers the story as a preparation for the Sinaitic revelation. God not only promises them the land and a great number of off-spring, but He also promises to be their God and that they are to be His children (Gen 17,4–8.19; Ex 6,4–7). The "God of the Fathers" will later be identified with God the Creator. The God of the Patriarchs assists them in all the moments of their life, and always shows His *presence,* which they can feel in different ways. The faith of the Patriarchs is not a blind faith, for it rests on the presence of God. This God Who is *present* is the faithful God.

e. *Christ and the Patriarchs.* According to Matthew (1,1), Jesus was the son of Abraham. St. Paul also identifies the Lord with the descendants of Abraham (Gal 3,16).

Christ is the true descendant of Abraham, Who will bring the Promise to fulfillment. Isaac is the figure and type of this other Son of the Promise, Who is the Lord Whom God has constituted heir of all things (Heb 1,2) and bearer of the promise of salvation made to Abraham and his descendants (Lk 1,55). Just as God brought His plan to fulfillment in a paradoxical way in the life of the Patriarchs, so today He exacts the acceptance of His inexplicable plan of salvation by means of the ignominy of the cross (Gal 3, 26; Rom 4,18–25).

The sacrifice of Isaac is the figure of the sacrifice of Christ on Calvary (Gen 22,12; Rom 8,32; Heb 11, 17–19). The son is delivered over, not pardoned, and must die, but Abraham receives his son back alive because of the strength of his faith. This recovery figures and anticipates the recovery of Christ by means of the Resurrection. In the Mass we ask God to accept the sacrifice like that of Abraham. And St. Thomas writes in the Eucharistic Hymn: "It was prefigured in type when Isaac was brought as an offering, where a lamb was appointed for the Pasch . . ." (Sequence of Corpus Christi).

2. *The Sinaitic Revelation*[22]

In the stage of preparation for the New Testament Revelation, the most marvelous intervention of God is without doubt the liberation of Israel from the slavery of Egypt and His revelation on Mount Sinai (Ex 12,38; Num 11,4). This divine intervention is so extraordinary that Israel will live by it in the rest of her subsequent history. Every other liberation will remind her of the liberation *par excellence,* and thus it becomes a type of the definitive salvation which is realized in the New Testament in the death and resurrection of Christ.

The book of Exodus gathers together different traditions existing in Israel since her beginning as a people. As they reach us

[22] Cf. H. H. Rowley, *From Joseph to Josuah* (Londra 1950); H. Cazelles, *Moïse* in Dictionnaire de la Bible Supplement, 5 (Paris 1957) coll. 1307–37; A. M. Dubarlé, "La signification du nom de Jahweh" in *Revue des Sciences Philosophiques et Théologiques* 25 (1951) 3–21; G. Lambert, in *Nouvelle Revue Théologique* 74 (1952) 897–915; H. Cazelles, "Les localisations de l'exode et la critique litteraire" in *Revue Biblique* 62 (1955) 321–364; C. De Wit, *The Date and Route of the Exodus* (Londra 1969); E. C. B. DacLaurin, "JHWH: The Origin of the Tetragrammaton" in *Vetus Testamentum* 12 (1962) 439–463; G. Auzou, *De le servitude au service. Etude di libre de l'exode* (Paris 1961); versione spagnola: *De la exclavidad al servicio. Estudio del libro del Exodo* (Madrid, Fax, 1967); IDEM, *El don de la conquista. Estudio del libro de Josué* (Madrid, Fax, 1967); A. Rolla, *La conquista del Canaan* (Roma 1962); W. F. Albright, *From the Stone Age to Christianity* (New York, 1957); R. de Vaux, *Le Istituzioni dell'Antico Testamento* (Torino, 1964); H. Cazelles, *Etudes sur le Code de l'Alliance* (Paris 1946); M. Noth, Die Gesetze im *Pentateuch in Gerusalemme Studien zum A.T.* (München 1957) p. 9–141; IDEM, *Historia de Israele* (Barcelona, Garriga, 1966); D. Daube *Studies in Biblical Law* (Cambridge, 1947); G. Mendenhall, *Law and Covenant in Israel and the Ancient Near East* (Pittsburgh 1955); E. Jacob, "Les bases théologiques de l'étique de l'A.T. in *Vetus Testamentum* 7 (1960) 39–51; J. J. Stamm, *Le Décalogue à la lumière des recherches contemporaines* (Neuchâtel 1959); R. Le Deaut, *La Nuit Pascale* (Roma, 1963); N. Lohfink, *Valores actuales del A/T/* (Buenos Aires, Ed. Paulinos, 1966); A. Rolla in *Il Messaggio della Salvezza,* vol. II (Torino 1967).

today, we recognize them as being several centuries later than the events about which they report. Present-day critics judge that at a later date the traditions of Sinai were introduced into other already existing traditions which described the wandering in the desert. At this time details were probably added, certain prodigious aspects of the original facts and the deeds of the people were exaggerated, and several laws and narrations were adapted to later needs and circumstances. But these additional new elements do not destroy the historical character of the narrated events. The historic substance of these events would be: Towards 1720 B.C., following the emigration of the Hyksos, Jacob's family goes to Egypt. After the expulsion of the Hyksos, under Seti I (1310–1290) and Ramses II (1290–1224) the Egyptians begin to persecute the Israelites. Then God intervenes, liberating His people and renewing the Covenant with them on Sinai. For the hagiographer, slavery has its roots in sin (Ex 2,23–25).

The Sinaitic narrations, which comprise a large part of the Pentateuch, are divided into two parts: the part which belongs to the J and E tradition (Ex 19–24), and the part which belongs to the P tradition (Ex 25–31, 35–40; Lev. 1–27; Num 1,1–10,10). Both traditions, JE and P, have in common the idea of the divine revelation at Sinai and Israel's reception of the fundamental laws for her religious and civil life. However, there are also clear differences between these two traditions. For JE the Sinaitic laws were rules for ordinary, secular (profane) life. The Decalogue was the proclamation of Yahweh's supreme right over all human life. On the contrary, the Priestly tradition (P) gives more consideration to what concerns the sacred order, i.e., it deals with everything regarding worship.

a. *Moses.* He was the man providentially chosen by God to liberate His people. All the history of Israel in fact will consider him the true liberator, the legislator and the religious head of the Chosen People. In the vision of the burning bush (Ex 3,1–4.17), the Bible narrates the vocation of Moses. His mission as liberator demands from him a total and unconditional faith. The great

40

vocations of other biblical personages are also born in a theophany: Josue will have an analogous experience (Jos 5,15); likewise, the prophets Isaias, Jeremias, Ezechiel (Is 6; Jer 1; Ez 1).

God presents Himself to Moses as "the God of the Fathers," the God of Abraham, of Isaac, and of Jacob (Ex 3,6). If He is the God of the Fathers, He cannot forget the Promise. Hence the vocation narrative of Ex 6,2–7,7 (P) recalls the Covenant with the Fathers in order to put the accent on the fidelity of Yahweh to His promises. The God Who reveals Himself to Moses is the God *Yahweh* (Ex 3,15), Who will be with Moses just as He was with Abraham, Isaac and Jacob, and will accompany him that he may free Israel (Ex 3,11s). With the liberation of Israel from the slavery of Egypt and with the Covenant on Sinai, Moses's mission reaches fulfillment. The narrations of Exodus insist greatly on Yahweh's divine help given for the liberation of the Chosen People.

b. *The Revelation of the Name of Yahweh.* The revelation of the sacred name of the God of Israel is found in the Priestly tradition (P), which in a certain way breaks the bond between the pre-mosaic religion of the Patriarchs and Yahwehism. In fact this Priestly tradition considers El-Shaddai the pre-mosaic God, while, according to modern-day critics, He would belong to the Chanaanite deities related to El. Instead the J and E traditions fuse the salvation history of these two periods, i.e., the pre-mosaic period and the Yahwistic period. In fact the narration of Ex 3 (where the revelation of the name of Yahweh to Moses is described) presents the revelation of this sacred name and shows that the revelation of Yahweh is intimately connected with the religious history of the Patriarchs. For the hagiographer, Yahweh is identical to the God of the forefathers of Israel (Ex 3,6. 13s). In Gen 4,26 (J) the cult and invocation of the name of Yahweh is attributed to a very ancient time.

A philosophic definition of God's essence must not be sought in the revelation of the name Yahweh. What God intends to manifest is this: from that moment He will be for Israel's help, her

41

protector and her liberator. Therefore the verbal root *hayah*, from which the word *Yahweh* is derived, is to be understood as *to be, to be present*. Indeed, one is dealing with an *efficacious presence of Yahweh*: "I will be there with you." This promise was made to the Israelites, who found themselves in great tribulation, and consequently needed divine help. The sacred author expresses this through the use of a popular etymology of the name of God.

The God Who reveals Himself in Exodus is the *personal God*, dynamic and active. He is the one God, Who has ordained the whole plan of salvation. He is the God of Abraham, Isaac and Jacob, the God Who saves us today. In 1 Cor 10,4, St. Paul teaches that Christ, pre-existent as Son of God, was already present in the Exodus. Furthermore, He is the God Who calls, and we must reply—like Moses—with firm faith and perfect self-donation. He is God the Savior, Who has liberated His people from Egyptian slavery, thus prefiguring future salvation. In short, He is the God Who saves all peoples, thereby prefiguring the Christian Church. Finally, He is the compassionate and saving God of love.

From this moment on, especially after the Sinaitic legislation, Yahweh wishes to be the only and exclusive God of the people of Israel. The Israelites must honor the name of Yahweh (Ex 20,7; Dt 5,11). The name of Yahweh must be honored above all with obedience to the precepts of God, i.e., "walking in the name of Yahweh" (Mi 4,5). Therefore, when Israel does not obey Yahweh, and honors other gods, she profanes the most holy name of God (Lev 18,21; 30,3).

Deuteronomy insists much on the name of Yahweh: Yahweh chooses Himself a place *to put His name* and *dwell there* (Dt 12,5.21; 14,24, etc.). Deuteronomic theology considers the name of Yahweh almost as the substitute for the image of the divinity. In fact, the name of Yahweh dwells in the Ark of the Covenant; it is present in the propitiatory of the Temple: it rests there as in sacrarium so that the Israelites can come to the Temple to invoke the name of Yahweh.

This is most important for the theology of the divine presence in the Old Testament.

c. *The Liberation from Egypt.* The liberation of Israel from Egypt constitutes the fundamental point of faith of Israel (Ex 20,2; Num 23,22.24,8; Jud 6,13; 2 Kgs 7, 7.23). Even the expression: "God has freed His people from Egypt", repeated many times in the Old Testament, is very ancient. Already in the earliest Creed (Dt 26,5–9), the liberation from Egypt constitutes the central point around which all the other historical facts are gathered. When the Israelites approached the Sanctuary to offer the first fruits to Yahweh, they used to recite an act of faith in which the principal motif was the liberation from Egypt. Even in the ordinary formulas; as in the doctrinal affirmations, the allusion to the exodus of Israel from Egypt is always the principal theme (Ex 1–14). The Old Testament narrations describing this event show that the exodus from Egypt of the people of Israel was not just a simple emigration of the Israelitic-tribes, but a powerful event of the God of Israel. Yahweh liberated His people from the slavery of Egypt in a marvelous manner. In this liberation God showed His mercy, His benignity, His faithfulness to Israel. The memory of the miracle of the passage through the Red Sea is also ancient. All of the succeeding history of Israel depends in some way on the event of the deliverance from Egypt, the historicity of which cannot be doubted.

The sacred author means to penetrate into the depths of the historical nucleus of the deliverance from Egypt in order to give us a theological interpretation of this deed, discovering thus its deep meaning, i.e., the intervention of God in favor of His people.

Moses and his brother Aaron act in the preparation of this deliverance. By means of them, the hagiographer intends to signify the priestly intervention in the liberation. Pharaoh is opposed to God's plan (Ex 11,14); in consequence the liberation also becomes the cause of judgment for the sin of Egypt. There begins a struggle between Yahweh and the Egyptians, represented by Pharaoh

43

and the magicians of Egypt (Ex 12,12). But Yahweh obtains a great victory, showing at the same time His power, His faithfulness, the love of His heart, and the rigor of His justice. This is seen in the plagues (Ex 7–11), which, although in many cases can be considered natural phenomena, have nevertheless a profound meaning: they are *signs* of God's action to judge Egypt and liberate Israel. In them shines the power, "the finger of God."

In the last plague, Yahweh "passes" (= Passover) through the land of Egypt in order to bring a judgment to an end. Hence, Yahweh's visit is one of judgment, condemnation, extermination for Pharaoh and his people, but a visit of grace, mercy, and salvation for Israel. In the actual narration, already influenced by the Paschal ritual, the liberation of Israel is attributed to the blood of the immolated paschal lamb, because that blood served to indicate the houses of the Israelites so that the angel of the Lord would strike none of them (Ex 12,13ss).

The deliverance from Egypt was forever united to the feast of the Passover (Ex 12,21–32), which existed before the exodus from Egypt. The feast is nomadic in origin. In it a lamb was offered as the first fruits of the animals in order to secure the Lord's blessing on the new year. The sprinkling of the blood on the doors and on other things was done to ward off evil spirits. The Passover therefore was a *redemption* in the decisive and dangerous moment of the renewal of things. The Hebrews re-interpreted that rite as a sign of protection in the moment in which Yahweh "passed" on the holy night of the Exodus (Ex 12,21–23). The blood of the lamb freed the Chosen People. These therefore continue to celebrate from generation to generation the immolation of the paschal lamb in commemoration of what Yahweh did for His people (Ex 12,26s). Later on in Israel the deliverance from Egypt was considered a *redemption* (Deut 9,26; 13,6; 21,8; Mi 6,4; 2 Kgs 7,23; Ps 78,42). This redemption is rendered present in the liturgy from year to year. The conjunction of the Passover with the salvific deed of redemption will be repeated in the fullness of time, at a more spiritual and ecumenical level. The

Mystery of Christ is therefore anticipated in the religious history of the people of Israel.

The liberation is the exclusive work of Yahweh (Ex 12,50; 13,3); but it will not be a perfect liberation, for the people immediately begin to complain against Moses and against Yahweh (Ex 14,11). They will need a future and better liberation. Whenever one goal is reached, a greater and more perfect one immediately appears (as we see throughout the history of salvation).

d. *The Exodus, Figure of Salvation.* The marvelous victory obtained by Yahweh over the Egyptians, enemies of His people, becomes in the Bible a sign of anticipation of another great and definitive victory God will one day obtain over his enemies. In this way the Exodus becomes a *type,* a figure of the future, full, and definitive *salvation.* Within the Old Testament itself, national calamities are compared to the slavery of Egypt. Only the intervention of God can liberate the Chosen People from these calamities (Is 11,16). For example, the return from the Babylonian exile is described in the same terms. This salvation, however, just like every new intervention of God, surpasses the preceding ones: it is more glorious, more marvelous (Is 43, 14–21; Jer 23,7–8). Nevertheless, the return from exile does not realize fully the salvific hope announced by the prophecy; this hope is realized fully only in Christ.

The life of Jesus, in fact, as the Gospel of St. Matthew presents it to us, repeats and realizes the authentic Exodus of Israel from Egypt. Jesus is called out of Egypt just like the people of Israel (Mt 2,25). Jesus is the new and authentic Moses, Who gives a law much more perfect than the ancient one (Mt 5, 7); He saves the people of God and organizes it; He nourishes it with the new manna (Mt 14,14). In John's Gospel Jesus is presented as the true paschal lamb, whose blood frees man from sin (Jn 1,17–29); (19,36). He realizes His own Passover, His own passage from this world to the Father, freeing man from sin and leading him into the Promised Land. The same perspective is dominant in St. Paul, who, speaking of the Exodus, says explicitly: ". . . these things came to pass as examples to us . . ." (1 Cor 10,6), and identifies Christ with the paschal lamb: "Christ, our passover, has been sacrificed" (1 Cor 5,7). The death of Christ becomes for Him—by means of His Resurrection—His "Passover," His passage from earth to the Father.

The "passage" of Christ to the Father is also ours, for although sin keeps us slaves, the blood of Christ our Lamb frees us from death. The Holy Spirit makes us pass through the waters of Baptism from death to life. Nevertheless, this salvation, although real and certain, is still only in hope.

e. *The Divine Revelation on Mount Sinai.* The agreement of Sinai constitutes the supreme and most decisive moment of the history of revelation in the Old Testament. Sinaitic revelation is, in fact, the coronation and end of all the preceding revelation. In the Sinaitic *Alliance,* Yahweh, Who has shown His power and His faithfulness toward the people of Israel in extracting them from the slavery of Egypt, takes Israel as His people and constitutes Himself as their guide. The Sinaitic Covenant forms the true nucleus of the entire history of Israel and the foundation of the faith of the Chosen People. Immediately after Josue's conquest of Palestine, the Covenant is renewed at Sichem with the intention of reaffirming the faith of Israel, and at the same time, of fortifying her against the dangers of the Chanaanite religion (Jos 24). During the period of the Kings, the Prophets often insist on the spirit and the demands of the Covenant. The King Josias renews the Sinaitic Covenant (4 Kgs 23). After the Babylonian exile, the Israelites, having returned to Palestine with a deeper awareness of the value of the Sinaitic legislation, renew the Covenant again (Neh 8–10). This Old Covenant will be replaced by the new *Covenant of Christ,* in which Revelation will be brought to its end.

aa. *The Form and Ceremonial of the Covenant.* The idea of a Covenant with God coincides perfectly with the social and cultural environment of the ancient Hebrews and of the Orientals, among whom the agreement between various individuals and clans was of great importance (Jos 9,3–21). Later it became the ordinary form for regulating the relations between different peoples or nations. Still extant are several formularies of these covenants between two kings of the same condition or between a victorious king and his vassal. In the light of these covenants, the elements that constitute and form the Sinaitic Covenant between Yahweh and Israel, as well as their peculiarity, are much more clearly understood, for the formulation of the Sinaitic Covenant follows the model of the other secular alliances of that epoch. In fact the covenant between a superior king and an inferior one has the following elements:

Preamble, in which the name and the titles of the sovereign who establishes the covenant are given. It is done like this in the books of Exodus and Deuteronomy. The formula: "I am the Lord, your God" (Ex 20,2; Deut 5,6), constitutes the preamble. First, He gives His name, Yahweh, and then the principal title in relationship to the people: "your God." This formula emphasizes the direct and personal relationship between God and the people of Israel. The same formula is found throughout Deuteronomy, Leviticus, and Ezechiel.

Historic prologue, which recalls the benefits the sovereign king has given to the vassal king either personally or through his ancestors. With this it is hoped to stimulate the gratitude of the vassal and urge him to accept the clauses. Yahweh too has given great benefits to Israel. The greatest of these was the deliverance from Egypt: "I, the Lord, am your God, Who brought you out of the land of Egypt, that place of slavery" (Ex 20,2; Deut 5,6). In Ex 19,4 it also says: "You have seen for yourselves how I defeated the Egyptians and how I bore you up on eagle wings and brought you here to Myself." Here God appeals to the testimony of the Israelites, who "have *seen*" His wonders. He reveals Himself as *Savior,* not as a static God. The Hebrew is lifted up to the Supreme Being through the contemplation of deeds and not through speculation. Therefore, the relationship that unites Israel with Yahweh is of an experiential order, not a speculative order. Israel *has seen* what God has done with them (Ex 14,30ss).

47

Stipulations or *clauses* of the covenant, are the expression of the will of the sovereign. These clauses impose upon the vassal king the obligation of helping the sovereign king in time of war, of paying him taxes, of being "the friend of his friends", "enemy of his enemies." They are unilateral stipulations that bind only the vassal king. They are always called *debarim,* "words" of the covenant, because they represent the will of the sovereign. According to the Bible, the clauses of the Sinaitic Covenant, contained in the Decalogue (Ex 20,3–17), are designated at times with the expression *debarim,* "words", or "ten words" of the Sinaitic Covenant (Ex 20,1; 34,28; Deut 4,13; 10.4). Hebrew theology has condensed the "theology of the Word" into the theme of the Covenant. If Revelation is manifested through salvific deeds; it is nevertheless gathered together in the form of the Word of God. For this reason the theology of the Word, much developed in the Bible, plunges its roots into the Covenant (Ex 20ss) and into the Promise (Gen 12ss). The Israelites always place the Decalogue and the entire Law within this historical context. In fact, the God Who delivered His people from the slavery of Egypt, could not disappoint them with a suffocating law. On the contrary, Israel adhered to the God of Life by means of the Covenant. Hence the Law of the Covenant was always considered by Israel as a source of life (Ps 19,119). The Word of God is dynamic and contains an energy that renders it fully efficacious (Gen 1,1ss; Ps 33,6; Jn 1,1ss).

This same Word reveals God's salvific plan to us. Thus, the Decalogue of the Covenant is not an asphyxiating letter; it is a Word of God which indicates to us the way of salvation. Ordinarily, the concept of "precepts" of the Decalogue presents us with only an unpleasant aspect . . .; but this is not the biblical perspective at all. Instead, "the precept" appears as the exigency of a loving reply to a gratuitous gift, the deliverance from Egypt. The salvific plan of God develops through a dialogue between God and man. It is God who first attracts man by showing him His goodness through deeds. Man must reply and commit himself.

48

Yahweh alone has brought Israel forth from Egypt. The Chosen People must admit this character of *oneness*. For this reason the Decalogue insists so much on the demand: "You shall not have other gods besides me" (Ex 20,3). The historical experience is what has made Israel know the one God. If Israel believes in Yahweh as the one and exclusive God, it is because Yahweh has manifested Himself as such to His people. Very rare in the history of human thought, monotheism is the fruit of a revelation.

Another exigency of the Covenant, which according to the critics comes from a later gloss, refers to the prohibition of images (Ex 20,4–6). Israel must know that no astral, terrestrial, marine god has done anything in her favor. For this reason Yahweh demands, as a reply, that the Israelites love Him and do His Will. In this sense Deuteronomy comments: "Hear, O Israel! The Lord is our God, the Lord alone! Therefore, you shall love the Lord, your God, with all your heart, and with all your soul, and with all your strength . . . take care not to forget the Lord, Who brought you out of the land of Egypt, that place of slavery" (Deut 6,5.12; cf. Hos 6,6). Furthermore, the sacred author means that no created thing is fit to represent the true nature of God. He reveals Himself as totally distinct from all creation and as a hidden and invisible God. Any worship given to creatures, including the stars, the sun, and the moon, is idolatry.

Love for God is expressed and manifested in respect for the name of Yahweh (Ex 20,7: Second Commandment) and in the sanctification of the Sabbath (Ex 20,8–11: Third Commandent). This is the day reserved for the recalling and celebration of the wonders of the Lord in favor of mankind and particularly in favor of Israel. The first divine wonder was creation and Salvation history constitutes its prolongation. The Exodus was a re-creation. For this reason Hebrew tradition based human activity and the law of weekly rest on the work of creation (Ex 20,11). For the same reasons, the history of salvation (Gen 12ss) was coupled with the history of the origins (Gen 1–11). Deuteronomy studies more the motivation behind the institution of the Sabbath. The reason for this institution was more humanitarian (Dt 5,14s).

The other clauses of the Covenant, or the other seven commandments of the Decalogue (Ex 20,12–17; Deut 5,16–22), regulate relations with one's neighbor. These are based on love and justice, and guarantee family and social life. Hittite pacts obliged the vassal king to be the friend of the friends of the sovereign: Hebrews must love and respect each other because all are "friends" of Yahweh. These clauses, which regulate the horizontal relationships with other men constitute the basis for the formation of the people of God.[23]

Invocation of the gods, as witnesses of the covenant made, and as a warranty of its observance. The Sinaitic Covenant lacks this fourth element. Israel did not recognize gods other than Yahweh, and He had already made His commitment. For the people His Word was enough guarantee of fidelity. In fact, one of the characteristics of the God of Israel was fidelity, fidelity accompanied by mercy from the moment in which the people broke the Covenant with Yahweh. In other biblical texts where the theme of the Covenant appears, the heavens and the earth are cited as witnesses. With this the hagiographers wish to remind the Israelites of the perpetuity of their agreement with Yahweh, for the immutability and the permanence of the heavens and the earth are a constant sign and commemoration of this perpetuity (Dt 4,26; 30,19; 31,28; Is 1,2s; Mi 6,2s; Jer 2,12).

Blessings and *curses,* for the vassal king, according to whether or not he is faithful to the stipulated agreements. These blessings and curses are guaranteed efficacy by the gods who witnessed to them. In the texts regarding the Sinaitic Covenant, blessings predominate (Ex 23,20–33), for in this first moment of generosity and enthusiasm of the engagement of Israel with Yahweh (Amos 5,25; Hos 2,16s; 12,10; Jer 2,2s; Ez 16,8–14), the hagiographer

---

[23] Cf. J. Salguero, "El mandamiento capital y las leyes específicas," in *Cultura Bíblica* 26, 1969, 259–293.

excludes the prospect of infidelity. There is an atmosphere of optimism. Nevertheless a veiled allusion to the possibility of infidelity, with its corresponding curse, is not lacking (Ex 23,21.33).

The curses take on a very great importance in later epochs, when Israel feels in her own flesh the suffering that the "curse of the Covenant" foretold (Deut 27–28; Lev 26). The prophetic oracles of punishment are inspired by the theme of the maledictions of the Covenant; those of salvation are like the prolongation of the blessings of the Covenant. The efficacy of the uttered Word of God is a guarantee of the fulfillment of the blessings or the curses for those who have been faithful or unfaithful to the agreements of the Covenant. In this initial period of the Covenant, the blessing and the malediction do not go beyond the material limits of this earth, for the ancient Hebrews did not believe in the future life nor in retribution after death.

Ceremony or rite of conclusion of the covenant. The vassal king had to make the *oath* of obedience to the agreements contracted. In the Sinaitic Covenant, the oath of the people is expressed in solemn form. "Everything the Lord has said, we will do" (Ex 19,8); "We will do everything that the Lord has told us" (Ex 24,3.7). This oath was accompanied by a symbolic ceremony: ordinarily an animal was slaughtered and cut into pieces to signify the lot of the transgressor (Jer 34,12–22); then the two negotiators walked between the victims (Gen 15,10.17s). Hebrew tradition puts the conclusion of the covenant into relation with a sacred banquet (Ex 24,11), symbol of communion of life with the divinity (Gen 26,28–30; 31, 44.54; Jos 9,11.14), and even more specially with the sprinkling of the blood of the victims. For the Hebrews, as for the Semites in general, the rite of the *sprinkling of blood* has the greatest importance for the blood is the "soul," i.e., the vital principle of man and of beast (Lev 17,14; Deut 12,33). After the acceptance of the clauses of the Covenant, blood is sprinkled on the altar, which represents God Himself, and on the people as a symbol of a communion of life between Yahweh and Israel. This vital communion is expressed even better by the image of a *sacred banquet* celebrated before Yahweh (Ex 24,9–11). Thus are expressed the peace and vital unity established by the Covenant between Yahweh and Israel: Yahweh is the God of Israel, and Israel is the people of God (Ex 24,4–8). In sprinkling the people, Moses pronounces these most important words: "This is the blood of the covenant the Lord has made with you in accordance with all of these words of His" (Ex 24,8). When Christ institutes the New Covenant, He will use this same kind of terminology (Mt 26,28. etc.).

bb. *The Scope and Essence of the Covenant.* The essence of the Covenant is made up of the relationship of vital communion between Yahweh and Israel. Its words express the exclusivism of the God of Israel and His moral exigencies. The Sinaitic Covenant was the true foundation of the constitution of Israel as a people, a community with a definite law, a cult, One God, and a precise religious conscience. Hence, from this moment, Israel is converted into a people directed by Yahweh Himself; she becomes intimately bound to the Will of God. From this moment, Israel knows that she finds herself in a dialogued existence: from one side God calls, demands, compels; from the other, man replies with faith and obedience.

The Sinaitic Covenant creates between Yahweh and the people a *community of interests,* such that Yahweh puts Himself as the guarantee of the safety of the people in every moment (Ex 23, 20.22).

The Covenant establishes *a relationship of property* between Yahweh and the people. In fact Yahweh is the owner of all the earth and of all peoples. However, He has wished to make, from a body of tribes, "His own people," the people of His own "possession" (Ex 19,5s; Lev 26,12). This changes Israel into a "holy" nation, a people dedicated to the exclusive service of Yahweh, a people, reserved for Him and separated from all other peoples. The task of this people here on earth will be to give to Yahweh and to Him alone the worship which is due Him; they are therefore a priestly people (Ex 19,6; Deut 7,6; 1 Pt 2,9).

The intimate relationship of Yahweh with Israel presupposes a special *presence* of God: "I will set my dwelling among you, and will not disdain you. Ever present in your midst, I will be your God, and you will be My people . . ." (Lev 26,11s). This divine presence in the midst of the people is made stable by means of the *Ark* of the Covenant, on which will dwell the glory of Yahweh (Ex 25,8). Within the Ark was the document of the Covenant between Yahweh and Israel. For the validity of every covenant it was required to put the document at the feet of the divinity. The Sinaitic Covenant created a relationship of love between Yahweh and His people, as of father for son, husband for wife (Os 2,14–21; Is 44,1s; 49,14s; Jer 2,2; 3,4.20). Yahweh's love demands from His people a reply of love, which is expressed and concretized through the law. True love for Yahweh is shown in the fulfillment of the Decalogue and of the entire Law. Hence Deuteronomy summarizes the whole of the Law in this precept: ". . . you shall love the Lord, your God, with all your heart, and with all your soul, and with all your strength. Take to heart these words which I enjoin on you today" (Deut. 6,5s). Later, Christ will summarize the Law and the Prophets in the love of God and of neighbor (Mt 22,37–40; Rom 13,10).

The Bible considers the Sinaitic Covenant as something totally gratuitous and willed by God because God Himself takes the initiative in it (Ex 19,3–5). According to Deut 7,7ss, the cause of the Covenant was not the merits of Israel, but the gracious love of Yahweh. Who "loved Israel and brought to fulfillment the oath made to the fathers." On His part, Yahweh did not impose the Covenant but left the free acceptance of the agreement up to the people (Ex 19,7s.10–12). Moses is the *mediator* of the Covenant; he is the *intercessor* of the people before God when Israel sins (Ex 32, 30ss; Nm 14, 13); he is her Savior (Ex 17,8–16; Deut 1–4), the *priest* who sprinkles the blood of the victims on the altar and on the people; he is the man involved with her people in suffering as well as in salvation (Deut 34, 1–5; cf. Deut 34,10–12).

cc. *The Sinaitic Covenant and Christianity.* The Israelites were unfaithful to the Covenant many times throughout their history. The prophets repeatedly recall them to the observance of the Covenant, but the people continue the way of infidelity. Then the prophets announce a new Covenant, in which the heart of men will be transformed so that it will always be faithful to God (Jer 31,31ss; Ez 36, 25–28). This presage becomes reality and presence in Jesus of Nazareth. Like Moses, it is He Who communicates the New Law to the New People of God (Mt 5–7), a law which does not intend to abolish the old one, but to perfect it, reduce it to its essential: love. With the outpouring of His Blood on the cross, Jesus, the new Moses, brings the New Covenant to fulfillment for the redemption of the world (Mt 26, 28). This New Covenant implies the presence of God among men in an unprecedented way: "And the Word was made flesh, and dwelt among us" (Jn 1,14). Furthermore, Christ brings to perfect fulfillment the commandment of love which is the true fulfillment of all the Law: "I give you a new commandment, that you love one another: that as I have loved you, you also love one another" (Jn 13,34). The presence of God among men, in the Word Incarnate, becomes an interior, spiritual presence in the faithful who through Baptism are incorporated into Christ (1 Cor 3,16). He makes Himself nourishment in order to bring the New People of God through the desert (Jn 6,30–32. 53–58). Like Moses, Jesus establishes the Covenant with God during a ritual banquet (Lk 22, 19s), and then He seals it with His own death and the shedding of His blood (Heb 10,5–10). Christ, therefore, has come into this world to fulfill all that the Old Testament prepared and announced. For this reason, the Christian should be able to find in the Sinaitic Covenant a lesson for himself, since the same God who made the Covenant with Moses also sent His only begotten Son into the world to bring the New Covenant to fulfillment. He is the holy, transcendent one, faithful God, the owner of all creation. He is the God of *love* Who calls us to a more intimate life with Him. The religion of the New

Covenant is a living, dynamic religion which should manifest itself in works of charity, it is a personal religion, but it is not individualistic and egoistic.

f. *The Journey of Israel Through the Desert.* The oldest Creed (Deut 26,5–9) presents the deliverance of Israel from Egypt as the unique salvific action of Yahweh. Very soon, this liberation will begin to imply the journey of the Israelites through the desert. In fact, a text of the book of Josue (24,76), very similar to that of Deuteronomy, attributes great importance to the wandering in the desert. Later the theme of the wandering in the desert will be found in all the historical hymns, e.g., Ps 136,16. In the liturgical hymns, the hagiographers attentively consider God's action during the journey through the desert. Israel is almost a mute and passive subject under the action of God. However, theological reflection soon begins to consider Israel's action in this salvific event. Two apparently contradictory tendencies are found in Sacred Scripture:

aa. According to the first tendency, the period in the desert constitutes the time in which the relationship between God and the people of Israel is most pure and perfect; indeed it is the time of the first love between Yahweh and Israel (Deut 29,5s; Jer 2,1–3). The desert is the privileged place of encounter with God. There Israel contemplates Him face to face, she speaks directly with Him, she feels His loving hand guide her, nourish her, defend her (Ex 16; 17; 33; 34). The Deuteronomic tradition insists on this aspect, and the Prophets make use of it to bring the people to conversion, so that they repeat in their own lives that which their fathers did in the desert (Deut 1,30–32; 4,25–40; Hos 2,14; Jer 2,1–3).

bb. According to another tendency, which begins with the prophet Ezechiel (c.20), the desert period becomes the prefiguration of the last judgment. As Yahweh judged the fathers that were unfaithful to Him, He will judge the present generation in the "desert of the peoples" (Ez 20,35). The desert is also a place of temptation: Yahweh subjects the people to a difficult journey through the desert with the intention of seeing their faith and their trust in God, and their willingness to be led by the Lord (Deut 8,2–6). On the other hand, the people tempt God: their infidelity, their murmuring and rebellion put Yahweh's patience, mercy, and faithfulness to the test (Ex 16,3; 17, 2s; Nm 11,13s; Deut 1,25–27).

The insistence of the prophets on the negative aspect of the period in the desert had its origin at the end of the Israelitic monarchy. The prophets realized that the people were in great danger, and indeed were already lost. Under the influence of this idea, they identified their own period with that of the desert in order to better incite the people to penitence. Thus the prophets of the Babylonian period begin to promise a new intervention of God. The same Yahweh will again free Israel from Babylonian slavery, and He will lead her through the desert into her own land (Is 43,16–21; 48,20s; 52,12, etc.).

The sources of the Hexateuch that tell us of Israel in the Sinaitic desert remain between the idea of Jer 2 and that of Ez 20. From one side they present us the mercy of God; from the other, they do not hide the infidelity of Israel. After the apostasy of Israel with the golden calf (Ex 32), Yahweh wanted to clarify His relationship with the people of Israel, because the sin of idolatry had profoundly modified it. God did not intend to abandon His salvific plan; however, from this moment on, He no longer wished to guide the people of Israel personally. For this reason the various traditions of the Pentateuch speak of Yahweh's substitutes.

   i. Yahweh sends an angel to take His place.
   ii. Moses builds the Ark of the Covenant to establish a bond between Yahweh and the people.
   iii. Yahweh accompanies the people by means of His *panim* = face.

All of these substitutes of Yahweh are at the same time the sign of God's salvific Will and the sign of His anger. Indeed the same holiness of God could have destroyed the Chosen People, in case He would have to guide them personally. From this moment on, the relationship between Yahweh and the people of Israel develops through a sign of mediation. The Yahwistic and Elohistic traditions describe the journey of Israel through the desert as a period full of the infidelity of the people and at the same time, full of the mercy of Yahweh.

In this period of the journey through the desert, the goodness, mercy, patience, faithfulness, justice, and loving providence of Yahweh are revealed in a special way.

cc. *Christ and the Religious Significance of the Desert.* We have already said that the psalmists and the sages celebrate the Exodus from Egypt and the journey through the desert (Ps 78; 105; 136; Wis cc.10–19). However, these two stages constitute only the initial realization of the divine salvific plan and the prefiguration of the redemption of the world in Christ.

The fact that Jesus is portrayed fleeing to Egypt and returning from there (Mt 2, 13ss. 19ss), being baptized in the Jordan and fasting for forty days in the desert (Mt 3,13ss; 4,1ss), does not mean that Jesus intended to follow the footsteps of the people of Israel like a pilgrim. What Jesus wants to do is to reproduce in His own life the spiritual itinerary of the Chosen People. When the temptation in the desert was overcome, Jesus manifested Himself as the faithful people, the authentic Israel, the Son of God. Indeed, Jesus did not do as Israel had done in the Exodus, but He overcame the temptation and remained faithful, preferring the word of God to bread, trust to extraordinary miracles, the service of God to the hope of earthly dominion.

Jesus is the Firstborn in Whom are fulfilled the characteristics of the people of Israel. In His own person the extraordinary gifts of the desert period are fulfilled. He is the living water, the bread come down from heaven, the way and the guide on the path, the light in the darkness, the serpent elevated on the cross giving life to all those that look at it, the paschal lamb (Jn 4,10.13ss; 3,14;

6,31–35; 8–12; 19,33–36). It can be said that Jesus Christ is our desert, for in Him we can overcome temptation, and in Him we have perfect communion with God.

dd. *The Church and the Desert.* The authors of the New Testament use the symbolism of the desert in relationship to the Church. The Church lives hidden in the desert until the coming of Christ (Rv 12,6.14). This desert is none other than the withdrawal from the world in which Satan dwells and rules, in order to live a life hidden with Christ in God (Col 3,3). In this desert, the Church will be preserved from pagan contamination, and consequently she will be able to develop a more intimate spiritual life with God. Christians will thus be nourished with the miraculous water of the word of God and with the bread come down from heaven, i.e., with the Eucharist, already prefigured by the manna (Ex 16,4–35; Ps 78,24s; 105, 40; Jn 6,31–35).

St. Paul considers the events of the Exodus figures of the New Testament. In fact God arranges the things of the Old Testament in such a way that they serve us as warning and example (1 Cor 10,11). The journey of the Israelites through the desert constitutes a figure of the journey of Christians through this life. Christians, like the Israelites out of Egypt, are baptized in the cloud and in the water; they are nourished with the bread of life and with spiritual drink. This drink issues forth from a spiritual rock which follows them—Christ (1 Cor 10,2–4). The manna which God gave the Israelites in the desert is for St. Paul and the first Christians a figure of the Eucharistic Bread; and the water issuing forth from the rock (Ex 17,6) constitutes a symbol of the Eucharistic Wine. Furthermore, St. Paul sees in the water (= sea) and in the Spirit (= cloud, symbol of the protective spirit of Yahweh) a symbol of Christian Baptism.

From all of this one can deduce that Christians still dwell in the "desert" but in a sacramental way, inasmuch as they participate in and live superior realities, i.e., grace given through the sacraments. In this world Christian life will always remain under the sign of trial and temptation. From the day in which the Christian enters the Church through Baptism until the day of his death, his life develops continually under the sign of temptation. He must wander through the "desert" of this life, and if he shows himself faithful in the various temptations of this desert, he will become worthy to enter the *Land of the Promise*.[24]

ee. *The figure of Moses in the Pentateuch.* According to Martin Noth (Pentateuch, p 172, etc.), later Israelitic theological reflection brought an idealization of the figure of Moses. In the historical compendiums belonging to the confessions of faith and to the liturgical hymns, Moses appears only occasionally, and does not occupy as predominant a place as he does in the J E D P traditions.

In the Yahwistic tradition Moses is found in all the events from the departure from Egypt to the end of the journey through the desert. But Moses's role in all the conflicts has no special theological importance. In this tradition Moses is in second place in comparison with Yahweh and His action. The narrator gives Moses an unimportant and inconspicuous role in many actions. Yahweh works the miracles alone without the intervention of Moses (Ex 7,17–25; 8,9.17; 9,6.18.33; 10, 13; 14,21b; 16,13ss; Nm 11,18, 31). Even in the miracle of the crossing of the Red Sea, Moses is presented as a spectator on the same level as the rest of the Israelites (Ex 4,20b—23; 14, 13s = J; instead Ex 14,15–18 = P). The purpose of his vocation is to instruct the Israelites in Egypt about the salvific plan of Yahweh (Ex 3,7ss; 16–20). Hence Moses's vocation is not to make him a leader, for in J this belongs exclusively to Yahweh. In short, in the Yahwistic tradition Moses is not a thaumaturge, nor a religious founder; nor a military leader, but a shepherd that God has called to expose the salvific plan of Yahweh to Israel. He is like a prophet (Ex 7,16s; 9,28).

In the Elohistic tradition, instead, the figure of Moses is very different. This tradition presents Moses as the true liberator of

---

[24] Cf. J. Salguero, "El tema bíblico del 'desierto' y su importancia teológica" in *Communion* 2 (1969) 263–274.

Israel from Egypt (Ex 3,10.12). He is God's instrument for bringing the Exodus to fulfillment. In this sense, the staff which Moses receives from God—symbol of the miraculous power that Yahweh has given him—is a characteristic note of the tradition E (Ex 4,17; 9,23; 10,13; 14,16; 17,9). For E Moses is always the initiator, the creator; Aaron is the executor, the mouthpiece (Ex 4,16). The Elohistic tradition also presents Moses as a prophet: Deut 34,10. This prophet does not limit himself to doctrine and to preaching. He is active and takes part in the events with great miracles. He is the greatest of the prophets (Nm 12,7ss). E also speaks to us of the intercession of Moses (Ex 18,19; 32,11ss).

The Deuteronomic tradition presents us a figure of Moses which, theologically speaking, is perfect. In Deut 18,18, Moses is the *nabî,* "prophet", *par excellence,* the figure and model for all prophets. But Deuteronomy says nothing of the miraculous intervention of Moses, or of any other intervention of Moses for that matter. On the other hand, Moses very rarely appears as a leader giving military orders (Deut 1,23; 2, 20ss; 3,18). The particular mission of Moses is the transmission of the word of Yahweh, which was revealed to him by God to preach to the people of Israel. Yahweh does not speak to the people except through Moses: Moses has the role of mediator (Deut 5,20–26); indeed, of patient mediator (Deut 1,37; 3,23–27; 4,21ss; 9,9.18ss; 25ss).

The Priestly tradition presents us with a figure of Moses quite different from that of Deuteronomy. Since this tradition proceeds from the priesthood, importance is given to Aaron. Thus the players of Egypt are executed by Aaron, not Moses (Ex 7,19s; 8,1ss, 12ss, etc.). The divine order is given to Moses and Moses transmits it to Aaron. It is Aaron who struggles directly with the Egyptian magicians. The rod, through which the miracles are accomplished, is now the rod of Aaron (Ex 7,9.19; 8,1.12). Only the last plague is executed by Moses. The P tradition attributes the oblation of sacrifices exclusively to Aaron, and in cases of rebellion it is Aaron, not Moses, who intervenes (Nm 16,4.22;

17,10; 20,6). In the P tradition Moses is not actually a priest, nor a thaumaturge, nor a prophet; he is something superior: Moses is considered a unique personage, the interlocutor with Yahweh, separated from other men (Ex 24,15b–18; 34, 29ss). However, P considers Moses a human being, since it speaks to us of his sin (Nm 20,8ss.12.24; 27,13ss; Deut 32,51).[25]

g. *Josue and the Conquest of the Promised Land.* The mysterious death of Moses does not impede the continuity of the history of salvation. Yahweh Himself brings it to completion, and as the mediators of one stage disappear, He elects new "envoys". Strengthening them with His spirit, He urges them to a new salvific task which is more appropriate to the new stage of history (Deut 1,37ss).

The conquest of Chanaan under Josue has a profound religious and salvific significance. In fact it constitutes the fulfillment of the promise made to the Patriarchs (Deut 1,6–8; Jos 1,2). The possession of the land of Palestine is a gift from God. Israel does not have to do anything but accept the gift, have faith in the word of Yahweh and await His intervention. This is how the crossing of the Jordan (Jos 4,19–25) and the conquest of Jericho should be interpreted, for they are performed through the power of Yahweh without the active intervention of the people (Jos 6).

The difficulties and the failures of the conquest are considered the fruit of the sin of the people. The hagiographer makes use of these circumstances to emphasize the mercy and fidelity of Yahweh (Jos 7). At the dismissal of the people, the sacred author puts into the mouth of Josue a discourse which summarizes perfectly the meaning of the conquest of Chanaan (Jos 23,3.11–14). The events of the conquest of Chanaan repeat the Exodus, as is seen even in the celebration of the first Passover, after crossing the Jordan (Jos 5,10ss; Ex 12–13). The Passover of Egypt has its complement in the Passover of Gilgal. The Promised Land already produces its fruits and blessings. The Hebrews have

[25] Cf. G. Von Rad, *Old Testament Theology,* vol. I, Edinburg-Londra, 1967, p. 289ss.

entered into the land of "repose". This entrance into "rest" prefigures the story of Christian hope (Heb 3,7–4,11; Ps 95, 7–11).

The book of Josue ends with a solemn Covenant, made in the sanctuary of Sichem, before the Lord (Jos 24,1ss). In it Yahweh renews His agreement with the people: He will be their God, their protector and savior; He will accompany them through life. And the people renew their agreement with Yahweh: " . . . we also will serve the Lord, for He is our God" (Jos 24,18). With the renewal of the Covenant of Sichem, the new Israelitic generation makes its own the covenant of the fathers. They are thus introduced personally into the history of salvation. A profound meaning is given to the conquest and possession of the land of Chanaan, which constitutes another step toward the supreme good of the Covenant—the communion of life with God.

The possession of the land of Chanaan given to the Israelites indicates that earthly realities are not incompatible with the history of salvation. On the contrary, man has an essential relationship with the world in which he grows up. Not only is he charged with transforming creation in collaboration with God's work, but he is also the element constituting the concreteness of salvation. However, no earth, no created thing can lead to the definitive and perfect repose. The Israelites who entered into Chanaan discovered this, and it made them think of another repose, another more lasting happiness, in another land where there would be no more suffering, nor death, nor war (Rv 21,4).

With Christ, the possession of the "new land" has become a possibility and a reality (Mt 5,4). This "new earth" is none other than the "kingdom of heaven" (Mt 5,3), in which the supreme good is that of "being with You," begun already here on earth. This therefore deals with a joy that constitutes the definitive "repose", which cannot be reached except through the fearing, loving, and obeying the word of the Lord (Jn 16,22; Heb 4, 1ss.11).

h. *The Epoch of the Judges. Punishment and Repentance.* The book of Judges affirms: "The people served the Lord during the

62

entire lifetimes of Josue and of those elders who outlived Josue and who had seen all the great work which the Lord had done for Israel" (Jgs 2,7). The following generation, however, was far from the salvific successes, and did not "know" Yahweh nor the marvels accomplished on Israel's behalf (Jgs 2, 10). Indeed, Yahweh, unlike Baal, reveals Himself through historical deeds. The experience of salvation history sustained the faith of Israel. A God Who does not manifest Himself remains unknown. For this reason the renewals of the Covenant were meant to recall to the people the soteriological deeds of Yahweh in favor of Israel. Then the fathers passed the historical sacred traditions on to their children.

The descendants of Josue's generation "abandoning the Lord, the God of their fathers, who had led them out of the land of Egypt . . . followed the other gods of the various nations around them, and by their worship of these gods provoked the Lord" (Jgs 2,12). Thus a break with patriarchal history as well as with the Exodus is produced. The constant themes of the book of Judges revolve around four points: infidelity, punishment, repentance, liberation. When Israel, oppressed by her enemies, cries out to Yahweh, He is moved by mercy and raises up a series of leaders to liberate His people. In reading the book of Judges, one gets the impression that God shows greater interest in saving man, than man shows in being saved. The faithfulness of Yahweh to His promises is an idea which dominates throughout the entire Bible.

The Deuteronomic author has a clear awareness that the figure of Josue closes the epoch of Yahweh's salvific interventions in favor of Israel. The *work of Yahweh* for Israel already begins to be considered as something preferred by the generation following Josue (Jos 24,31; Jgs 2,7). Nevertheless Yahweh continues His work in Israel after the occupation of the land of Chanaan. He grants her His protection against her enemies in the difficult periods of the 12th and 11th centuries B.C. The Spirit (= *ruah*) of Yahweh raises up valiant men who become the leaders of His

People, freeing them from their enemies. Yahweh Himself takes active part in the battles in favor of Israel. This new experience of the divine help, with which Yahweh reveals Himself anew to Israel, is expressed in the canticle of Deborah (Jgs 5).

3. *The Monarchy and Divine Revelation.*[26]   After two centuries of existence as a people in Palestine (XII–XI centuries B.C.), because of the threat of the Philistines who had settled along the Palestinian coast almost at the same time the Hebrews settled in Chanaan, Israel feels the need to unite. And so, the various tribes elect Saul as the first king (c. 1020 B.C.). National unity is consolidated under his successor David (1000–970 B.C.). The year 1000 marks a great turn in the political and religious history of the Hebrew people. Under the monarchy Israel becomes a cultured people. The most ancient pages of the Bible, the Yahwistic and Elohistic narrations of the patriarchal origins, the Exodus and the conquest of Chanaan, go back to this time. The monarchy represents the golden age of Hebrew civilization and therefore also the golden age of biblical literature. Biblical theology becomes more elevated and purer; the morality preached by the prophets is more demanding.

In this period, too, God renews with Israel the promises made

---

[26] Cf. J. De Fraine, *L'aspect religieux de la royauté israélite* (Roma 1954); J.S. Croatto, "La institución de la realeza en Israel a la luz de recientes documentos acádicos" in *Revista Bíblica* (Argentina 1959) 71–74; D. N. Freedman-E. F. Campbell, "The Chronology of Israel and the Ancient Near East" in *The Bible and the Ancient Near East* (Londra 1961); A. M. Brunet, "La Théologie du Chroniste" in *Sabra Pagina* (Paris, 1231–1256); G. Ricciotti, *Storia d'Israele,* I, pp. 296–496; H. Van der Bussche, Le texte de la prophétie de Nathan sur la dynastie davidique" in *Ephemerides Theologicae Lovanienses* 25 (1948) 354–394; M. Simon, "La prophétie de Nathan et le Temple" in *Revue d'Histoire et de Philosophie Religieuses* 32 (1952) 41–58; S. Porporato, "Il 'tronno eterno' promesso a Davide nel suo avveramento in *La Civiltà Cattolica* (1949), III, 130–139.265–275; F. Vattioni, "La caduta di Samaria" in *Rivista Biblica* 6 (1958) 368–371; A. Conzales, *Profetas, sacerdotes y reyes en el antiguo Israel* (Madrid Marova, 1962); Y. M. Congar *El misterio del templo* (Barcelona, estele, 1964); G. Von Rad, *Theologie de l'A.T.* (Gioebra, 1963), II/C; M. Tsevat, "The House of David in Nathan's Prophecy" in *Biblica* 46 (1965) 353–356; R. de Vaux, "Jérusalem et les prophètes" in *Revue Biblique* 73 (1966) 481–509.

to the fathers, although in a form corresponding to the new situation. He addresses Himself more particularly to the king, i.e., to the "corporate personality" of another kind [i.e., different from the Patriarchs and Judges] he is responsible for the Covenant and natural mediator for the people He represents. In fact, the figure of the king, idealized and projected into the future, becomes the first vehicle of the blessings promised to Abraham and to his descendants. The cycle of salvation history from Abraham to Josue pivots around the idea of the Promise of the land and descendants. This new cycle pivots instead around the idea of the *Savior King*. The king becomes the vice-ruler for the divinity and the representative of the people. For this reason the covenant of Yahweh with the people is replaced by the new Covenant with the king; with David and his family (2 Kgs 7). In the interpretation that the Bible gives us, God establishes this Covenant with David after "the Lord had given him rest on every side from all his enemies (2 Kgs 7,1). The content of the Davidic Covenant is the election of David and of his descendants as depositories of the kingship in Israel (2 Kgs 7,8–16). Through the prophet Nathan God announces to David a most glorious future, a permanent posterity on the throne of Judah, and the establishment of a paternal relationship with this posterity (2 Kgs 7,5.9.11ss).

This promise, which in David's own mind surpasses himself and Solomon (2 Kgs 7,19ss; 23,5), was already prepared for by the events of his life and by his military conquests. The identification of the king of Israel (David) with the future Messiah begins with Nathan (2 Sam 7,12–16), but even the oracles of Gen 49,10. "The sceptre shall not depart from Judah . . . until he comes to whom it belongs" and that of Nm 24,17: "A star shall advance from Jacob," are only understandable in the light of the military successes of the king or kings of Judah. Until the end of the monarchy (586 B.C.) the oracle of Nathan is retaken and re-specified. The kingly Psalms speak of a king, guardian of the sanctuary, son of Yahweh, ruler (Ps 2,6ss), priest (Ps 110,4), redeemer, and source of blessing (Ps 21,7.9ss), peace and justice

(Ps 72,7.17). The Prophets keep to these same lines, now and then bringing surprising additions (Mi 5,1ss; Jer 23,6; Ez 34,2ss). At times they describe the future Davidic king, i.e., the Messiah and His kingdom with characteristics hard to attain in this world. Isaias, for example (c. 100 B.C.), predicts a Davidic King extraordinarily gifted with the greatest virtues (Is 9,5ss), full of the prophetic spirit, who establishes justice on the earth, communicates to men the knowledge of Yahweh, and for that reason restores the paradisiacal era (Is 11,209). Fortified by such promises, Israel awaits their realization every time a new reign begins (Ps 45,72).

The monarchy therefore offers to God a model for the future configuration of salvation. The Messiah, restorer and redeemer, will be a monarch, and His rule will have the form of a kingdom (2 Kgs 7,12; Nm 24,12). Kingly or Davidic Messianism is one of the first, most precise ideas that God reveals to Israel concerning His future projects. For about 500 years the history of salvation moves along this one precise line: its bearers and propagation are the prophets, preachers, and writers (Is 7,14; 9,11; Jer 23,5; 30,2, etc.).

Beginning from David's own son Solomon, with whom Yahweh renewed the Covenant (3 Kgs 8,62–66), many Davidic kings from David to the Babylonian captivity abandon the Covenant rather than observe it. God punishes the guilty kings. The punishments are in proportion to the gravity of the faults. Yahweh does not permit Israel to become totally perverted through the fault of her princes. He sends punishments which aim at teaching that trust in earthly goods (riches, chariots, horses, forts, political alliances, etc.) should not replace trust in His power. He does not wish to be supplanted in the hearts of His people by earthly things and foreign gods (Is 2,6ss). The various punishments that God sends to unfaithful Israel (epidemics, droughts, schism, civil wars, invasions by foreign arms, Babylonian exile) aim only at re-establishing within the Chosen People the atmosphere favorable to the realization of the Covenant. They prepare the purification of the contaminated mass; the formation of the "Remnant" (Amos 3,12; 5,15; 9,8ss; Is 4,2ss).

Christ, Son of David. The descendant of David, the Messiah King, is Jesus of Nazareth. He is the definitive liberator of the people of Israel from all her enemies. He will bring her to the perfect "repose." Jesus often appears in the Gospels and in the rest of the New Testament as the "Son of David" (Mt 1,1,20; Lk 1,27,32). The simple people recognize Him as the Son of David (Mt 2,1-6; 21,9). But since this title has political implications at the time of Jesus and could compromise His divine mission, the Lord tries to make the people understand the transcendent character of His salvific mission, of his Messianism which is not of this world (Jn 18–19). The death-resurrection-ascension of Jesus constitutes His enthronement at the right hand of God (Ps 2,110) as King (Acts 2,22–36; Phil 2,5–11). Although His kingdom is established, it awaits its final consummation in the heavenly Jerusalem, where God has placed His throne forever (1 Cor 15,23s; Col 3,1; Rv 22,4s,16).[27]

4. *Pre-exilic Prophetism.*[28] Prophetism constitutes another im-

[27] Cf. L. Rubio Moran, *El misterio de Cristo en la Historia de la salvación* Salamanca, Ed. Sígueme, 1968, p. 182; J. Cantinat, *La pedagogia di Dio nella Bibbia,* p. 80ss.

[28] J. Chaine, *Introduction a la lecture des prophétes* (Paris 1932); G. Ricciotti, *Storia d'Israele,* I (Torino 1932) pp. 31–395; G. Rinaldi, "Sintesi della dottrina religiosa dei Profeti" in *Aevum* 25 (1951) 193–209.305–323; J. M. Gonzales Ruiz, "La restauración de Israel en los Profetas" in *Estudios Bíblicos* 11 (1952) 157–187; O. Eissfeldt, "Thé Prophetic Literature" in *The Old Testament and Modern Study* (Oxford 1951); A. Neher, *L'essence du prophétisme* (Paris 1955); J. Gilbert, "Prophétisme et attente d'un Messie prophète dans l'ancien Judaisme" in *L'Attente du Messie* (Paris 1954) p. 85–130; H. H. Rowley, "Ritual and Hebrew Prophets" in *Journal of Semitic Studies* 1 (1956) 338–360; Id., "The Nature of the O.T. Prophecy in the Light of Recent Studies" in *The Servant of the Lord* (Londra 1952) p. 89–126; B. Vawter "De justitia sociali apud prophetas praeexilicos" *Verbum Domini* 36 (1957) 93–97; A. Gelin, "Messianism" in *Dictionnaire de la Bible Supplément,* 5 (Paris 1957) coll. 1165–1212; E. Massaux-P. Grelot, *La Venue du Messie. Messianisme et Eschatologie* (Paris 1962); C. Tresmontant, *La doctrine morale des prophétes d'Israel* (Paris 1958); S. Garofalo, *La nozione profetica del "Resto d'Israele"*

portant moment in the history of Revelation in the Old Testament. In this period Hebrew theology undergoes a great evolution. The different prophets, contemporary as well as successive, concur to perfect, deepen, and spread among the people the religious faith, the idea of God, and Messianism. Prophetism accompanies almost all the religious and civil history of Israel. It is the soul of biblical history. Indeed God reveals Himself, intervening in the life and in the history of the people of Israel. It is He Who dominates all of history and directs it towards His plans of love. But with their words the prophets explain and clarify the historical events, presenting to the people above all their religious meaning. The prophets are nothing but preachers who speak in the name of Yahweh. Under divine light, they discover the Will of God in events, and thus they present to Israel and to the other nations what the Lord wants from them. The message to be communicated to men is at the center of the existence of these chosen men. The prophets speak with absolute divine authority, as authentic interpreters of the Will of God. Their mission is always confirmed by a perfect conformity of their teaching with the Yahwistic religion (Deut 13,2–6) by the fulfillment of the things they announce (Deut 18,21s), and by the attitude they assume before the poor and the oppressed, defending them against the kings and the rich. Their words, often in contrast with the customs of their times and the interests of the mighty, stir up persecutions against them (Amos 3,8).

Among the numerous prophets enumerated in the Bible, we have groups or corporations of prophets called "sons of the prophets," types of confraternities which under the guidance of Elias and Eliseus work for the purity of the faith and of the worship of Yahweh. These develop principally around the

(Roma 1952); A. Gonzales Nunez, *Profetas, sacerdotes y reyes en el antiguo Israele* (Madrid, Marova, 1962); J. Lindblom, *Prophecy in Ancient Israele* (?Oxford, 1962); G. Von Rad, *Théologie de l'A.T.*, II (Gioebra 1963); S. Granild, "Jeremia und das Deuteronomium" in *Studia Theologica* 16 (1962) 135–154; W. F. Albright, *Yahweh and the Gods of Canaan* (Londra 1968).

sanctuaries, like those of Rama, Bethel, Gilgal. They are young volunteers who dedicate themselves spontaneously to the service and to the cause of Yahweh. Then among the prophets properly called there are some that have left no writings. The most important are Samuel, Nathan, Elias (the champion of monotheism against the idolatry introduced into Israel by Achab, at the urging of his wife Jezabel: (3 Kgs 17; 4 Kgs 2), Eliseus, Micheas ben Yemla (4 Kgs 2–8;22). The prophets who wrote are Isaias, Jeremias, Ezechiel, Daniel, and the twelve Minor Prophets.

The Israelite prophets are men of action. Their life is a struggle which requires much courage because it is exposed to many dangers (3 Kgs 22,26s; Jer 1,7s; 20,2s; 37,15s). They are considered heralds of Yahweh and announce His Will and His Word. They judge happenings in the divine light, they stigmatize hypocritical and formalistic worship, idolatry, social injustice and corruption of customs. They announce divine punishments which, in the perspective of the Covenant, are not an end in themselves, but an attempt to bring about the conversion of the people and lead them back to God. Finally they open up a horizon of restoration and salvation.

Amos appears around the year 750. He is a shepherd of Thecua, near Bethlehem. He preaches and prophesies in Samaria under Jeroboam II, vigorously denouncing the injustices (oppression of the humble, corruption of the judges), the dissoluteness of customs and the formalism of worship (Amos 2,6ss; 5,12.21s; 6, 4ss). He foretells punishment, the day of the Lord (Amos 5,16ss). Nevertheless Amos unveils a Messianic perspective, and for the first time in prophetic literature the "remnant" is spoken of (Amos 5,15).

Osee, just a little after Amos, denounces the same abuses, but he insists more on religious life and worship. He combats the formalism of the sacrifices in the temple and foretells the punishment of Israel (Osee 6,6; 8,13). The punishment will serve for the purification of the Chosen People, and all the trials will be a calling from the divine love for the people to return to the Lord.

The love that Yahweh has for Israel is represented by the symbol of conjugal love and by the image of Yahweh's paternal and maternal love (Osee 11,4). The second chapter of Osee, dedicated to the God-Spouse, is one of the most beautiful pages of the Bible. In spite of all the infidelities of Israel, Yahweh, Who has punished her, will pardon her with His great mercy (Osee 11,9). *Osee is the prophet of God's love.*

Isaias is a cultured man of a good family in Jerusalem; he carries on his ministry in the capitol from the year 740. His message is characterized by the faith and holiness of Yahweh: "the holy one of Israel"; he preaches constantly on justice and devotion, without which worship has no value (Is 1,15–17; 29,13). One must put one's entire trust only in God and not in political alliances which put fidelity to Yahweh in danger (Is 8,12s). He announces punishment, the day of the Lord, but at the same time he foretells the perseverance of a remnant (Is 10,12).

Isaias presents the word of God as full of dynamism: "The Lord sent a word into Jacob and it lighted upon Israel" (Is 9,8). The prophet considers the word of God as an arrow that falls from heaven and produces its effect (Is 55,11). According to Isaias, the divine word contains a great energy which fulfills in a progressive way: it stirs up, moves and interprets history. God is the absolute sovereign of all of history and of the politics of the kingdom of Judah. Consequently, every search for human alliances is an attempt against this sovereignty. This concept springs from Isaias' basic theological idea: *Yahweh is the Holy One of Israel* (Is 1,4, etc.). The holiness of God implies also in Him a great richness of life, power and goodness. In Is 6, God appears as the "King of tremendous majesty," Whose glory fills the earth. His intervention is not a judgment of condemnation, but, through purification, the offering of salvation to the "holy seed" (Is 6,13). God's action corresponds to a plan laid down by Him (Is 5,12; 10,12; 14,24; 18,24), and this plan is irrevocable (Is 31,2). The God Who establishes it is Yahweh, the God of Israel, the living God of the history of salvation. Man must reply to God's plan with faith. Faith in God is indispensable for life (Is 7,9; 28,16; 30,15). The people must live in the trustful certainty that help and salvation can come only from God (Is 8,17; 25,9; 26,8). He is their only support and defender (Is 10,20; 31,6). Sion is the stronghold and refuge of His people (Is 14,32). Yahweh lays in Sion "a chosen stone, a cornerstone, a precious stone as a foundation. He who believes will not be shaken" (Is 28,16). Isaias is the prophet of faith. He awaits a national awakening, which coincides very well with his kingly Messianism (cc. 9–11).

Isaias presents us with a Messiah who will be the ideal king of a universal kingdom with its center at Jerusalem (Is 1,26s; 2,2s; 9,5s; 11,10ss). The idea of a future reconstruction of Israel is expressed by the notion of the "remnant." The "remnant" will be as a sprout, a "holy seed" (Is 4,2s; 6,13). The seed of Jacob, the new Israel, must blossom and bear abundant fruits (Is 27,6ss). The Messianic prophecies of the "book of Emmanuel" (Is 9–11) are famous. A descendant of David, the Messiah will make justice and peace reign upon the earth, and He will diffuse the Knowledge of the Lord (Is 9,5a). He is not only the successor of David, but also Emmanuel, i.e., "God with us" (Is 7,14). "And the spirit of the Lord shall rest upon Him." (Is 11,2s). At His side, in the place of the sword, He will carry justice, and He will be the Prince of Peace. Within His boundaries no evil shall appear, neither will anyone be hurt, for with the breath of His lips He shall slay the wicked. Just as in the beginning, the animals will be at peace with man. The wolf and the lamb, the cow and the bear, the lion and the ox shall pasture together (Is 11,4–7). Hence, His kingdom does not seem to be of this earth, and the Messiah, more than a king of Palestine, seems to be king of an earthly paradise.

Micah, a contemporary of Isaias, insists strongly on divine judgment (Mi 2–4; 6,1–2), on the destruction of Samaria (1,6s; 6,16), and on the ruin of Sion (3,9–12). Because of his humble country origin (in this and in the content of his book he shows a great resemblance to Amos), Micah feels very deeply the injustice and hypocrisy of the rich of the land (2,1s; 3,1–12; 6,10–12; 7,1ss), who are bringing the people of God to ruin. At the same time, with a highly appropriate formulation, he presents the ideal of life proposed by the preceding prophets: justice, faithful love, humble submission (cf. Am 5,24; Hos 6,6; Is 2,9–19).

The message of Micah is not only a prophecy of misfortune, he also speaks of the hope of the Messianic future. From the little town of Bethlehem "shall come forth He who is to be the ruler in Israel: His going forth is from the beginning, from the days of eternity" (5,1–5). Micah also speaks of the "remnant of Israel" (4,6ss; 5,2.6s). His writings are later enriched in the exilic and post-exilic periods, during which the hope of a Messianic restoration is translated into the promise of a permanent reign of Yahweh in Sion (4, 1–5; 7,8ss).

Zephaniah, Nahum, Habakkuk. In the 7th century B.C., in which these prophets live, the Assyrian empire is ruined. Even the Kingdom of Judah, the only one left, undergoes the difficulty of that period. Josiah undertakes an energetic religious reform (4 Kgs 23,4ss), but it is only an ephemeral restoration.

Zephaniah emphasizes above all the theme of the "day of the Lord," which assumes cosmic dimensions (Zep 1,14–18). He stresses the judgment and punishment of Yahweh against Judah because of sin, particularly idolatry. But the end of his book opens up a vision of hope with the themes of the "remnant" (3,11ss), the promise concerning Sion (3, 14–18), and the return from exile (3,19–20).

Nahum intones an enthusiastic hymn to Yahweh, the Lord of History, Who saves Israel (2,3) and guides all of history with power (2,14). This idea is important for his time.

Habakkuk knows of the invasion of the Babylonians and he lives its consequences in anguish. This stirs up in him a theological problem analogous to that of Job: how can one reconcile the piteous condition of Israel with the justice of God (1,2ss). He synthesizes the answer in this expression: ". . . the just shall live by faith" (2,4; cf. Gal 3,11; Rom 1,17). The openness of man to the plan of God is the condition and guarantee of God's fidelity to His Covenant. Habakkuk's deep trust in the faithfulness of God inspires the hymn of 3,1–19, which ends with a cry of jubilation in God the savior (3,18).[29]

Jeremiah has a great importance and influence on the theological reflection concerning the fact and the nature of Revelation in the Old Testament. He is called by God to the prophetic ministry, and the Lord Himself constitutes him a prophet with a kind of rite: the Lord puts forth His hand and touches his mouth, signifying that the Lord places His word into the mouth of Jeremiah (Jer 1,9). From this moment on he remains under the influence of the omnipotent word of God. At times this is pleasant nourishment for the prophet; at others, it is reason for his suffering and persecution (Jer 20,8–9). His prophetic ministry begins about the year 627 B.C. and he follows it with exemplary fidelity throughout the rest of his life. Jeremiah is a great patriot and because of the exigencies of his prophetic mission, he finds himself obliged to always announce calamities. He is of a peaceable character and must struggle continually against ruthless enemies, he is affectionate, and suffers persecution and solitudes. His life seems an apparent failure, but in reality Jeremiah has an extraordinary influence on Israel's religious evolution during and after the Babylonian captivity. He foretells and lives a more spiritual, interior, profound religion. He is the father of personal prayer with God, of trusting dialogue with Yahweh.

The tragedy of Israel, which terminates with the exile, is first felt by Jeremiah as a personal suffering and is expressed in his "confessions" (11,18–12,6; 15,10–21; 17, 12–18; 18,18–23; 20,7–18). His life of isolation, misunderstanding, sorrow and persecution is a figure of Israel, who must be purified in the crucible of suffering. Jeremiah has an acute sense of sin, which he analyzes in a profound manner. By sinning, Israel has abandoned God, giving herself over to idolatry (1,16; 2,13–19; 16,11). The people refuse

[29] Cf. A. Rolla, I Profeti su *Il messaggio della Salvezza* (Torino 1967) p. 483ss.

to "know Yahweh" (4,22; 9,23); this leads to violence, theft, extravagant luxury, lying, deceit, social injustice. The prophet shows a deep perception of the almost hopelessly sinful situation of the people of Israel. Israel's sin is not considered a simple rebellion against God (13,23), but rather a rupture of the divine plan in which the Chosen People have been given an extraordinary mission. Jeremiah emphasizes the exceptional destiny of the Chosen People and Yahweh's love for Israel at the time of the Sinaitic Covenant and the conquest of the Promised Land (2,2ss; 3,18; 10,16; 11,4s; 13,11; 14,21). In Jeremiah God presents Himself with characteristics analogous to those of Osee: He has the tenderness and love of a spouse and of a father (2,2; 3,4.19; 31,9.20). But at the same time, He is God the Creator (27,5); the Lord of History (1,15; 18,5–10; 28,14), just and merciful (3,12; 11,20; 31,3; 32,18). Hence the prophet insistently invites to conversion, which is considered as a return to intimacy with God, a purification of the heart (3,12ss; 4,1ss,14). The messages of salvation which Jeremiah (cc.30–33) addresses to Israel are among the most vivid pages of the Old Testament. Salvation is a work of Yahweh, for He is the absolute Lord of history (7;26). After the purification of the exile, His intervention will be crowned by a return to Sion, which is to be rebuilt (31,1–22). The return of the exiles will establish a union with God more marvelous than that of the Sinaitic Covenant (31,22; 23,7s). It will be a new Covenant, "written in the heart," which will give an intimate knowledge of Yahweh (31,33s). It will be the universal restoration, for all the nations will take part (3,17; 12,15–17; 16,19–21); it will be brought about by a "just shoot," a descendant of David (23,5s; 33,15–22). Hence the Messianism of Jeremiah is still Davidic.

Deuteronomy. Besides the prophetic writings already mentioned, other books of the Old Testament were gathered and published while the effects of the Babylonian exile were still being felt. The most important perhaps was Deuteronomy, which seems to come from the nothern kingdom of Israel. The *Deuteronomist* is the author of four great discourses, which he attributes to Moses in order to give them greater importance and authority. Deuteronomy shows a generous devotion towards God and a great benevolence towards society and towards man. Even the duties of man are presented with profound and tender sentiment. For the Deuteronomist the other gods have no power; Yahweh is the source of all power, all authority, all creation. He is just, and nothing escapes His justice. His nature is different from that of any other being; therefore He cannot be represented by any created being. No place is worthy for His worship, if He Himself has not chosen it. Yahweh makes His Will and His thought known through the prophets. The basis of the relationship between Yahweh and Israel is the divine election, which is not founded on juridical rapport but on the mercy and love of God. On this love rests the entire history of Israel. The fundamental precept of Deuteronomy is love towards God and towards men. This love is shown in worship and in the observance of the law.

Two tendencies meet in Deuteronomy—the prophetic and the legalistic, which come from the prophetic-priestly class. Under the new historical-doctrinal perspective of the time, the traditional concept of the word of God undergoes a certain modification. In the Sinaitic documents the word *debarim* is first used to designate the Decalogue (Ex 20) or the Code of the Covenant (Ex 20,22–23,19) or the legislation of the Exodus (20,1; 24,3s.8; 34,1.28). The Deuteronomist instead calls the Decalogue: the *ten words* (Dt 4,12ss; 5,19; 10,2.4) and extends this designation to all the clauses of the Covenant (Dt 17,19; 27,3.8.26; 28,58; 69), i.e., this expression designates the whole complex of moral, civil, religious and criminal laws. Thus the expression *dabar*, "word," comes to designate the whole Mosaic law (Dt 4,2; 28,69; 30,14; 32,42). And in this way *dabar* and *Torah* come to designate the same thing. In Deuteronomy there is also the equalizing of the legislative word and the prophetic word. In the last books of the prophets and in the sapiential books *dabar* and *Torah* complete all of Revelation. This means that the *debarim* of Sinai assumes its full significance if it is considered in the complex of all the Deuteronomic laws. Besides the precept, Deuteronomy offers historical evocations, promises and threats (4,32), that aim at stirring up love and reverence for the law. This way of acting offers us an analogy with the prophetic exhortation. In fact, Deuteronomy presents similarities to the prophetic genre, especially in regard to religious interiority, importance attributed to the idea of the Covenant, and future sanctions for the infidelity of the people.

5. *Revelation in the Period of the Babylonian Captivity.*[30]

The destruction of the Davidic monarchy, the fall of Jerusalem (586 B.C.) with the ruin of the Temple, and the exile, represent the most critical time in the history of Israel. A series of anxious questions oppresses the hearts of the Israelites. What happened to the word of God? Where are the promises made to David, to the Holy City and to the Temple? Where is the power of Yahweh before the gods of Babylon? Have they beaten Him? Are these gods "vanity" as the prophets preached? Where is the justice and faithfulness of Yahweh? The people found themselves in danger

[30] C. J. Gadd, *The Newly Discovered Babylonian Chronicle* (Londra (1923); D. J. Wiseman, *Chronicles of Chaldaean Kings* (Londra 1956); F. VAttioni, "I settant'anni della cattività" *Rivista Biblica Italiana* 7 (1959) 181 ss; J. B. Pritchard, *Ancient Near Eastern Texts* (= ANET, Princeton 1950); F. Spadafora, *Collettivismo ed Individualismo nel VT* (Rovigo 1953); M. Noah, Daniel und Hiob in Ezechiel XIV" in *Verbum Testamentum* 1 (1951) 251–260; A. M. Dubarle, "Le don d'un coeur nouveau" in *Bible et Vie Chrétienne* Ch. 14 (1956) 57–66; J. Steinmann, *Le prophète Ezéchiel et les debuts de l'exil* (Paris, Cerf, 1953); C. Stuhmueller, "The Theology of Creation in Second Isaiah" in *Catholic Biblical Quarterly* 21 (1959) 429–467; J. Coppens, "Le Serviteur de Yavé: Vers la solution d'une énigme" in *Sacra Pagina,* I (Paris 1959) 434–454; H. H. Rowley, *The Servant of the Lord* (Oxford 1965); P. Grelot, "La dernière étape de la rédaction sacerdotale" in *Verbum Testamentum* 6 (1956) 174–187; A. Gelin, *Les pauvres d'Israel* (Paris, Cerf, 1953); versioni italiana, spagnola, ecc.; J. Salguero "Finalidad del dolor según el A.T.: Soluciones definitivas del problema del dolor" in *La Ciencia Tomista* 90 (1963) 369–395; IDEM, "La cautividad de Babilonia y la espiritualidad del dolor" in *Selecciones de Teologia* 4, n. 16 (1965) 305–311.

of losing faith and hope (Ex 37,11). However precisely in the moment when all seems lost, Israel's faith surges forth with greater power. In the plans of Divine Providence the exile is a trial that serves to purify the Chosen People. What should be annihilation is converted into a wonderful renewal. This "turning of the tables" is influenced by the prophets: Jeremiah, Ezechiel and Deutero-Isaiah.

Reading the writings of Jeremiah, the exiles reflect on past history in order to deduce the explanation for their present situation. At the same time they find in the writings a presage of consolation based on hope in the future. The prophets of the exile insist on seeing in it the punishment for the sin of infidelity to the Covenant of Yahweh. Even the exile had a purpose: to purify the people in their faith. It is necessary that the people feel themselves deprived of all the material institutions: city, monarchy, temple, in which they have placed their trust. Thus they are obliged to trust in Yahweh alone. In this way, reflecting on their past, the people will return to Yahweh; and be converted to their God (Jer 3,25; Lam 5,21).

a. *Ezechiel.* His prophetic activity takes place between 593 and 570. Ezechiel's personality is very complex. Like Jeremiah, he is a priest and a prophet. Ezechiel's message is addressed to a difficult and hostile environment: for him Israel's fault is that of having profaned God's holiness through idolatry (5,11; 8,7ss; 14,3ss; 22,23ss; 24,6ss). The central idea of Ezechiel's message is the magnificant concept of the divinity of Yahweh Who is the God of glory, Whose power has cosmic dimensions. In the vision of Ezechiel's vocation (cc. 1–3) we find the highest expression of the majesty, power, and omnipotence of Yahweh. This absolute sovreignty of God is manifested in the history of Israel: Yahweh is indeed the Lord of History, Whom Israel must recognize (10, 5–20; 20,38–44). In spite of Israel's obstinancy, Yahweh will rule over her, showing the power of His arm (20,33). Yahweh has loved Israel with the solicitous care of a mother and of a spouse; therefore, when this love is betrayed, it is transformed into passionate jealousy (16,38; 23,25). The two themes of sanctity and of divine jealousy increase the efficacy of the recall of the Sinaitic Covenant and of the Promised Land. On the other hand the knowledge of the infidelity of the people and the highest concept of God are at the basis of the prophet's mission (33,1ss). The theme of conversion also returns insistently in Ezechiel.

There is a new and original aspect in Ezechiel: the idea of individual responsibility (14,12–23; 18,1ss; 36,10–20). After the destruction of Jerusalem (33,1–20), Israel no longer exists as a nation. For this reason the word of God is addressed to the exiles as individuals, in order to invite them to penitence and to lift up their spirits. This explains why Ezechiel insists on individual retribution and on the formation of the conscience of men as individuals. Almost as a spiritual director he intends to form a new people of Israel (9,14–21; 33,1–9).

After the destruction of Jerusalem and the exile, Ezechiel assumes a new attitude towards Israel: it is the message of consolation and hope. The exiles will make up the "Remnant" of the new Israel (11,13–20; 20,32ss). The theme of the "remnant" is deepened through the projection into eschatological times, when Yahweh will realize the restoration of Israel (37,1–14) in the renewed land (36,33ss), liberated of the unfaithful (20,38; 34,20). In the members of the new Covenant Yahweh will place His spirit which will transform their heart (36,23–38). This transformation will be worked by Yahweh through "His servant David" (34,23). The renewed Israel will be the living witness of the holiness of God's name (36,22s). His conception is nationalistic. In Ezechiel post-exilic theocracy assumes a strong priestly and liturgical coloring, the vital center of the new kingdom will be the Temple (40,1–43; 17); divine cult will be the means of showing their exclusive belonging to the God of the Covenant (43,18–46; 24); the Promised Land, irrigated and fertilized by the water issuing forth from the Temple (47,1ss), will be the place of Israel's happy existence.

For Ezechiel the necessity of an integral purity is the indispensable condition for being able to value the Messianic Jerusalem, under its new name, "Yahweh is there."

The book of Ezechiel has a marked apocalyptical character. Perhaps this explains the great number of visions and symbolic actions that we find in it (1,1ss; 2,8–3,9; 8,11; 37; 40,1–48,35). Another characteristic of Ezechiel is the pastoral way of presenting the prophetic word.

b. *Deutero = Isaiah.* In the so-called Deutero-Isaiah (40–66) two parts are distinguishable: Is 40–55 = the "Book of Consolation," and Is 56–66 = "Trito-Isaiah." These two parts belong to the period of the Babylonian Captivity, or they are subsequent to it.

The sacred author addresses himself to the skeptical and discouraged exiles, and to give them courage he invites them to look at the heavens. Yahweh has created the stars and He calls them each by name. All of them obey Him, for they follow in every way the order the Creator established (Is 40,26; 45,12; 48,13). His absolute power over all creation constitutes the foundation of His omnipotent action in history (Is 44,24). The transcendence of Yahweh is manifested first of all by the order of the universe. Yahweh is the Lord of the nations and of the forces of nature, for He has created everything from nothing by His word. This idea which attributes creation and even the preservation of the world to the omnipotent word of God seems to have begun in the more developed theology of the Deutero-Isaiah (48,13). Its classical exposition is found in the narration of the priestly tradition (Gn 1,1–2, 4a), which was formulated in this same period. The "Book of Consolation" considers the divine *dabar* in its historic and cosmic dynamism. The word of God dominates all of history and shows us its course and its meaning (45,19; 48,16). What God has said is true and irrevocable, for He has sworn thus (45,23).

In Is 42,9 and 48,3–8, the fulfillment of the preceding prophecies is an argument in favor of the fulfillment of the future things already foretold, i.e., the deliverance from the Babylonian Captivity, the return to Palestine and the restoration of Israel,

79

eschatological universalism. For Deutero = Isaiah, history has an aim and a determined finality, for God keeps in His hands the two extreme poles of history (41,4; 44,6; 48,12). Thus the word of God predicts events, stirs them up and fulfills them. History itself then is intelligible because it is progressively revealed to men according to the Divine Will, and it is explained with the words of the prophets. Deutero = Isaiah teaches the infallible efficacy of the word of God which fulfills the Divine Will with the same fidelity as the elements of nature (55,10s). Here the divine word is represented as a dynamic reality and the creator of history. In a certain way, the divine word is also personified (cf DBS, 5, 708s).

The "Book of Consolation" has a very lofty concept of God the Creator-Savior. Its theocentrism has an essentially salvific character. Yahweh is God, the only Creator (40,4.12.21ss; 42,5; 43,7; 45,9ss, 18). The hagiographer passes from the creative intervention to the salvific intervention of Exodus. The constant repetition of the formula: "I the Lord," "I am the Lord," is already a reminder of that period, which is also found in many references to the election-liberation-Covenant of God with Israel (41,8ss; 43,1ss; 44,1ss.21ss). The divine name, "Yahweh is the Holy One of Israel," (41,14.16.20; 43,14s) is also very common. Nevertheless, Exodus is only one stage in the history of salvation, and it will be surpassed by the future intervention of God. It will be the Messianic kingdom, eschatological in character, into which Yahweh will gather all the dispersed from the four corners of the world (43,5s; 49,17s.22s). Yahweh Himself will march before His people, as in the days of the Exodus, and then the God of Israel will manifest Himself to every man (40,5; 52,10). The loving intervention of God will create "a Covenant of peace," "an eternal Covenant" (54,8.10), a definitive renewal of the Davidic Covenant (55,3). This will bring peace and prosperity to Israel, instructed and protected by Yahweh Himself, Who will write His law in their hearts (48,17.19; 51, 3.7; 54.1ss).

Deutero-Isaiah emphasizes insistently Israel's privilege in being the Chosen People (45,1; 51,16.22; 52.4ss). Yahweh is her Spouse, who in spite of the infidelity of His partner does not demand divorce (50,1). But the salvific work of Yahweh is not founded on a God who lives in Jerusalem but on the Lord God of nature and history. This brings Deutero-Isaiah to consider salvation with a universal spirit (40,15.20.23; 41,1.5.9; 42,10ss). All men of good will are invited to the banquet of the new Covenant (55,1s).

Isaiah recalls the vocation of Israel: she is a witness and a mediator. She gives witness to the one living God, Who is the Creator and universal Savior, Who guides toward eschatological fullness. Furthermore Israel is the mediator in the conversion of the nations, both because God is glorified in her, and because proselytism was beginning at this time (45,22ss).

With the exception of the Servant of Yahweh passages, the Messianism of Deutero-Isaiah is presented without the Messiah. Yahweh works without intermediaries (43,15; 44,6; 52,7). But in the canticles of the Servant of Yahweh (42,1–4; 49,1–7; 50,4–9; 52,13–53,12) the doctrinal progress concerning the preceding Messianic prophecies is very perceptible and evident. Who is this Servant of Yahweh? Is he perhaps an idealization of the "Remnant of Israel?" (41,14ss; 46,3). Or is he a personage that synthesizes and transfigures the features of the life of Moses or even of Jeremiah? It is very probable that it is this way but these features are immensely surpassed in the mysterious description of the Servant of Yahweh. He will stipulate the definitive Covenant with Israel (42,6), but at the same time his mission will be universal, for it will be a light to the nations (49,6). His teaching mission (50,4) will be carried on in spite of strong opposition (50,5–9). His sufferings and his death will have a redemptive and expiatory value (53.5.10). Hence the Messianism of the canticles of the Servant of Yahweh is not a royal messianism, but an expiatory one. The Servant must bear the sins of the people and expiate them in his own flesh in order to obtain the forgiveness and liberation of the people of God: The Messiah is no longer a warring deliverer, who defeats His enemies with the strength of His arm, but a gentle and humble Servant Who will liberate His people and convert the world to God through His own sufferings and humiliation.

In these canticles the Messiah becomes a poor and humble Messiah. He is presented covered with confusion and shame. He will repeat in His life not the glorious feats of David, but the experience of Jeremiah, the martyr prophet; of Job, the just man who suffers innocently; of the exiles, persecuted and despised for the sins of the entire nation. In His life He will endure every repugnant, humiliating, upsetting thing that Israel has tasted. "Despised and the most abject of men," struck hard, indeed "a man of sorrows and acquainted with infirmity" (Is 53,3), the Servant of Yahweh does not turn away from anyone, neither does He withdraw from His unjust lot (Is 50,6). But through sufferings, weakness and powerlessness "He will see the light" (53,12). "Humble and poor" (Zec 9,9), "He will bring the gospel to the poor," He will heal the contrite of heart, He will console the "afflicted," He will judge with justice and will utter "just sentences on the wretched of the earth" (Is 66,1–2).

The canticles of the Servant of Yahweh, i.e., of humble and suffering Messianism, find their historical setting only in the Babylonian Exile. We are at the most tragic turn of the history of Israel, but also at the most salutary point of the history of Revelation. The new Israel which returns from exile is a remnant of poor, humble, prostrated people. Earlier Zephaniah had already invited them to find safety and salvation in making themselves "poor and small" before the Lord (Zep 3,12; 2,3). "To make one's self poor" is the new motto that is born from the environment of the Babylonian exiles. Prophets (Is 57,15; 66,1s) and psalmists (Ps 9–15; 20,22,25–26,34,37,69,74,76,86,103,149) announce it with their pressing invitations. Future salvation is by now in the hands of the "humble." They have taken the place of the great and powerful (Is 57,15; 66,1s). The voice of the "poor" exiles will be silenced no longer. It reappears in the sapiential writings (Sir 3,19s; Bar 2,18; Dn 3,38.87), in the apocalyptic writings (Is 25,1–5), in the Lamentations (c.3), in the Qumran literature (1 QH5,21s; 11,32s; 18,14; 1QS 11,9–13; 13,13.14; 14,17; 1 QpHb 1,2s.6.10), and flows directly into the New Testament (Lk 4,18; Mt 5, 3; 11,28). Without the "poor of Yahweh" we would not have the "poor in spirit" of evangelical spirituality.

The spiritualization of Messianism, offered by the poems of the Servant of Yahweh, makes the pages of Isaiah among the most profound texts of biblical Revelation. Indeed, in Isaiah's Servant of Yahweh, the primitive Church sees Jesus, Who fulfills this mission completely. The Acts of the Apostles call Christ "the Just One," the "Holy One," the "Servant of the Lord" (3,13ss; 4,21–30; 7,52).

c. *The Priestly Tradition* (P)—This tradition comprises different codices which were later united and expanded (cf. DBS5, 505). In the priestly tradition the divine *dabar* is often found in a legalistic sense. This is true not only in the legislative or juridical part, but also in the historical narratives. The narrated events often carry in themselves a normative value, or they give occasion to the promulgation of a law (Gn 1,29.17,23; Ex 12,1; 25,1; 40,1; Nm 5,4; 17,1; 26,52; 35,1). But even though the priestly tradition does give great importance to legislation, the priestly history looks first of all at its theological meaning. For this reason the hagiographer dwells longer on certain more significant facts, above all in the narration of creation. This deals with an action completed in time, but the sacred author intends to affirm that all the things of the universe, even man, exist only because of the free Will of God. This explains the much repeated formula: "And the Lord said . . ." (Gn 1,3.6.9.11.14.20.24.26). The word of God is a creative word, which produces its effect immediately and without any opposition. Hence, God's command and its realization are expressed as a word: God said, 'Let there be light,' and there was light" (Gn 1,3). In this way the hagiographer signifies that the world is an effect of the divine wisdom, for it clearly manifests His perfection. For this reason the sacred author often affirms the goodness of creation: "And God saw that it was good." (Gn 1,10.12.18.21.25.31). The flood, which also belongs to the priestly tradition, is considered a cataclysm of a punitive character, which God had already preannounced (Gn 6,13).

In the priestly tradition, the Sinaitic Covenant is considered the ultimate perfection of the Covenant with the Patriarchs. God reveals His true name to Moses (Ex 6,2–8), and through the plagues of Egypt, as well as through the Exodus from Egypt, Yahweh shows Himself to be the true God of all events and all physical reality (Ex 7,19; 8.1,12; 9.22; 11,9). Yahweh also stirs free wills (Ex 6,10.13; 7,8; 14,1; Nm 2,1; 20,7; 34,1.16) and announces the future (Ex 7,22; 9,12.35; Nm 20,12.23).

The priestly tradition gives great importance to the divine manifestation. Consequently the hagiographer lingers on the description of the Dwelling (Ex 25,27) because Yahweh's "constant presence is there." The "Ark of the Covenant" is already spoken of in the Yahwistic (Nm 11,16) and Elohistic (Ex 33,7; Nm 12,4) tradition, but in the priestly tradition this expression often has the character of a technical formula which is perfectly in accord with the theology of this tradition. When He resides in the Dwelling, Yahweh Himself directs the steps of the people of God through the desert (Ex 40,36s; Nm 9,23; 10,11). In these and in other texts the idea of the constant communication between Yahweh and the people of Israel is taught. God often speaks directly to His people (Ex 25,22; Nm 7,89; 14,10ss), but generally He speaks through Moses, the mediator of the revelation.

d. *The Evolution of Theological Ideas During the Babylonian Captivity.* With their religious and national structures destroyed and annihilated, the Israelite exiles in Babylon, begin to seek a more intimate religion, separated from the political and religious structures of Palestine. Since they have no temple or sacrifices, the religion of the exiles seeks interior life, intimate contact with Yahweh. Properly speaking, the religion of interior prayer begins now. From the ruins of ancient Israel, a new one springs forth.

The "remnant" chosen by God will become the salvation of Israel itself and of all other nations.

As we have already said, the prophets, especially Jeremiah, Ezechiel and Deutero-Isaiah, exercise a great influence in this change. Under their guidance the "small remnant" of Israel is formed, becoming the leaven that will transform the mass of the Chosen People. Even in the heart of this "Remnant" a deep transformation is wrought through suffering. The exiles begin to meditate on the ruins of Israel and on the reason why they themselves have to suffer so much for the whole nation. . . . Then comes the idea of *individual retribution,* abandoning the idea of collective and national retribution. If then the just suffer like the unjust, this means that the just, through their sufferings, cancel out their sins. Thus they obtain from God the ability to be the true "Remnant" of Israel, from which will come salvation for all of Israel (Ez 18; 36,24–28).

A most important solution to the problem of suffering is found in Deutero-Isaiah (cc.40–55). Here the sufferings of the just are considered as the redemption of the sinful people of Israel. In fact, because of their sufferings the just purge the sins of the people and hasten the hour of salvation. This idea is expressed best in the oracle of the Servant of Yahweh (Is 52,13–53,12).

In Trito-Isaiah (cc.56–66), the sufferings of the just are no longer considered a means of expiation for sinners, but rather a means to hasten the divine intervention for salvation and for judgment. The just who humbly and patiently bear suffering and persecution are called *anawim.* They make expiation for others and with their prayers hasten the advent of the time of mercy (Is 63,7–64,11; cf. Ps 78; 105; 106;136; Neh 1,5ss, Ezr 9,6). From this time on the humble man, the poor man, the persecuted man is no longer the cursed, but the beloved of God (Is 25,6; 55,1–6; 61,1–3; Prv 9,1–6). God Himself wishes to dwell with the poor and the humble (Is 57,15; 66,2).

Jeremiah initiates a movement of renewal, which influences post-exilic Judaism. Indeed Jeremiah will be the *anaw par excel-*

lence, the *father* of the "poor and the humble." He is the first to consider religion as a personal and interior relationship with God Himself. For this reason Jeremiah can be considered the *father of prayer.* Persecuted and rejected by all, the prophet begins to dialogue with God in the intimacy of his heart. This kind of interior religion of Jeremiah is expressed in his prophecy of the New Covenant (Jer 31,31–34). In the New Covenant, God works directly on the heart and on the will of men (Jer 24,7; 32,39s). One is dealing with a new Pact, a more interior pact, which joins the individual with God. Therefore the future religion, i.e., the religion of the New Covenant, will be a personal and interior religion. However this religion will be the religion of the people of Israel, for the aim of the new pact is to produce good for the nation and for the individual.

The fundamental disposition of post-exilic piety is *contrition of heart,* which constitutes an authentic disposition for a more perfect acceptance of God. When God liberates Israel or the faithful after a trial, this liberation is converted into a motive of hope for the establishment of the kingdom of God in the world. Just as the sufferings of the Servant of Yahweh obtain the establishment of the Messianic kingdom, so the sufferings of the *anawim* hasten this establishment. In the same way the liberation of the just man who suffers, like the liberation of the Servant of Yahweh (Is 53,11s) and the liberation of Israel herself from the Babylonian Captivity (Is 40–55), will constitute the reason for the conversion of the nations and the triumph of monotheism. In fact, the *missionary theme* will be a basic idea in the post-exilic prophets (Is 45,14s; Zep 3,9s; Jon 1,1; Zec 14,16s; Mal 1,11).[31]

6. *Revelation in the Post-exilic Prophets*[32]

To the repatriates from Babylon, who return to Palestine in 538, complaining of their small number, of the return accom-

[31] Cf. J. Salguero, in *La Ciencia Tomista* 90 (1963) 369–395, e in *Selecciones de Teologia* 4, n. 15 (1964) 305–311.

[32] Cf. A. M. Brunet, "Le Chroniste et ses sources" in *Revue Biblique* 60

plished without miracles, of the difficulties of the new settlement (Hg 1; Zec 1; Esr 1–6; Neh 1), God formulates again His best promises through the postexilic prophets. The unification of the people will be accomplished (Is 57,19; Zec 8,7; 10,10; Ps 79,36); the nations will be converted and they will serve Israel (Hg 2,7s. 22; Zec 2,15; Is 60,5ss); the conditions of existence will be transformed (Is 65,1.3; 6,20–25).

The peace of the Persian Empire (538–332) favors the Judaic interest in its religious patrimony and facilitates the work of collection undertaken by the various schools. At the same time new books appear with a new literary form. Here we have the theological history with the first and second books of Chronicles, the edifying or prophetic history of Ruth, Tobit, Judith and Jonah.

a. *The work of the Chronicler* (*1–2 Chronicles*) presents Israel as the ideal community of Yahweh. This is its central idea. Israel is seen as the *community*—fruit of the eternal Covenant of God with David (2 Chr 13.5). The books of *Ezra* and of *Nehemiah,* which are a continuation of the Chronicles, specify ulteriorly the characteristics of this community. The different personages of the post-exilic restoration, such as Zarubbabel, Ezra and Nehemiah, show no desire to restore the monarchy (Neh 6,6–8). The community of the repatriates assumes an eminently religious character:

(1953) 481–508; 61 (1954) 349–386; IDEM "La Théologie du Chroniste" in *Sacra Pagina* I (Paris, 1959) 384–397; Id., "Paralipomènes" in *Dictionnaire de la Bible. Supplément.* 6 (Paris 1960) coll. 1231–1256; R. T. Siebeneck, "The Messianism of Aggaeus and Proto-Zacharias" in *Catholic Biblical Quarterly* 19 (1957) 312–328; A. Fernandez, *Un hombre de carácter, Nehemias* (Jerusalén 1940); E. Olavarri, "Cronologia y estructura literaria del oráculo escatologico de Abdias: in *Estudios Bíblicos* 22 (1963) 303–313; H. Cazelles "Jérémie et le Deutéronome" in *Recherces de Science Religieuse* 38 (1951) 33–36; L. Dennefeld, "Les problèmes du livre de Joël" in Recherches de Science Religieuse 1924ç1926; J. Bourke, "Le Jour de Yahwé dans Joël" in *Revue Biblique* 66 (1959) 5–31. 191ç212; H. Cazelles "La mission d'Esdras" in *Verbum Testamentum* 4 (1954) 138ss; T. Chary, *Les Prophètes et le culte ápartir de l'exil* (Paris 1955) A. Lefèvre, "Néhémie et Esdras" in *Dictionnaire de la Bible. Supplément,* 6,401ss; M. Delcor, "Les sources du Deutéro-Zacharie" in *Revue Biblique* 59 (1952) 385–411; P. Lamarche, *Zacharie IX–XIV. Structure littéraire et messianisme* (Paris 1961).

everything tends to create a people belonging wholly to Yahweh and separated from the other nations. Their ideal is to realize that type of unique and isolated community which perfect Yahwism seems to require. Two things serve to express the spirituality of the "community of Yahweh": the Temple and the Law. The Chronicler emphasizes often that the repatriates are in fact "every one whose spirit God had raised up to go up to build the temple of the Lord, which was in Jerusalem" (Ezr 1,5; 2,68; 5,8–17; 6,3–12, etc.). The new community is gathered around the Temple, where the resumption of worship gives a new religious energy to the life of the people of God (Ezr 6,13–22). Even the Law has a central importance for all of this period and for the construction of Judaism. At this time it receives its definitive draft, and can therefore be posted as the foundation of life for the new community. The reform of Esdras and Nehemiah, which aims at the renewal of the Covenant with Yahweh, poses the observance of the Law as the condition for the Covenant (Ezr 9–10; Neh 8–10).

The post-exilic reform also emphasizes another particular in order to create the separation of Israel from the other nations: endogamy (Ezr 9–10; Neh 10,30s; 13,1–3.25.27). Thus Israel is taut in the effort to realize the divine ideal of not mixing "the holy seed with pagan people" (Ezr 9,2). This preoccupation is chiefly of a religious nature, but it does smack of a "Judaic racism." Nevertheless, the contemporary prophets: Haggai, 1 Zechariah (cc. 1–8), Trito-Isaiah (57–66), Malachi, Jonah, Joel, Obadiah, and 2 Zechariah (cc. 9–14), establish equilibrium, pointing out the universal aspect of the divine message.

b. *Haggai* and *Zechariah* (1–8) are the first prophets to encourage the repatriates to build the Temple. The message of the two prophets has an identical thought, although from different perspectives: the cultural re-awakening in the Temple as the foretaste of the Messianic temple. For Haggai the new Temple will have a greater glory than the first one (2,9). He announces a particular "election" of Zerubbabel, which follows along the same line of Davidic Messianism. For the realization of these promises the purification of the people is necessary (2,10–14.23).

Zechariah considers Yahweh as the transcendent God, Who acts and speaks to men through the angels (1,8ss; 2,2ss) and Who demands the complete conversion of His people (1,3s; 8,16s). Zechariah insists on moral purification as a necessary premise to salvation. The divine transcendence is greatly highlighted by the various prophets during this period. Since Yahweh is considered almost inaccessible, one has recourse to intermediaries like the angels, the interpreters and executors of God's orders. For this reason Zechariah multiplies the angel interpreters who are the intermediaries between the prophet and God. Also in Zechariah a great importance is given to nocturnal visions (Zec 1,7–6,15). The first part of Zechariah (1-8) can be considered the first apocalypse of the Old Testament (cf. RB, 1906,69). In Zechariah there is a predominance of announcement of the consolation that Messianic times will bring to Israel. God will intervene and will punish the oppressors (1,14s; 2,1–4); Sion will become the dwelling of Yahweh (1,16s; 2,8.14ss; 8,3–5); Jerusalem and the Temple will be the center of the Messianic restoration (1,16; 8,9). The Messianic peace will be extended even to other peoples (2,15; 8,20–23). Thus Zechariah gives a note of universality to the somewhat nationalistic vision of salvation found in post-exilic theology. The idea of a liturgical theocracy centered at Jerusalem and at the Temple had limited the universal Messianism of Is 40–55. Zechariah seeks to combine love for the Temple, the liturgy and the priesthood with the Messianic-prophetic annunciation. This tendency is manifested in the idea of the Messiah as prince and priest (3,8; 6,11–13).

c. *Trito-Isaiah* (Is 56–66) is the most representative prophetic writing of the period of the post-exilic restoration. It manifests clear connections with Is 40–55 and the undoubted influence of Ezechiel. For Is 56–66, Yahweh is the Holy One of Israel. He is "the High and the Eminent that dwells in eternity: and His name is Holy" (57,15; 60,14). His majesty, glory and power are manifested in His universal dominion over nature (65,17ss) and

89

history (64,1ss). No one can resist Him when He intervenes to save or punish (63,1ss; 66,15ss). The holiness of the people must correspond to the holiness of God, for Yahweh loves justice and hates iniquity (61,8). Trito-Isaiah strongly denounces idolatry (65,3.11; 66,3.17) and inculcates the obligation of the true worship of Yahweh (58,3ss; 59,13; 66,22s). Besides holiness, Isaiah emphasizes three other ideas: the paternity of God, the theme of the "Remnant" and that of the *anawim,* "the poor." The title of God as "Father" re-enters into the perspective of the history of Israel (63,16), in order to indicate the glorious power and the salvific mercy of Yahweh (63,15s). For this reason, it becomes the most cherished title among the people's invocations (64,7). The divine love surpasses every expectation (65,24; 66,7ss). The theme of the *anawim,* common to all of Isaiah (1,17.23; 3,14s; 41,17; 49,13) is more accentuated in Trito-Isaiah. The prophet himself has been sent to the "poor" (61,1ss). God loves them and protects them. He consoles them, and He will make an eternal covenant with them (57,15.18; 61,8; 66,2).

The Messianism of Trito-Isaiah has its center at Jerusalem and the Temple. The City will be renewed and will be called "the City of Yahweh," "Sion of the Holy One of Israel" (60,14; 62,2). The theme of the centrality of Jerusalem recalls Ezechiel. It also exalts the magnificence and the splendor of the Temple (60,7.13), which makes it a worthy habitation for Yahweh (63,15; 64,10). Israel will be clothed with the priestly character (61,6) so that worship may be more perfect. The prophet does not exclude the other nations from this Messianism: everyone will be conducted by Yahweh to His holy Mountain (56,7). Unlike Is 40–55, the practice of the Mosaic law is a necessary condition. The new cult will bring a universal renewal extended to all peoples (66,19ss); nevertheless the centrality of Jersusalem and of the Temple and the pre-eminence of Israel (60,10; 65,18ss; 66,7–14, 20) place a certain limit on this universal vision.

d. *Malachi and Jonah* represent respectively the nationalist movement and the universalist movement. Malachi affirms that

Israel is impure and has profaned the Name of Yahweh. For a true renewal she must abandon her mixed marriages (2,10–16) and return to the true worship of Yahweh (1,7ss). "The day of the Lord" will realize the perfect worship (3,4). In the eschatological perspective he insists on the spiritual character of the people of God (3,14ss): the observance of the commandments will be the measure for the choice of the members of the Messianic kingdom. Yahweh is considered a king (1,14). Malachi also foretells a new cult, diffused to all peoples (1,11), which only the sacrifice of Christ continued in the Eucharistic sacrifice will be able to fulfill completely (Denz. 939; DBS 5,744s).

The characteristic message of the book of Jonah is the doctrine of universalism. It has an evident polemical scope against the rigid nationalism so common among the Jews. According to Jonah, the prophecies are a call to conversion, the threats of God therefore are conditioned by the reply of man (3,10; 4,1ss). The God of Jonah is the God of mercy. Therefore, He accepts the sacrifices and hears the prayers of the Phoenician sailors (1,14–16). But above all, He pardons even the most ruthless enemies of Israel, the Ninevites, if they are converted to Him (4,1ss). The book of Jonah is the most picturesque anticipation of evangelical universalism.

e. *Joel and Obadiah* have a nationalistic tendency. Joel's message is eschatological in character, and everything converges toward the "day of the Lord." Two signs show the imminence of the "day of the Lord": the effusion of the Spirit (3,1s; cf. Acts 2,16ss) and astronomic wonders (3,3–4): "Yahweh is judge" and he will pronounce "judgment" in the valley of Josaphat. God's intervention is described in dramatic terms as the punishment of the wicked (4,1–17). Instead the community of Judah will finally find Messianic peace, symbolized by the prophetic images of fertility and prosperity (4,17–21).

The supremacy of Judah is the central idea of Obadiah's prophecy. Edom will be severely punished for her ruthlessness against Israel (1,1–15). The People of God, instead, will extend her dominion with Jerusalem as the center (1,16–20) and "the kingdom shall be for the Lord" (1,21).

f. *Zechariah* (9–14) is of uncertain date, although connected to the others through content. He presents interesting eschatological ideas: the extraordinary intervention of Yahweh to punish the wicked and save Israel is expected (10,2–11,3); Jerusalem will be liberated and the house of David revalorized (12,2–13,1); a liturgical theocratic kingdom will be established (c. 14). Zechariah conceives the Messiah as a "just, victorious, humble king," who "will speak peace to the Gentiles, and his power shall be from sea to sea" (9,9s). Furthermore, the mourning of Israel for him "whom they have pierced" (12,10) is foretold. The similarities between this Messianic figure and the Servant of Yahweh of Isaiah are very clear.[33]

A greater optimism is found in the prophets of the post-exilic period than in the prophets of pre-exilic period: the promises surpass the threats. As we have seen, under the influence of Ezechiel a liturgical tendency is present, the Temple is considered to be the center of the entire community of the restoration. The prophets of this period progressively determine the eschatological doctrine with increasing accuracy: the last judgment (Jl 3,4; Zec 12–14), the return of Elias (Mal 3), Gehenna (Is 66,24), the resurrection of the dead (Dn 12,1–3).

7. *Revelation in the Sapiential Books of the Persian Period*[34]

The originality of the wisdom of Israel comes from the fact that it is derived from an experience conducted in the environment

---

[33] (Cf. *Dictionnaire de la Bible. Supplément* 5, 1187s; *Revue Biblique* 69, 1962, 590s; *La Ciencia Tomista* 92, 1965, 49–62).

[34] Autori Vari, *Le Psautier. Ses origines. Ses problemes littéraires. Son influence* (Lovanio 1962); L. Alonso Schoekel, *Estudios de poética hebrea* (Barcelona, 1963); G. Castellino, *Libro dei Salmi* (Torino 1955); R. Tournay, "Recherches sur la chronologie des Psaumes" *Revue Biblique* 1958–1959; *Recherches de Science Religieuse.* 35 (1961) 225–256; A. Colunga, El Mesianismo en los Salmos regios" in *Studia Anselmiana* 27 (1951) 208–230; A. Feuillet, "Les Psaumes eschatologiques du régne de Jahweh" in *Nouvelle Revue Théologique* 73 (1951) 244–266.352–363; H. J. Franken, *The Mystical Communion with*

of the religious Yahwistic life of the people of God. Human wisdom is an endowment of the human soul which brings it to act rightly. Ordinarily it is a simple technical skill: ability in work (Sir 9,17; Is 3,3; 40,20), prudence in managing private, commercial and political affairs (Sir 10,1–5; Ez 28,1–10). At times wisdom assumes a moral aspect and becomes synonomous with "virtue" and "probity"; then "prudence" and "understanding" are her crown. This human wisdom gives man the orientation to be happy and prosper (Prv 14,8–14) and draws its origin almost exclusively from experience or from tradition (Prv 22,17–21; Sir 8,9; Jb 15,10–18). After the exile, however, this human wisdom is always presented with increasing insistence as the gift of God (Sir 39,1–8; 24,23ss). Even in the sapiential literature the prophets gave rise to a movement which considered wisdom a divine prerogative, communicated by God to men. Wisdom was made synonomous with the spirit of Yahweh and also its effect (Is 11,2). Israelitic wisdom has an eminently practical and concrete character, alien to any philosophical and theological speculation.[35]

Jahvé in the Book of Psalm (Leyden 1954); A. Miller, "I Salmi nella visione cristiana" in *Rivista Biblica Italiana* 5 (1957) 1–16; A. Gelin *La prière des Psaumes* (Paris 1961); Versione spagnola: *La plegaria de los Salmos* (Barcelona, Estelam, 1965); H. Cazelles, "Bible, Sagesse, Science" in *Recherches de Science Religieuse* 48 (1960) 40–54; R. Murphy, "La literatura sapiencial del A.T." in *Concilium* n. 10 (Diciembre 1965) 121–133; A. Gonzalez Núñez, *El libro de los Salmos* (Barcelona, Herder, 1966); D. Gallucci, "Il concetto di 'Dio' nel libro dei Proverbi" in *La Scuola Cattolica* 58 (1930) 337–51. 417–32; 59 (1931) 364–370; 60 (1932) 36–37; A. Robert, "Le Yahwisme de Prov. X, 1–SSII, 16; XXV–XXX: in *Memorial Lagrange* (Paris 1940) 163–82; G. Ricciotti, *Il libro di Giobbe* (Torino 1924); A. Feuillet, "L'énigme de la souffrance et la réponse de Dieu" in *Dieu Vivant* 17 (1950) 77–91; H. H. Rowley, "The Book of Job and its Meaning" in *The Bulletin of the John Rylands Library* 41 (1958) 167; H. Duesberg, *Les scribes inspirés* II (Paris 1939); H. L. Ginsberg, *Studies in Qohelet* (New York 1959); C. C. Forman, "The Pessimism of Ecclesiastes" in *Journal of Semitic Studies* 3 (1958) 336–343; F. Vattioni, "Niente di nuovo sotto il sole" in *Rivista Biblica Italiana* 7 (1959) 64–67.

[35] (A. Rolla, "La sapienza nei libri sap.: in *Il messaggio della salvezza* vol. 2, Torino, Elle Di Ci, 1966, p. 597–602; D. F. Festorazzi, *Ibid.*, p. 720–723).

Although there is a certain unitary line in resolving the problems of Israel, the sapiential literature confronts them from an aspect different from that of the historical and prophetical books. There are three fundamental themes of sapiential literature: the problem of the destiny of the individual, a re-examination of Israel's history in the light of the sorrowful experience of the exile, and the singular contribution of the mysterious doctrine of the wisdom of God.

a. In its oldest part, *The Book of Proverbs*, presents the earthly solution of the problem of retribution based on a profound trust in the intervention of God. For Proverbs *word* and *wisdom* are synonomous terms. But the *dabar* of which the sapiential books speak is the word of God inasmuch as it contains the prescriptions of the Torah. The wise, *hokamin,* know that they are simple interpreters of the word of God or of the Torah. They know very well that all comes from God (Prv 10,22). Therefore what does not please God is to be avoided (Prv 11,1; 12,22; 15,3.8; 16,1–9). The fear of God is the beginning of wisdom and of justice (Prv 1,7; 14,2). Wisdom, *hokmah,* is sometimes personified: to it are attributed the functions that are reserved to the spirit of Yahweh. Wisdom is the active principle of the creation and governing of the world; it has a divine and eternal origin; it is the omnipotent spirit of God which permits Him to penetrate all things. Like the ancient prophets, it preaches in the squares, it threatens, it presents Messianic promises (Prv 8,22–31; Sir 24,3; Wis 7,24–28; 8,1; 9,9). Wisdom is the educator of humanity, of individuals, of kings, it is the guide of Israel in the accomplishment of her special mission (Wis 10–12; Sir 44–50). It is a gift similar to the Covenant and to the Law, with which it is identified (Sir 24,22–31). Wisdom issues judgments and promises rewards (Prv 1,26.28; 8,18–21). In Prv 8,22ss, the idea of the sacred author seems to go beyond the limits of simple poetic personification (cf. Sir 24). Is he dealing with an hypostasis or with a literary personification? Numerous authors have seen an anticipation of trinitarian revelation. But it seems more logical to see only a strong poetic personification of the wisdom of God. One finds among the Hebrews the innate fondness for personifying the divine attributes, which was done in Mesopotamia and in Egypt. However, the rigid monotheism of Hebrew theology did not permit them to go beyond a simple poetic personification.

Modern authors find a parallel between the description of Wisdom and that of the Messiah-King. Like the Messiah, Wisdom also was "created" by God, invested with the royal investiture of the Messiah (Prv 8,22s; cf. Ps 2,6). Its mission assumes the same qualities and tends to the same scope as Is 11,1ss (Prv 8,12–18); furthermore its task has a universal range like that of Is 40–55. Another parallel between this sapiential "Messianism" and prophetical Messianism is the image of the banquet which is found, for example, in Is 55,1ss (Prv 9, 1ss). Sirach presents the same image in c.24, under the influence of Prv 8–9, but the role of Wisdom in creation and as guide of Israel stands out more clearly. Hence we can affirm that there is an enrichment of Messianism through the introduction of this mysterious personage, Wisdom, who possesses the characteristics of the Davidic Messiah and also participates in some way in the transcendence of God Himself. The book of Wisdom will continue in that direction, thus preparing the way to the *Logos,* "Divine Word", of St. John (Jn 1,1ss).[36]

b. *The Book of Job* has a great importance for what regards the problem of *individual retribution.* The prophet Ezechiel had already spoken of such a problem, limiting himself to the earthly retribution, without saying anything about future individual retribution. Like Ecclesiastes, Job studies this problem more deeply, reaching a great development even in the area of piety (cf Ps 16; 49; 73; Dn 12,1–3; 2 Mc 7,9.11.14.23; 12,43–46; Wis 1–5).

Job considers suffering and punishment as providential warnings from God (Jb 33,19; 36,15), not as punishments for sins com-

---

[36] Cf. D. F. Festorazzi, "Teologia della Storia della Salvezza," in *Il Messaggio della Salvezza* vol. II, 1956, p. 723.

mitted. Job hurls himself violently against the traditional theory that he who has sinned will be punished and he who has led a just and virtuous life will be rewarded by God (Jb 21,1ss). Nevertheless, his own life speaks to the contrary (Jb 6,9–30). The book of Job does not reach a true solution of the problem, however. The answer given is found in Jb 40, 1–6: God is just, although His ways of justice are mysterious; man must recognize the absolute sovereignty of Yahweh, Lord of nature and of history. Suffering is a mystery of Divine Providence, which God is not obliged to reveal to anyone (Jb 40,3–5; 42,1–6).

c. *Ecclesiastes* also speaks of the same problem but in a different way. Qoheleth not only deals with the problem of retribution, like Job. He considers more the problem of human life which he presents with unequaled force. The experience of every day is at the basis of a merciless criticism of the traditional explanation. He harshly refutes the idea of earthly retribution and decisively rejects the "cyclical" solution of the mystery of history. Qoheleth does not consider himself blessed with earthly happiness (all in this world is vanity!) but rather he seeks eternal good (Eccl 2,16–21; 5,14; 6,6; 9,5.10). Life on earth is disappointing (Eccl 2,1–17; 3,16–21); the ways of God are obscure, unreachable. Hence man must content himself with the unsatisfying joys of the moment (3,22; 8,15, etc.).

Qoheleth's book has great influence on the evolution of the idea of retribution. Indeed, it rejects the traditional theory and considers it totally inadequate to the facts of reality (Eccl 7,15; 8,14; 9,2).

d. *Sirach.* In regard to the problem of evil and of suffering, *Sirach* emphasizes the idea of trust in God without, however, ignoring the mystery of His action towards man and his history. Sirach can be defined as "the poem of the faith of Israel". A part of the book is dedicated to the history of the Chosen People. This book has an interesting and original concept of the History of Salvation: creation (Sir 42,15; 43,33) and human history (44,1–50,21) form the one History of Salvation. In fact, creation and history are derived from the same salvific activity of God, fruit of the same love as in the Covenant of Sinai (cf. Ps 135; 136). The wisdom of God, which guides all salvation history, will bring a final solution to the problem of evil. In the meantime Israel can wait trustingly for the eschatological intervention of God the Savior. The book of Sirach also gives great importance to the theme of Wisdom, at times presenting her as personified (24,3). The mission of this wisdom is to guide Israel and educate mankind (cc 44–50). She is a sublime gift, similar to the Covenant and to the Law (19,18; 24,22–31). She teaches, exhorts, speaks to her disciples with divine authority. In fact, the worship rendered to her is rendered to God, and the eternal destiny of men depends upon their attitude towards her (4,11–19). Sirach 24,1–32 is a hymn to wisdom. In person she begins to speak to Israel and declares that she has come from God and is the intermediary in creation (v. 3–6). She identifies herself with the personified word of God and with the divine spirit stirring above the primordial waters (v 3). The Creator orders her to establish her dwelling in Israel (v 7–8). This dwelling does not destroy her transcendency and her divine character (v 9). Then the hagiographer speaks of her beneficent effects on Israel and on mankind (v 10–21), and affirms that the wisdom communicated to the Hebrews is identifiable with the Book of the Law (v 22).

Although the sacred author presents wisdom as a divine attribute, he does not affirm wisdom as a divine person. Belonging to the post-exilic movement of prophetic origin, the hagiographer uses a simple poetic personification to exalt the antiquity and the authority of the Mosaic Law. To achieve this aim there was nothing better than presenting it as the manifestation and incarnation of divine Wisdom.

From all this it can be seen that this wisdom can be applied only in a typical sense or in a full sense to Christ, *Verbum,* Incarnate Word and Wisdom (1 Cor 1,24.30; Col 2,3). On the other hand the things that are said of wisdom can be very easily referred to Mary most holy. Having possessed this divine gift of wisdom in an eminent way, Mary well deserves to be called "Seat of Wisdom."

e. *The Psalms,* composed at various times, also show different aspects of Old Testament Revelation. Very often the divine word (revelation) coincides with the prescriptions of the Law given by Yahweh Himself to His people (Ps 17,4; 107,11). For this reason the psalmists identify the Law (Torah) with the word of God. This appears clearly in Ps 50,17 where there is perhaps an allusion to the *debarim* of the Decalogue, and even in Ps 147,19, which is nearer to the Deuteronomic notion of the word of God.

Psalm 119 insists very much on fidelity to the Mosaic Law. In this psalm the divine word is considered as the light that shows us the way to follow (v 105,130,133). The same Psalmist considers the Law as the divine revelation delivered through Scripture.[37]

The faith and security that the psalmist places in the divine word comes without a doubt from faith in Sacred Scripture (Ps 33,4; 105,8; 111,9; 119,25.28,42.49.65.74, etc.). However, there are also psalms in which the divine word is considered an expression of the Will of the Creator: in the creation of the universe, in its ordination, and in its moderation (Ps 33,6.9; 90,3; 107,20; 147,15–18). In Ps 104 the greatness of God as Creator and His providential activity in the universe are exalted. According to Ps 29, nature obliges all creation, which has become a "sanctuary" of the Lord, to sing His glory. A motive for praising God is offered to the psalmist in Ps 8; 19; 104, through the contemplation of His masterpiece: man. The hagiographer affirms his profound gratitude to the mercy of Yahweh, Who bends lovingly over man. There are very interesting Psalms (19,33; 74; 89; 135–136) in which the motives for praising God spring forth from the meditated union of the creative work with the salvific. Psalm 19 teaches that creation sings the glory of God, but the Law does so

[37] Cf. A. Robert, in *Revue Biblique,* 1937, 5–25.

even more. The holiness and power of God are shown above all in Salvation History; indeed creation itself is a preparatory part of it. Man should sing hymns to Yahweh because He is good, and His Name is sweet; He has chosen Israel as His own possession (Ps 135–136). Praise expresses faith in divine goodness, which demands man's correspondence. This goodness arising from the gratuitous and stable initiative of God's love in the covenant with man is expressed by the word *hesed*. The central work of the love of God is the Exodus, but the story of this love begins already with creation (Ps 136,5). God therefore saves with His faithful love. His repeated interventions in the past are not only a guarantee of His actual Presence, but they also inspire certainty in His final intervention in Messianic times. The divine action of the Old Testament is prolonged in the salvific action of the Messiah. Man realizes his mission as image of God through the ideal image Who is Christ.

In the face of sufferings, persecutions, and sorrow, the psalmists turn to God with trust, asking help and protection. Confronted with sorrow, the psalmists follow the concept of retribution diffused throughout all of the ancient Middle East: the good man must be rewarded here on earth, the wicked man punished (1, 52; 112; 119; 127–128). Since a true Yahwist could not admit injustice or caprice in Yahweh, when they were conscious of being innocent, although persecuted or ill, they ask of God liberation from and punishment of their enemies (Ps 5,11; 7; 14; 16; 28,4; 31,18s; 35,4–6; 58, 7–11; 69,23–29; 109,6–19; 140,9–12). At other times the psalmists are not intimidated by the dangers of their enemies, for they feel themselves solidly anchored in God: their prayer then assumes the tone of a serene effusion of soul (Ps 3,11; 16; 22; 41; 62; 131). One does find attempts to resolve the problem of the suffering of the just. Indeed some Psalms (16; 36; 37; 91; 139) deny any value at all to the prosperity of the wicked and affirm that the true good of the just man consists in enjoying God and in being approved by Him. Other Psalms

(17,15; 49; 73,23s) seem to foresee the solution of the problem in as much as they affirm, although in a veiled way, retribution in the next world.

Different Psalms celebrate the Law, its gift on Sinai, and fidelity or infidelity to it. The Law is the concrete expression of the divine Will and the condition through which the divine promises and guarantees are actuated (Ps 119). Numerous Psalms (42–43; 63; 84, etc.) express joy for their sojourn in the one Temple of Jerusalem; others however condemn empty ritualism and demand, besides the external cult, the faithful practice of the Law (Ps 40,7–9; 51,18s,69,30ss). For the psalmists, the word of God is contemporaneously law, promise, and dynamism which develops in nature and in history. As promise, the word of God constitutes a very important aspect in the psalms: in anxieties the psalmists hope in the promises of the word of God. The divine word is the nourishment of eschatological hope.

The Psalter is strictly monotheistic. God shows His power and wisdom especially through natural phenomena (Ps 19; 29). The power and the glory of God shines through in the glorious theophanies (Ps 18,8–16; 50,1–4). God is the creator of all things (Ps 104). Although He is above creatures, God is in intimate rapport with them. He is Providence, for He assures order through the natural laws and through justice. More than any of the other creatures, man manifests the divine wisdom and experiences its benevolence, mercy, and love. Above all, the divine attributes of omniscience and omnipotence are emphasized (Ps 139). In speaking of God, the psalmists attribute to Him human members and sentiments. Through these anthropomorphisms and anthropopathisms, the psalmists emphasize the personal character of Yahweh.

After the Prophets, the Psalms have the most references to Messianism. The Messianic doctrine, however, is presented in only a fragmentary manner and under different aspects that should be harmonized. Furthermore the Messianism of the Psalms is expressed in categories and images taken from Hebrew institutions.

In fact the Messiah is described as "son of God" and priest (Ps 2,18; 110; 72), "son of man" (Ps 8, 16, etc.), and as a suffering just man (Ps 22; 69; 109, etc.). The Messianic kingdom will be universal because all peoples will spontaneously submit themselves to Yahweh (Ps 66,2; 72; 102, 16). Ordinarily this conversion is attributed to Israel. Nevertheless, it must also be realized by an individual who will spread the worship of Yahweh everywhere, who will make injustice cease, who will give the world peace and who will be uncontestedly recognized by everyone (Ps 2,110). Yahweh Himself intervenes without intermediaries. And thus we have a Messianism with a Messiah. All of these different types of Messianisms are also found in the Prophets.

In many Psalms the intense desire of union with God is found. Because of their ardent and ever deepening spiritual piety, some psalmists experience an interior impulse for a stable union with God (Ps 16,8–11; 73,23.26). The promoters of this interior piety are the *anawim,* i.e., the humble, the poor, the afflicted, the pious of whom the psalmists speak (Ps 9–10; 34; 37). In some psalms (16,8–11; 49,16; 73,23–26) which seem to express the hope of remuneration after death, which reaches the peak of Judaic piety, the psalmists place themselves before God and under His protection; they want an intimate union with God and they want it to be eternal.

The Psalms in the Christian Church. It seems that from the beginning the Church did not accept in total the block of the Psalms of the Old Testament into her official office [of prayers]. Instead she made use of a collection of poetic Christian hymns. Only later, when these hymns fell into discredit because of abuses and gnostic influences, did the Church take up the Psalter. To make the Psalms express the piety of the faithful and of the Church, they were subjected to a process of adaptation and transfiguration. From the beginning the Church considered the Psalter a book totally centered in Christ. For her the psalms either speak of Christ or they speak to Christ, or else in them the Church listens to Christ speak to the Father or to her (Riv.B 61 Tr. 145

1957, 8s). In this total and unconditional Christologization of the Psalms, the Church was inspired by the method used by Christ and by the Apostles in the N.T. (Mt 21, 16; Jn 13,18; Acts 7, 59: where Stephen addresses to Christ the same words that Christ addressed to the Father.)

8. *The Last Books of the Old Testament*[38]

The political situation of Israel in the last two centuries before Christ takes a step backwards. At the fall of the Persian Empire (330 B.C.) the Palestinian horizon is dimmed by the Syrian domination (199–163 B.C.). With Antiochus Epiphanes the Hellenistic eruption reaches its most exasperating form. The Judaic

[38] J. Henning, "The Book Tobias in Liturgy" in *Irish Theological Review* 19 (1952) 84–90; J. Goettmann, "Le Livre de Tobie" in *Bible et Vie Chrétienne* 28 (1959) 20–33; A. Lefèvre, "Judith" in *Dictionnaire de la Bible Supplément* 4 (Paris 1949) 1315–1321; A. M. Dubarle, *"Judith. Formes et Sense des diverses Traditions,"* vol. I–LL (Roma 1966); H. Cazelles, "Note sur la composition du rouleau d'Esther" in *Lex tua Veritas,* Festschrift für H. Junker (Treviri 1961) 17–29; S. Talmon, "Wisdom in the Book of Esther" in *Verbum Testamentum* 13 (1963) 419–455; W. H. Brownlee, "Le livre grec d'Esther et la royauté divine" in *Revue Biblique* 73 (1966) 161–185; A. Vaccari, "Il Cantico dei Cantici nelle recenti pubblicazioni" in *Biblica* 9 (1928) 443–57; 14 (1933) 361–66; 29 (1948) 416–424; A. Feuillet, "La Cantique des Cantiques et la tradition biblique" in *Nouvelle revue théologique* 74 (1952) 706–733; IDEM, *Le Cantique des Cantiques. Etude de Théologie biblique et réflexions sur une methode* (Paris 1953); P. Grelot, "Le sens du Cantique des Cantiques" in *Revue Biblique* 71 (1964) 42–56; G. Rinaldi, *Daniele* (Torino 1952); H. H. Rowley, "The Composition of the Book of Daniel" in *Verbum Testamentum* 5 (1955) 272 ss; A. Feuillet, "Le fils de L'homme daniélique et la tradition biblique" in *Revue Biblique* 60 (1953) 170–202. 321–343; J. Coppens, "Le fils d'homme daniélique . . ." in Ephehemrides Theologicae Lovanienses 37 (1961) 5–51; P. E. Testa, "Daniele" in *Il Messaggio della Salvezza,* II, Parte II (Torino, 1967) pp. 109–184; F. M. Abel, *Les livres des Maccabées* (Paris, EB, 1949); A. Penna, Libri dei Maccabei (Bibbia Garofalo, Roma 1953); A. Lefèvre, "Maccabés" in *Dictionnaire de la Bible. Supplément* 5 (Paris 1957), 600 ss; M. Laconi, *Primo e secondo libro dei Maccabei* (Padova-Torino, 1960); P. Van Imschoot, La Sagesse dans l'AT. est-elle une hypostase?" in *Coll Gand* 21 (1934) 89–92; IDEM, in *Revue Biblique* 47 (1938) 34–49; D. Colombo, *Doctrina de providentia divina in libro Sapientiae* (Roma 1953; P. Grelot, "L'eschatologie de la Sagesse" in *Melanges A. Gelin* (Le Puy 1961) 165–178.

religion is prohibited. The center of this last period of the Old Testament is the heroic testimony of the Maccabees. The persecution, instead of arresting hope, however, serves to sharpen it. The persecution leads to the development of a new literary form which is the exasperation of prophetism: the apocalyptic form which becomes predominant in the Hellenistic-Roman period. The persecution of Antiochus Epiphanes intensifies the need for a direct divine intervention in the history of salvation. It will be the way of arriving at the concept of a transcendent Messiah. It is necessary to arrive at the brink of desperation and misery in order to feel the unsuppressible need for such an intervention. It is the time of the Apocalypse of Isaiah (cc 24–27), Judith, Esther, Daniel and the books of the Maccabees; but above all, of extrabiblical authors: "Book of Henoch," "Assumption of Moses," "IV Book of Esdras," "Baruch," "Book of the War of the Children of Light Against the Children of Darkness" (Qumran), etc. The exasperated situation leads to the invocation of the coming of Yahweh the Judge before that of Yahweh the Savior, when ordinarily there is not one without the other.

In the first clash with paganism, polemical apologetic writings— 2 Maccabees, the Letter of Jeremiah, the letter of Baruch, the Wisdom of Solomon—appear along side of the apocalyptic writings.

a. *The Book of Tobit.* The three books of Tobit, Judith and Esther, today considered as *midrashim,* attempt to stir up trust in the salvific intervention of God. The whole post-exilic period is subject to the temptation of mistrust in God. This is especially true of the Hellenistic period during which the above mentioned books were probably compiled. The efficacious reply to this skepticism is given by the divine assistance in the most difficult moments in the history of the Chosen People. The book of Tobit presents the typical case of the just man faithful to God in spite of misfortunes. To this corresponds the idea of the justice of God which always triumphs over evil. The observance of the Law is the sign of Tobit's justice (1, 3ss, 10ss; 2,1ss, 10ss). In spite of the many misfortunes that come upon Tobit, he hopes in the Lord for he knows that God is just, that His ways are mercy and truth, that He will judge with truth and justice (3,2). The words of the angel (12,6ss) and the prayer of Tobit (c.13) are a clear announcement of the Providence of God, even in the most difficult moments. The life of man is like a long and difficult way, that must be traveled with the conviction: Yahweh is my good."[39] The last words of Tobit (14,3–7) are an invitation to Messianic hope: Jerusalem and the Temple will be renewed and all the nations will be converted to the one God. The ruin of Nineveh is already a prefiguration of the final triumph of Yahweh (14,15).

b. *The Book of Judith* teaches unconditional trust in the help of God. Israel's faith in God, based on history, is announced in the discourse of Achior (5,5ss), which is like the center of the book. The God of this people is the God of heaven (v.8), Who guides history. If Israel is faithful to Him, no army will be able to defeat her, for her God protcets her (v.17–20). Judith is presented as an ideal model of fidelity to Yahweh. The hagiographer forcefully points out the power of God (7,19ss). He is the omnipotent Lord, the Lord our God (8,13s; 16), the God of the humble, the help of the poor, the defender of the weak, the refuge of the disheartened, the savior of the desperate (9,11), the God of their Fathers, the God of the heritage of Israel (9,14). The book of Judith would perhaps acquire a particular value and meaning, if it were paralleled with apocalyptic literature: it would deal with the struggle without quarter between good and evil, which the episode of the advance of Holofernes and the siege of Bethulia only prefigure. Thus the lesson offered to the People of God, who are beginning the heroic period of persecution by the Seleucids, would be: Israel must fight against the introduction of the pagan religion, relying on God the Savior, the Lord Who stops wars, the powerful Lord (16,2.5).

c. *Esther* recalls a terrible moment for Israel in exile. At first sight it can seem a simple exaltation of hate and thirst for ven-

[39] Milik, in *Revue Biblique* 1956, 60.

geance against her enemies. The Hebrew text avoids every explicit mention of a religious character. Nevertheless, for the hagiographer, it is God Who guides all the action: Esther is chosen as queen precisely for this. If she is not worthy, help and salvation will come for the Jews from another place (4,14). This trust in the divine intervention explains the penance of Mardochai (4,1) and the fast of Esther and the Jews (4,16). Mardochai's confession, taken from the Greek text is an exaltation of the work of God, the Savior of His people (10,3ss).

d. *The Song of Songs* offers an optimistic vision of the rapport between God and the community of Israel. It was probably composed at the end of the Persian epoch. It lives in expectation of the idyllic union between God and Israel. It treats of an ideal to reach rather than a reality already actuated, as the uncertainties, the hardships and the fluctuations of the love of the spouse towards the Spouse (2,6s; 3,5; 5,4-6, etc.) seem to indicate. Perhaps the book represents a translation of the history of Israel, in which the untiring love of God seeks union with His people. The passionate movement, made up of admiration, desire, recall, response, is resolved in loving union (2,6; 3,4; 5,1; 6,2). This mutual possession of the two spouses, however, is complete and definitive; it is an expectation of the ideal union that will be realized in the future (8,3–7).

e. *The Book of Daniel* is an apocalyptic writing. When it speaks of the divine word, it commonly refers to the prophecies of Sacred Scripture (Dn 9,2.6.12), but it also often refers to the Revelation actually communicated. This Revelation is given in dreams and in visions (7,1.28). In Daniel 9,23 the word is identified with the vision. The book exhorts fidelity to the Law, offering Daniel as an example. It consoles in present tribulations, announcing the inauguration of Messianic times as imminent, the "kingdom of the saints," in which there will be no more sin but perfect justice. It presents the God of the Jews (it never calls Him Yahweh) as the one God, all-powerful, omniscient, Who protects and liberates His faithful servants. He is the God Who directs universal history, which is conceived as a great struggle between God, Who wants to establish His "kingdom," and the powers of this world (incarnated in the great empires) who are opposed to its establishment. God dwells in the heavens and governs the world through angelic agents who help and protect the faithful.

The Messianism of Daniel is totally dominated by the eschatological and apocalyptical idea of the book. All the earthly empires are destroyed so that they can be supplanted by the "kingdom of the saints" (2,45; 7,13). The "son of man" receives from the Ancient of Days (God) "power, majesty and the kingdom." The Messianic doctrine of Daniel presents us with a great evolution in comparison with preceding prophecies. The Messiah is no longer the son of David, but is conceived as a mysterious son of man who will come with the clouds of heaven (7,13s). Here one is dealing with a transcendent Messianism which directly prepares the way for the New Testament.[40]

The book of Daniel is the first to speak explicitly of the lot of the just and of the wicked after death (12,1–3). The sacred author looks toward the last day of the world, which will be the beginning of the Messianic kingdom. On this day many will rise from the dead: some, i.e., the faithful Israelites, will rise to eternal life; others instead to eternal shame. The eternal life which is spoken of here presupposes the happy life which is obtained through intimacy with God in heaven. The idea of punishment after death is also clearly announced. This text of Daniel is the first of the entire Old Testament which speaks clearly of the idea of the resurrection, of the individual judgment after death, and of the final separation of the good and of the bad. Nevertheless, it must be noted that Daniel speaks only of the Jews. Nothing explicit is said of the pagans.

f. The Two Books of the Maccabees. The heroic time of the

[40] (cf. A. Feuillet, in *Revue Biblique* 1953, 170ss).

Maccabees is perhaps the period of the Old Testament in which the tension between the divine promise and its fulfillment is most greatly perceived. It is in fact the moment of the hardest and most insidious trial against religion and the people of God. From this arises the urgency of the extraordinary intervention of God as a reply to the trusting expectation of Israel. The environment is prepared for the Messianic advent. 1–2 Maccabees have a different perspective.

1 Maccabees emphasizes in a particular way the importance of the Law as a guarantee of membership in the people of the Covenant (2,27). Hence the Law is the center of the struggle and the measure of separation. It also presents a religious nationalistic concept of an earthly character. The Messianic terms, like "peace," "immense joy," the "humble of the people," etc., also have a nationalistic and earthly resonance.

2 Maccabees is much more religious and interesting from the theological point of view. God demands a total religious purity of His people. Jonathan's prayer (1, 14–29) expresses the idea of God very well. He is presented as Creator and Savior, terrible, strong, omnipotent and eternal, just, merciful, the only good king, the only provident king (v.24–25). Here we observed the union between creation and salvation, which form one single history. The idea of God the Creator, Who made all things out of nothing (7,28), becomes the first step of the history that has the Chosen People as its protagonist (1,25ss). Israel must trust in the help of God (8,18), Who will intervene if not because of the merits of the contemporary Hebrews, at least because of "the Covenant that He had made with their Fathers" (8,15). Yahweh, however, is an exacting God. He is the holy of all holies (14,36), Who sanctifies the people by means of the holy laws (6,23.28) and by means of a deep love of the Temple as a sign of the divine Presence. The Temple constitutes the center of 2 Maccabees (c.3, 5,15ss.20; 6,1ss). The triumph of Judaism has its most significant manifestation in the purification of the Temple (10,1–9; 13,23; 15,34–36). God's action is developed through frequent extraordinary interventions which make this period somewhat similar to the period of the Exodus (3,24ss; 5,2ss, 8,20; 10,29s, 11,8).

The persecution of Antiochus Epiphanes is the period of the martyrs. I Maccabees sees these events as a consequence of the wrath of God towards Israel (1,64); II Maccabees considers these sacrifices as a font of salvation for the people (7,37). The witness of the martyrs stirs up a very grave question: that of their lot after death. 2 Maccabees is a fundamental document of the Old Testament for the solution of the problem of retribution and of evil: the martyr will rise again (7,9). Faith in the God Who overcomes death (6,26) is here transformed into the doctrine of the resurrection (7,9.13.23.29.33.36; 14,46). As far as faith in the resurrection of the dead is concerned, the sacred author admits two kinds of men: the wicked who are punished in this world, and the good, or the just, who can contribute much to the salvation of the people by bearing with the sufferings inflicted on them by their persecutors. The good do not fear the shadow of Sheol, because Sheol is only a place of transit, the intermediate state before reaching eternal happiness. Thus the ideas of 2 Maccabees concerning the just correspond perfectly to those of the book of Daniel. However, the ideas concerning the wicked still remain in their ancient stage: the wicked are punished in this world. Nothing is said of their future lot.

The text of 2 Mc 12,43–46 is of maximum importance for the clarification of the intermediate state between this life and the resurrection. The sacred author thinks that the just who have died without the complete remission of their sins can be liberated through the prayers of the living. Hence, it admits the possibility of the satisfaction of unexpiated sins after death. This comes about through the prayer and intercession of the living. Another interesting point of doctrine on the hereafter concerns the intercession of the dead for the living (15,11–16).

Hence the idea of retribution is being outlined little by little. Towards the end of the Old Testament faith in the future life is a truth diffused throughout the Israelitic ideological environment. It is admitted that the true retribution of the just will come about only in the future life, the resurrection will be at the end of time. In the meantime the just live in a transitory state until the resurrection.

g. *The Book of Wisdom*. During the Babylonian exile the anti-idolatrous polemic is accentuated, as Is 40–55 and Jer 10,1–16 indicate. These writings coincide in exalting the power of God Who guides history and in emphasizing the absolute nothingness of idols. The *Letter of Jeremias* (last period of the Old Testament) and the description of idolatry in Wisdom follow the same line.

Wisdom (c. 50 B.C.) connects the description of idolatry with the central idea of divine wisdom, and especially with its action in salvation history (9,1–18). In order that the memory of the benefits offered to Israel and the punishment of the other nations (11,1ss) will not seem a lack of goodness or justice on God's part, the book of Wisdom also shows the divine mercy towards pagan peoples (11,15–12,17). The hagiographer accentuates the impotence of the idols, and thus at the same time, accentuates the salvific might of God, Who manifests Himself in the history of Israel (19,22).

In the book of Wisdom, life after death appears as a prolongation and completion of the present life. The problem of future life is directly confronted in the first five chapters. Mankind is divided into two camps. There are the wicked, for whom the certainty of death as an end without hope is a stimulus to the most intense enjoyment possible of earthly life, realized in injustice (2, 1–20). The just on the other hand have their "hope full of immortality" (3,4). Life on earth is only a period of trial, which will end with their reward (3,1–8). The sufferings that the just must bear in this life are trials willed by God for their purification. Death will be only a moment of passage to the new life, where God will reward them greatly (3,5–4,19). The traditional opposition between suffering and virtue is abandoned. The good and the bad will receive their recompense in the future life: the good will be happy near God; the wicked will be punished in Hades. Hence the book of Wisdom throws full light on the problem of suffering and retribution. The just, freed from this corruptible body, will rule forever with the Lord (3,9; 5,15, 9,15), and their reward will be very pleasing in the Lord's temple (3,14; 5,5.16). The happiness of the just is the fruit of a special intervention of God (3,7.13; 4,15; 14,11; 19,15). With the establishment of the eternal kingdom of God the problem of evil is definitely resolved (Dn 12,1ss, 2 Mc 7; Wis 3,7s).

9. *Conclusions.* From all that has been said, we can summarize the ideas of the Old Testament in this way:

a. God reveals Himself in the Old Testament in a *noetic* and *dynamic* form. In fact, although the divine word is directed to the mind of prophets and men, at the same time it constitutes the testimony of the presence and continual action of Yahweh in the Chosen People. Thus God slowly and progressively reveals His plan of salvation, the mystery and the attributes of the Divine Being.

b. God reveals Himself in the first place in creation. For the hagiographer all of the universe is the expression of the Will of God, Who through the stars, the seasons, determines the liturgical times, the Sabbaths and the feasts (Gn 2,2s).

c. Historical Revelation begins with Abraham. Revelation becomes a *personal encounter* of the living God with man. God in fact speaks with man, questions him, associates him with His salvific plan. The Law, the prophetic word, the historical deeds, and the events constitute the different ways of presenting this Revelation. The Law, like prophecy and wisdom, constitutes the expression of the Will of God, the way of salvation and life.

d. The God of the Old Testament reveals Himself above all as the living and personal God (Jer 10,10). The personal encounter with Abraham (Gn 12,1ss) is only the beginning of biblical revelation. Yahweh also presents Himself as the living

God (Dt 5,23; 3 Kgs 17,4; Ps 42,3) and His vitality is shown in the dynamism of His action. This specifies the nature of the God of Israel and differentiates Him from the gods who are devoid of life, inactive and defenseless, i.e., "a vanity" (Jer 2,5). The fact that Yahweh reveals Himself as the "living God" is at the basis of two other attributes: the eternity and the oneness of God. God is not living because He is eternal; He is eternal because He is living.[41]

e. The God of Israel also reveals Himself as the one God (the "vitality" of God, through which He is the fountain of life: Ps 36,10 [also] renders Him the one God: Dt 32,39). He is omnipotent, the living God Who thinks, wills, and directs history. Deutero-Isaiah is the one who best expresses the extraordinarily active presence of God, and His eternity and oneness (Is 40,28s, 44,6). Yahweh is the omnipotent God, the Lord of the universe and of all nations, Who manifests His moral laws and at the same time demands obedience to them. The God of Israel also reveals Himself as the merciful God, full of love for the Chosen People.

f. With the prophets, Israel little by little arrives at a more perfect and profound understanding of the attributes of God. Amos presents the justice of God; Osee, His tender and zealous love; Isaiah, His majesty and transcendence; Jeremias preaches a more interior religion; Ezechiel insists on the exigencies of the holiness of God; Deutero-Isaiah teaches a more universal religion and insists strongly on the holiness of Yahweh (40,25). At the same time that Israel is presenting the divine transcendence, the idea of the nearness and intimacy of God is also developing.

g. The word of God has an *objective* and *dynamic* character; in fact it is full of the power which comes from God (Jer 20,7–9). The prophetic word is creator and interpreter of history, since Israel and the prophets themselves always consider their relations

---

41 Cf. E. Jacob, *Théologie de l'A.T.*, p. 29.

111

with God within the sphere of history. Thus the divine word completes history and makes it comprehensible: in fact, the word of Yahweh stirs up and directs events and interprets their meaning (Am 3,7). God reveals to the prophets His salvific Will in the reality of history. The prophet perceives the meaning of the events and announces it to his contemporaries. In fact, he interprets history in a divine light. For example, through the events of the Exodus, interpreted by Moses himself, Israel knows that Yahweh is the living God, personal, one, omnipotent, faithful; the God Who saves the Chosen People and makes a Covenant with them (Dt 6,20–24). From this, one deduces that the attributes of God are revealed concretely, not abstractly, in history and through history itself. Thus we have Revelation the event and Revelation the word, which constitute the two forms which the word of God assumes in the prophets.

h. When God speaks, man must listen. God speaks to men through His word, through their conscience, through deeds. Man must reply not only passively, but also actively. The divine word which is heard must be assimilated with faith and with submission (Gn 15,7; 24,7; Mi 6,8). Israel has known God by means of Revelation, and thus has been admitted to a certain communion of thought and life with Yahweh. For man, this knowledge implies a total bond with God through faith, obedience, will and love. Whoever listens to the word of God must put it into practice. This is the constant preaching of the prophets (Hos 6,6; Mi 6,8; Jer 5,1–9; 9,2–5; 22,15s). Already from the time of Abraham, for the Hebrews "to believe" was equal "to obey" and to place trust in Yahweh, the one God of salvation.

i. Old Testament Revelation is essentially *interpersonal,* i.e., it does not deal with the manifestation of something, but rather with the manifestation of one person to another. Yahweh, the living and personal God, puts Himself into interpersonal relationship with man. Yahweh is at the same time both the subject and the object of Revelation. The word of God introduces man into a certain *communion* with God which is ordered to man's salvation.

God has made His Alliance with man as an owner with his servant, then as a father with his son, then as a friend with his friend, and finally as a husband with his wife.

j. In biblical Revelation, it is always God Who takes the *initiative*. It is also God Who reveals Himself when He wants and to whom He wants. God is *absolute liberty*. This liberty is shown in His different ways of revelation: in creation, in human nature, in history, in the prophets, in the priests, in the kings, in the shepherds, in the wise, etc. Hence Revelation is a divine intervention—*gratuitously and freely given*.

k. Revelation comes about through *deeds* and *feats* especially in history. Therefore the progress of Revelation is intimately connected with history. In fact, the manifestation of the various *attributes* of God depends on the different historical circumstances: in the Exodus, God reveals Himself as Savior; in the period of the conquest of Canaan, as God the omnipotent warrior; in the prophets, as the just, holy God, full of love.

1. The aim of Revelation is the salvation of men through communion with God Himself (Is 55,2). The hope of future salvation gives all of Revelation its own meaning; indeed all biblical history tends to the fullness of times, i.e., to Christ. Biblical time is not cyclical, but linear. . .

m. The People of God both in the Old and in the New Testament consider and study their own history in the light of new historical events, and thus incessantly perceive new dimensions and meanings. In this way Revelation grows quantitatively and qualitatively.

CHAPTER 3

Revelation in Judaism at the Time of the New Testament

After the Babylonian captivity the sages and scribes take the place of the prophets. For this reason, wisdom and the Law (the Torah) are studied more than the divine word. This explains why the doctrine of the divine word does not have a substantial development in this period. Nevertheless, in the non-canonical Judaic writings the divine word is represented according to two new aspects.

1. Palestinian Judaism and the Memrâ.

In Palestinian Judaic literature, there are different examples of the use of the divine word. For example, in the Syriac Apocalypse of Baruch 21,4, it says: "O You Who have made the firmament with *Your Word*. . . ." Still more important is the use of the word in the place of the name of God, in the *Assumption of Moses* 8,5: ". . . because of the wicked, one is forced to blaspheme the *word*. . . ." In this text, in the place of the word perhaps there was *Memrâ*, even though Charles thinks that it was probably *dibbar* (we have extant only the Latin text). This text of the *Assumption of Moses* is most important because the *word* is used in an absolute manner and without a complement.

Rabbinical theology always tries to stress the divine transcendency. For this reason, it uses different expressions to designate the name of Yahweh, like: "Merciful," "Holy," "Most High," "Heavens," "Glory," "(*Memrâ*) word of the Lord," "Shekina." The tendency to hypostatize the creative word of God is also found in rabbinical Judaism. Nevertheless, *Targum Onkelos* and

Yerushalmi I intentionally exclude from the narration of creation in Genesis the term *Memrâ,* so that the listeners in the synagogue do not see in it a hypostases of the creative power of God. Generally, when *Memrâ* is used in rabbinical theology, it is a synonym of the name of Yahweh. From this it does not seem that *Memrâ* is the immediate and direct origin of the Word (Logos) of St. John, which is related to the idea of the "word sent by God to men." See Strack-Billerbeck, II, p. 306, 333.

When the rabbis speak of *Memrâ,* it does not seem that they go beyond the purely poetic personification, just as happens in the rest of the Old Testament with the divine wisdom. In the liturgy of the synagogue, St. John could often have heard the expression "Memra Adonai," and the memory of this expression could have favored at least unconsciously the choice of the expression Word of God ("Logos tou Zeou").

2. The Doctrine of Philo Concerning the "Logos."

The Judaic-Alexandrine philosopher, Philo, uses the term Logos to designate a certain intermediary between God and created things in order to better preserve the divine transcendence. In order to explain the harmony existing in the universe, Philo establishes a principle of order that he himself calls *Logos of God,* or *Divine Word.* He considers this principle the instrument of God in the creation of the world, the image of God, the firstborn son of God. In the world, he dwells as a high priest in the temple; he is the intercessor of men before God, he constitutes the ideal according to which men should live, and the guide which brings them to the knowledge of God.[1]

St. John the Evangelist could have heard these ideas of Philo and perceived their similarity with the Christological doctrine. Indeed, Christ is the perfect image of the Father; He is His only-begotten Son; through Him God created all things; He is the true

[1] Cf. Filone, *De Cherubim,* 125–27; *Quod Deus immutabilis sit,* 57; *De somniis,* 1, 125; 2, 45; *De Fuga* 109–118; *Quis rerum divinarum heres,* 205s; *De confusione linguarum,* 147; *De migratione Abrahami,* 174.

and only High Priest and mediator before God. Christ is the way, the truth and the life. All of these similarities could have influenced St. John in his choice of the word and title of "Logos".

Nevertheless, we must also note the great differences between the Logos of Philo and the Logos of St. John.

a. The Logos of Philo is an intermediary subordinate to God, the Logos of St. John is similar to the Father in all things.

b. The Logos of Philo is called "son of God," but in the sense in which all creatures are called children of God; the Logos of St. John is really and truly the Incarnate and Eternal Son of God.

c. The Logos of Philo is not the Messiah whom he considers a great conqueror; the Logos of St. John is clearly represented as the Messiah.

d. In Philo's system, there is no possibility of the Incarnation of God, for God cannot have contact with matter without contamination; indeed matter is the principle of evil. For this reason, he seeks intermediaries between God and matter. On the contrary, the Logos of St. John becomes man, and is not contaminated by contact with matter.

e. The Logos of Philo is only the exaltation of human reason. The Logos of St. John comes into this world to bring us supernatural revelation; He Himself is the object of faith.

From what has been said, it can be concluded that apparently St. John has been influenced more by the doctrine of Wisdom in the Old Testament than by the doctrine and ideas of Philo. Nevertheless, he uses the expressions of Philo, which are known in the Judaic-Christian ecclesiastical circle, in order to express and present the doctrine of the Incarnate Word.[2]

[2] Cf. J. Salguero, "Il divino 'Logos' de San Juan" in *La Vida Sobrenatural* 66, 1965, p. 257ss.

CHAPTER 4

Divine Revelation in the New Testament

INTRODUCTION

The letter to the Hebrews (1,1) begins with these words: "God, Who at sundry times and in diverse manners spoke in times past to the fathers by the prophets, last of all in these days has spoken to us by His Son. . . ."

Christ constitutes the fullness of all Revelation. This full Revelation in Christ is described in different ways in the New Testament. Every book insists on this Revelation under a certain aspect. The Synoptic Gospels describe especially the historical manifestation of Christ, and intimately join His mission of Revealer with the title of Messiah, or doctor (rabbi), or teacher. The Acts of the Apostles present the Apostles as witnesses, ministers, and representatives of the word of Christ. St. Paul develops the idea of revelation, beginning from the theme of the mystery and gospel of Christ. The letter to the Hebrews compares the Economy of both Covenants and exalts the excellence of the Revelation of Christ. For St. John, Christ's true function as revealer is strictly connected with His quality as Word (Verbo = Logos) and as Son.

All of these different features of the Mystery of Christ are parts of the same reality, and they fulfill it and bring it to an end.

I. *The Synoptic Gospels*[1]

1. The Origin of the Gospels.

Modern critical studies have shown that the books of the New

---

[1] Cf. A. Bea, *La historicidad de los Evangelios* (Madrid, Razóy Fe, 1965);

Testament have all risen up in an atmosphere of faith; this constitutes one of their principal characteristics. We cannot assume the attitude of the historiographers of the past century. They were looking for "the pure historical source," free from every allusion, free from external influences. Such a source should report events in the precise, objective way in which they happened. This is not possible. In order to interpret and gather the true meaning of a biblical text, one needs an attitude of understanding and an effort to enter into syntony with the man speaking to me through a certain document. We will be able to gather the whole truth of a biblical text only if we seek to understand it in the vital situation of its original environment (= "Sitz im Leben"). Historical knowledge does not imply the gathering of "facts," so much as the reading, interpretation, hermeneutics of "human facts." Any kind of hermeneutic, besides scientific research, needs a connaturality with the object, an elective affinity, in which the awareness of the historian is involved in its existential components (affectivity and liberty).

Moving in an environment of faith—when one reads or studies the Gospels—is not an obstacle to the credibility of our documents; indeed, it points out their sound character. One is dealing with a preaching and a faith whose intimate exigency is to rest "on ab-

---

X. Leon-Dufour, "Les Evangiles Synoptiques" in *Introduction à la Bible, II: Nouveau Testament* (Tournai, 1959) p. 323 ss; M. J. Lagrange, Evangile selon *Saint Matthieu* (Paris 1927); B. C. Butler, *The Originality of St. Matthew* (Cambridge 1951); L. Vaganay, "Matthieu" in *Dictionnaire de la Bible. Supplément.* 5 (1957), 940–956; S. Munoz Iglesias, "El Evangelio de la infancia en San Mateo" in *Estudios Biblicos.*17 (1958) 243–273; J. Schmid, *L'Evangelo secondo Matteo* (Brescia, Morcelliana, 1965); IDEM, *L'Evangelo secondo Marco* (Brescia, Morcelliana, 1961); E. Trocme, *La formation de l'Evangelo secondo Luca* (Brescia, Morcelliana, 1957); V. Pisanello, *Il segreto messianico del vangelo di Marco* (Rovigo 1953); E. Rasco, Hans Conzelmann y la "Historia Salutis". A propósito de "Die Mitte der Zeit" y "Die Apostelgeschichte" in *Gregorianum* 46 (1965) 286–319; O. Da Spinetoli, *Introduzione ai Vangeli dell'Infanzia* (Brescia 1967); D. Laurentin, *Structure et théologie de Luc I–II* (Paris 1957); S. Munoz Iglesias, "El Evangelio de la Infancia en S. Lucas" in *Estudios Biblicos* 16 (1957) 329ss.

solutely certain facts," i.e., the facts of the life, death, and resurrection of Jesus. Only the certainty of these facts, guaranteed by witnesses, gives the preaching its reason for existence. The problem of the historicity of the Gospels is resolved in that of their origin. Indeed the Gospels are not originally passages of literature, but of preaching, of catechesis, of liturgy. For this reason, they are not works of one source, of one author only, but a group of numerous writings of various, and often anonymous authors. The incubation period of the actual Synoptic Gospels embraces about 30 years of time, from 35 to 65 A.D. In order to understand well the rapport between the primitive nucleus and the successive developments, adaptation, interpretations, or "forms" that they have assumed, one must know the protagonists of the actual compositions.

The environment that influenced the first expression of the teachings of Jesus is the biblical Old Testament tradition. Without the Old Testament and the traditions, the spiritual and cultural movements that give the setting for the preaching of Jesus and the Apostles, neither the formulation nor the content of the New Testament would be understood. Another key to the explanation of the actual physiognomy of the Gospels is the primitive Christian community with its problems, its apostolic preoccupations, its liturgical life, its internal and external difficulties.

2. The Three Stages of Revelation in the New Testament
   According to the Second Vatican Council.

For the comprehension of the Gospels and their doctrine of Revelation, it is of maximum importance to consider the three times of tradition through which the doctrine and life of Jesus have come down to us. The Church speaks to us of these three stages of tradition in certain documents; first, in a decree of the Biblical Commission (April 21, 1964) entitled: "Instruction on the Historical Truth of the Gospels;" and then in the "Dogmatic Constitution on Divine Revelation," *Dei Verbum* of the Second Vatican Council (November 18, 1965).

119

a. *The Decree of the Biblical Commission* exhorts the interpreter of Sacred Scripture to study and to follow diligently the three stages or times of the tradition of the New Testament through which the life and doctrine of Jesus have come to us: i.e., the *time* of *Christ,* the time of the *Apostles,* and the time of the *Sacred Writers,* so that the exactness of those things given to us through the Gospels may be established.

Christ the Lord wrote nothing, but He preached and He acted. In their non-literary, i.e., not written, first phase, the Gospels blend in with the salvific deeds accomplished by Christ more than they announce them. In this period there are Christ and His preaching, but not the Gospels. When Jesus presented His doctrine orally, He followed the methods of reasoning and explanation proper to the time, adapting Himself to the mentality of His listeners and doing it in such a way that the things He was teaching would be impressed in the mind and easily remembered by His disciples. In spite of His originality, Jesus Himself kept to the biblical tradition and was influenced by the environmental traditions. He could not go into many deep studies for which His audience was not prepared. More than once the Apostles confessed not having understood Jesus's discourse (Jn 2,17–27; 7,37–39; 12,13–16). Nevertheless the Apostles understood the miracles and the other events in Jesus's life in the right way, as deeds so prepared and arranged that through them men would believe in Christ and embrace the doctrine of salvation with faith. Jesus's richer and more profound preaching was undoubtedly that which He did after the Resurrection, in the forty days in which He remained to speak of the kingdom of God (Acts 1,3).

During His public life, Jesus had to establish the first guidelines for the Apostles and disciples, sent out to preach in Galilee. Hence there exists a "tradition of Jesus" even before He was able to fulfill His work. It probably collected the themes of the end of time, of conversion, of the kingdom, of the paternity of God, etc.

The *Apostles* begin their ecclesiastical activity around the message of Christ. From the simple testimony, or attestative repetition, of the salvific deeds, we pass to the preaching or internal teaching within the primitive community itself, i.e., to the *catechesis* and to the *didaché,* and from these to the *kerygma,* or announcement or proclamation of salvation to the pagans. From these elements is born the Apostolic Tradition, which gathers them together and channels them into one stream. But in the thirty years that pass between the Ascension and the appearance of the first Gospels, the "tradition of Jesus" is broken up into a vast multiplicity of local and personal communitary and particular formulations that will become the basis of the actual written compositions. The Apostles were not simple repeaters but witnesses authorized by Christ. Therefore, in preaching and in handing on the "tradition of Jesus," they initiate their own tradition, destined to be superimposed on the first. This is the *Apostolic Tradition,* which assumes various forms according to the preaching of the different Apostles. The preoccupation of the Twelve was to ". . . faithfully hand on what Jesus Christ, while living among men, really did and taught . . ." but, ". . . with that clearer understanding which they enjoyed after they had been instructed by the events of Christ's risen life and taught by the light of the Spirit of truth" (*Dei Verbum,* n. 19). Indeed, after Jesus had risen from the dead and after His divinity was clearly recognized, the Apostles began to venerate Jesus as Lord and Son of God. Their faith, however, did not cancel the memory of the events in the life of Jesus, nor did it deform His doctrine or His person. Instead, faith increased and clarified their memory. "Just as Jesus Himself, after His resurrection had interpreted (Lk 24, 27) the words of the Old Testament as His own" (Lk 24,44c; Acts 1,5), in like manner, they also explain the deeds and the words according to the exigencies of their hearers. Constant in the ministry of the word (Acts 6,4), they preached using methods of exposition adapted to their specific end and to the mentality of the hearers. . . . These methods of exposition, used in preaching the theme of Christ, are specified and divided into catechesis, nar-

121

rations, testimonies, hymns, doxologies, prayers and other similar literary forms which appear in Sacred Scripture and which were in use among men of that time."[2]

Easter revolutionized the minds of the Apostles. The gestures and words of Jesus, which had not been understood, were re-thought and meditated on in the light of the resurrection. To rediscover the Lord and to bring Him to the knowledge of everyone is the anxiety of the apostolic community. The Christian message is not a doctrine, but a program of life. It is not enough to accept it; it must be lived, and lived in such a way that others welcome it and translate it into practice. The important thing is not to precisely recount Jesus's life and the deeds that fill it, but rather to recount their salvific value. This pastoral preoccupation left the interest for history or chronicles in second place. It was not necessary to prove that Jesus had really existed (preoccupation of later times), but to show Who He was, the meaning of His coming, the value of His work, His historical influence.

Anti-Judaic apologetics, brings the evangelical preachers to look for constant comparisons between the prophecies of the Old Testament and the events of the New Testament. The narrations of the Passion, according to modern authors, are reconstructed on the bases of comparisons with the Servant of Yahweh (Is 52,13–53,12) and with Psalm 22. Different episodes of the infancy of Jesus have lost their primitive and original structure in order to be inserted into Old Testament or pre-existing popular schemes (cf Lk 1–2: annunciations to Zachary, to the Blessed Virgin, to the shepherds). For the primitive generation the temptations of Jesus are a retracing of the trials of Israel during the Exodus. The "coincidence" moves the real modalities of the events into second place, to the advantage of its meaning and its theological bearing. The evangelical message is transmitted through preaching but also through the liturgical action and sacramental life of the Church. The texts which describe the institution of the Eucharist

[2] *Instruction on the Historical Truth of the Gospels*, 2.

122

are drawn from the primitive Canon of the Christian Mass as well as from the memory of the Last Supper.

This is sufficient to make us understand the origin and range of the Gospels: they are a gift, but they are also a product of the apostolic community. The parenetic, catechetical, liturgical aims of the Church are not always equal to her historical preoccupations. The accommodation, the stylization pertain to the very nature of the liturgical celebration. Thus the Gospel, passed into the hands of the Church, although retaining its documentative value, assumes an external dress which is more devotional, edifying and theological than historical.[3]

When the *sacred authors* or *evangelist compilers* received this material, which had become increasingly more amorphous and dissimilar to the original, they subjected it to a final formulation and enrichment. The evangelists emerge through their personality, culture, and literary aptitudes. They are writers, but above all they are preachers of the Word. Thus their work has an eminently practical, parenetic, edifying character. This explains why the written Gospel, just like the oral one, is above all a work of faith rather than of erudition. One is dealing with narrations that seek to convince, to move and to instruct in order to lead to faith in Christ.

The evangelists do not limit themselves to simply re-transmitting the traditional data. Instead, they enrich them with their own personal memories, studies, comparisons, etc. Each one has written down the deeds and doctrine of Jesus with a method corresponding to the end proposed. Of the many things handed on, they chose some; at times they compiled a synthesis, at other times, seeing the situation of the individual churches, they developed certain elements . . . In fact, from all the material available to them, the hagiographers chose particularly that which was adapted to the various conditions of the faithful and to the end they proposed. . . . Actually, the fact that the evangelists referred to

---

[3] Cf. O. Da Spinetoli, *Bibbia parola umana e divina* (Bologna, 1968), p. 144.

the words and the deeds of the Lord in a different order and expressed His words, not according to the letter but according to the meaning, does not contradict the truth of the narration.[4] The Dogmatic Constitution *Dei Verbum* makes the same idea ever more precise: "The sacred authors wrote the four Gospels, selecting some things from the many which had been handed on by word of mouth or in writing, reducing some of them to a synthesis, explaining other things in view of the situation of their churches . . ." (*Ibid.*, n. 19). The choice, the synthesis, the explanation show the work and the personal contribution of the individual authors in the actual evangelical formulation. The necessity of choosing and of making some things emerge in preference to others is innate in whoever must sustain a particular thesis. The originality of the evangelists is manifested in the weaving, in the plot, in the orientation of the single events and the single teachings of the Lord. The culture and the personal learning of the evangelist serves to amplify the original discourse. Matthew comments on Jesus's mission with references to the Bible and to the popular Judaic traditions (*Midrashim*). But the ulterior study comes from the new situations which are created in the heart of the community. For example, the Beatitude of the poor, pronounced by Jesus in a Messianic sense, as the fulfillment of Is 58,6; 61,1, acquires a new meaning in Matthew and Luke. Matthew, who wants to establish the requirements of Christian "justice" or spirituality, intends poverty as an interior disposition to welcome the paradoxical goods of the Kingdom, i.e., poverty of spirit would be more or less equal to humility. Instead Luke, who writes for a community in which the rich take advantage of the poor, presents the Beatitudes as a warning to the one group and as a word of consolation to the other. The parable of the lost sheep was originally pronounced by Jesus against the accusation of the Pharisees that He was the friend of sinners (Lk 15,1–5). In Matthew it is addressed to the Christian community as an exhortation to forgive an erring brother (Mt 18,12–14). Actually, there-

[4] *Instruction on the Historical Truth of the Gospels*, 2.

124

fore, it is an appeal to the heads of the Church to be diligent shepherds.[5]

At times not only the primitive enunciation but also the primitive intention of Jesus can be forgotten, or passed over, when the catechetical-liturgical preoccupation of the Church or the aims of the evangelist do not coincide with those of the first author. Every evangelist has his own reconstruction and interpretation of Jesus's doings. Matthew, for example, sees Christ Who conquers temptations, as the new Israel; for Luke, He is the new Adam. For Matthew, the transfiguration is like the enthronement of Jesus as universal legislator; for Luke it is the preparation for His ascension and celestial exaltation. Thus the Gospel becomes a theology as well as a history. This is particularly clear in St. John where the symbolism, the liturgy, the theology have almost made the primitive historical nucleus forgotten. In the miracle of Cana, he emphasizes certain particulars which indicate his secondary intentions: the miracle "happens" after three days, "during a banquet," through the change of the Judaic ablution water into wine, near the time of the Passover. These details can be historical, but they are mentioned only for their symbolic value. St. John wants to show that the teachings of Christ are superior to the water of the Judaic amphora; the banquet is converted into the Eucharistic banquet. The Incarnate Word, Who wrought the miracle of Cana, is the same Who distributes His spiritual food in the Christian agapes and in the Eucharistic celebrations. There is no solution of continuity in the history of salvation.

The narration of the miracle of Cana is not therefore, the chronicle of a nuptial banquet, but a page of theology and sacramental liturgy. And as such, the hagiographer would not wish to give us the exact way in which the episode happened, for this would be the work of a chronicler, not a theologian. St. John and St. Paul are, first and foremost, theologians.[6]

[5] O. Da Spinetoli, *op. cit.* p. 117–119.
[6] O. Da Spinetoli, *op. cit.* p. 120–122.

b. The Second Vatican Council presents and teaches this same doctrine, just discussed, with these words:

"Holy Mother Church has firmly and with absolute constancy held, and continues to hold, that the four Gospels just named, whose historical character the Church unhesitatingly asserts, faithfully hand on what, Jesus Christ while living among men, really did and taught for their eternal salvation until the day He was taken up into heaven (Acts 1, 1–2). Indeed, after the ascension of the Lord the apostles handed on to their hearers what He had said and done. This they did with that clearer understanding which they enjoyed after they had been instructed by the events of Christ's risen life and taught by the Spirit of truth. The sacred authors wrote the four Gospels, selecting some things from the many which had been handed on by word of mouth, or in writing, reducing some of them to a synthesis, explicating some things in view of the situation of their churches, and preserving the form of proclamation but always in such fashion that they told us the honest truth about Jesus. For their intention in writing was that either from their own memory and recollections, or from the witness of those who themselves from the beginning were eyewitnesses and ministers of the word we might know the truth concerning those matters about which we have been instructed (Lk 1,2–4)".[7]

3. The Personality of Jesus.

During His human life, Jesus acted as a normal man, showing Himself to be like to us in all things except sin.

After the conception, the Madonna showed the external signs of maternity (Mt 1,18, Lk 2,5–6).

After birth He was wrapped in swaddling clothes like any other baby (Mt 1,25; Lk 2,6–12).

On the eighth day He was circumcised and then presented in the Temple as a male Hebrew (Lk 2,21–23).

[7] Cost. dogmatica *Dei Verbum*, cap. 5, n. 19.

He was persecuted and had to flee (Mt 2,13–18). Later He had to hide Himself in order not to be stoned (Jn 8,59).

Jesus grew in all senses, just as it happens in adolescence (Lk 2,40–52).

He was baptized like many others by John the Baptist (Mk 1,9).

He fasted and because of it felt hungry, and then was tempted by the devil (Mt 4,1–11).

In walking the ways of Palestine, he became tired and felt thirsty (Jn 4,3s).

He had relatives everyone knew, who felt ashamed of Him and considered Him mad (Mk 3,21.31).

He took part in secular feasts and was considered a glutton and a drinker (Mt 11,16ss; Jn 2,1ss).

He knew the human limitation of ignorance (Mk 9,21–33; 10,36; 13,32).

He rejoiced over the triumphs of the disciples, and He was saddened by misfortunes (Lk 10,17; 19,41; Jn 3,29; 11,3).

He loved with delicacy and He was moved to pity by the hungry crowd (Jn 11; Mk 6,34; 8,1).

He was irritated by unworthy actions (Jn 2,15s; Mk 8,11–13; 11, 15–19).

He was discouraged (Lk 22,43) and anguished in the face of death (Mk 11,33 ss; Lk 22,44).

He experienced death with all the sufferings of an unjust condemnation (Mk 15,44; Jn 19,34).

All of these features show us that Jesus is not a legendary or mythological personage, nor just the appearance of a man. He is an authentic man like anyone else born of a woman. Nothing that is human is extraneous to Jesus: "For which cause He is not ashamed to call them brethren" (Heb 2,11). Although Jewish by race, His life and attitudes indicate that He does not feel Himself coerced by the conventional limits of His time. He breaks the political, religious, social barriers then existing. Everyone— poor and rich, women and men, just and sinners, well and sick, children and adults—are received and treated with supreme goodness and mercy. He proclaims love for all men, be they Jew or pagan, and forgiveness for all, for everyone is our neighbor (Lk 10). Cf Heb 2,14–18.

4. The Mystery of Jesus Christ.

The historical existence of Jesus of Nazareth, together with the survival of His community, obliges all men sensitive to religious reality, to pose to themselves the problem of Jesus: Who is this extraordinary man? The Christian Church confesses that Jesus is truly and really the *Son of God*.

Indeed, during His public life everyone who approached Jesus found in Him something mysterious (Mk 3,31ss; Lk 2,48ss; Jn 6,15; 7,1–9.33–36; 10,24; 16,17–18,25). Jesus Himself at times lets some aspect of this mystery appear. The names by which He is designated by contemporaries and which He Himself uses, constitute images to express this mystery. The Synoptic Evangelists use different terms to express the personality of Jesus and His action of Revelation. Jesus is the Rabbi, the Teacher Who interprets Sacred Scripture with the maximum authority. He is the Prophet, Who preaches the word of God and works marvelous things; He is the Messiah foretold by the prophets in the Old Testament; He is the Son of David. . . . Nevertheless, it is not Jesus Himself Who attributes to Himself these titles, for He is something more: He is the Son of God. After the Passion, and especially after the Resurrection, which revealed the true identity of Christ, the Apostles and the faithful of the primitive Church abandoned these titles, and in their place substituted others, like: *Christ, Lord, Son of God*. The Synoptic Gospels however, still retain those titles (Rabbi, Teacher, Prophet, etc.). This shows the historical fidelity of the Synoptics.

a. Christ inaugurates His ministry like the prophets of the Old Testament: preaching good news and repentance (Mk 1,14s; Mt 4,17). He acts like a prophet, for He announces the coming of the Kingdom of God, reveals the mysteries of the final time, the punishment of the nations, and urges conversion (Mk 1,15; Mt 24). The crowds consider Him a prophet (Mk 6,15; 8,28; Mt 21,46; Lk 7,16; 24,19), and at the same time they ask if He is not "the prophet" par excellence, who is to come at the end of time (Mt 21,10–11; Jn 6,14; 9,17). At times, in a veiled manner, Jesus identifies Himself with the prophets when He says that He must accept the same lot (Mk 6,4). In the synagogue of Nazareth, Jesus applies to Himself the words of Deutero-Isaiah which present the Messiah Who preaches to the poor (Lk 4,18; Is 61,1–2). And in Mt 11,5, Christ considers the preaching done to the poor as the sign of the authenticity of His mission.

Jesus is the last of the prophets (Dt 18,18), Who fulfills and completes all of Revelation. Hence when He invites repentance, He is dealing with the last notification, the last eschatological invitation of God. Nevertheless, the unique and final character of Christ's prophetism is not sufficient to express the mystery of Jesus adequately: indeed Jesus is more than a prophet. Jesus is the fulfillment and the consummation of the Law and the Prophets (Mt 5,17); thus He does not say, like the ancient prophets: "the Lord says," but "I say to you" (Mt 5,22.28.32). He not only announces the coming of the Kingdom, He also indicates its presence (Mt 11,12; 12,28.32; Lk 17,21; 23, 42s). This presence is identified with His own person (Mk 3,22; Mt 11,6; Lk 7,23). He not only promises the forgiveness of sins, He also forgives them Himself: "Son, your sins are forgiven you" (Mt 9,2; Mk 2,5; Lk 5,20; Jn 5,1). "Young man, I say to you, arise" (Lk 7,14). These affirmations are of the greatest importance; indeed, the remission of sins and the resurrection of the dead constitute the exclusive privilege of God. Jesus is not a simple transmitter of the word of God, the way the prophets of the Old Testament were; He is the Word of God Himself sent to men: "And the Word was made flesh, and dwelt among us" (Jn 1,14; Heb 1,1–2).

b. In the Gospels, Jesus teaches often, and like the rabbis, He also has disciples (Mk 4, 34; 6,37–41; 11,1–6), and He inculcates in them new moral principles: poverty, humility, charity. However, Jesus' doctrine has a unique character (Mk 1,22; 11,28; Lk 4,31; Mt 7,28s), far superior to the doctrine of the most famous Jewish rabbis, for Jesus is not just a Rabbi: He is the Teacher par excellence (Mt 23,19). Jesus does not make a commentary on the Law like the Jewish rabbis; He interprets it, corrects it, and gives it a more profound meaning. "Heaven and earth will pass away, but My words will not pass away" (Mt 24,35). Hence Jesus possesses an *absolute* and exclusive authority, not coming from a human creature, which He claims for Himself and exercises. This supreme authority of Christ emanates from His Person. The mystery of this divine authority, which flows from the Person of Jesus, constitutes the mystery of Christ inasmuch as He is the executor and the completer of Revelation. The authority of Christ is the authority of God Himself. When Jesus speaks, God speaks, when Jesus works, God works.

c. The contemporaries of Jesus often give Him the title: Son of David (Mk 10, 47s; Mt 21,9). Jesus never attributes this title to Himself personally, but neither does He reject it (Mt 9,27–29). This attitude of Jesus seems to signify that He accepts what is true in the title, in Him are fulfilled the promises made to David. However, the title "Son of David" could be interpreted in a political sense, and therefore Jesus shows Himself cautious, oriented towards a higher and more mysterious origin (Mt 22,41–46). Instead the primitive community attributes this title to Christ often, for by this time there is no danger of interpreting it in a political sense. With it, the community expresses its faith that in Christ the hope of the liberation of Israel is fulfilled (Mt 1,1; Lk 3,23ss; Acts 2,34–36; Rom 1,3; 2Tim 2,8; Apoc 3,7).

d. Seeing the miracles of Jesus, the Jews ask themselves: Is this the Messiah? Jesus never uses this title to designate Himself. When they ask Him if He is the Messiah or not, He responds with an evasive answer (Jn 10,25). If anyone publicly proclaims His Messianism, Jesus orders Him to keep quiet (Mk 8,29s; Lk 4,41; 5,43; 7,36). Nevertheless, Jesus does not refuse the title of Messiah, but He does correct it, as we see when He is before the

Sanhedrin and before Pilate. To Pilate who asks Him in a political sense, "Are you the king of the Jews?" (Mk 15,2s; Jn 18,33), Jesus replies: "My kingdom is not of this world" (Jn 18,36). Before the Sanhedrin Jesus affirms that He is the Messiah (Mt 26, 62–64), and adds in explanation: ". . . I say to you, hereafter you shall see the Son of Man sitting at the right hand of the power and coming upon the clouds of heaven" (Mt 26,64). Therefore Jesus rejects earthly, political Messianism, giving to His own Messianism an interior, spiritual, heavenly character.

After the Resurrection and the coming of the Holy Spirit, when there is no longer any danger of misunderstanding the Messianism of Jesus the primitive community uses the title the Messiah-Christ to designate Jesus. This led to the followers of Jesus being called Christians, i.e., disciples of Christ, the Messiah (Acts 2,31; 3,18s; 4,26; 11,26).

e. When Jesus speaks with His disciples and wishes to make them understand His true mission in this world, He uses terms that recall to us the Servant of Yahweh (Is 42,1–4; 49,1–7; 50,4–11; 52,13–53,12), although He does not use the title itself. The noted characteristics of the Servant of Yahweh are His humble bearing, His voluntary acceptance of sufferings and death in substitution for the people, with the aim of obtaining the salvation of all and of re-establishing the Covenant with Yahweh.[8]

Jesus announces to His disciples that He is going towards death and that this is part of His mission (Mk 2,19s; 10,38s; Mt 12,39s; Lk 12,50; 13,31–33). Jesus accepts this death willingly (Mt 17,22s; 20,18s; Jn 10,17s; Heb 10,5–7), in substitution for the people (Mk 10,41–45). In the institution of the Eucharist, the allusion to Jesus' sacrifice is clear: He will hand over His body and He will shed His blood for many for the remission of sins (Mk 14,22–24; Mt 26,26–28). At the moment of Jesus' baptism, the evangelists apply to the Lord the words that allude to the

[8] L. Rubio Moran, *El Misterio de Cristo en la Historia de la Salvación*, p. 292–95.

Servant of Yahweh (Mk 1,11 = Is 42,1; Mt 12,15s = Is 42,1–4). The Gospel of St. John expresses the same idea by calling Jesus the *Lamb of God* Who takes away the sins of the world (Jn 1,29; Is 52–53).

The primitive Church continues to designate Christ with the title of *Servant of God* (Acts 3,13; 26,4,27; 1 Pt 2,21–25), but this seems to be only in small circles, influenced principally by the preaching of St. Peter. The title is soon abandoned, for the Christians understand this title defines the earthly mission of Jesus, without serving to explain His actual mission in heaven and in the Church.[9]

f. *The following of Christ.* Since Jesus is the fulfillment and coronation of all Revelation, He invites us to leave all and follow Him. But such an invitation demands a complete and total renunciation so that one can participate in the same life and in the same lot as Jesus. "To follow Jesus" is the new principle of moral action. Jesus is converted into the norm of human action and into the criterion for the Last Judgment (Mt 25,40). This explains very well why Jesus demands belief in His own Person, and why final salvation or damnation depends on man's attitude towards the Person of Jesus (Mt 10,32s; Mk 8,38; Lk 12,7).

If Jesus declares Himself greater than the Temple of Jerusalem (Mt 12,6), the "Son of Man," and the "Lord of the Sabbath," (Mt 12,8), these different formulas signify that in Jesus there is "still more," i.e., that the Revelation of the Old Testament is surpassed and all of Revelation is fulfilled.

g. In His preaching, Jesus announces the *Kingdom of God* and its "supremacy," i.e., the supreme power and importance of the Kingdom of God. The theme of the Kingdom of God constitutes the central theme of His preaching. Nevertheless, He frees this doctrine from its political, nationalistic, and earthly meanings, and gives it a religious, universal dimension. Jesus announces His own mystery in parables; indeed the Kingdom of God is already present in Him. Furthermore, the miracles and the virtues reserved to God do not constitute only the fulfillment of the Messianic

[9] L. Rubio Moran, *op. cit.* p. 294s.

prophecies (Mt 11,4–11). They also signify that in Jesus Himself God's dominion over the world and over the devil has already begun, and through it, sickness, death, and sin will be destroyed (Lk 11,20; Mt 12,28). Indeed the power to forgive sins and to cast out demons are signs that the Kingdom of God has already come into the world, that it is already in our midst (Mt 9,1–9; 17,20).

h. Jesus, *Son of the Father*. The fulfillment of Revelation and the mystery that surrounds the Person of Jesus of Nazareth are expressed even more deeply with the affirmation of the divine *filiation* of Jesus: "All things have been delivered to Me by My Father; and no one knows the Son except the Father; nor does anyone know the Father except the Son, and him to whom the Son chooses to reveal Him" (Mt 11,27). In this text Jesus reserves for Himself a knowledge similar to that which the Father has of Jesus Himself. This presupposes that Jesus belongs to a divine order and also possesses the divine essence. Therefore the knowledge Jesus has of the Father and of divine things surpasses all other knowledges, be they human or divine.

Thus Christ is the perfect revealer of the Father. In fact only Jesus knows the Father and His secrets perfectly (Mt 11,25–30).[10] The Father also reveals the Son; and this He does especially to the *little ones;* for no one can know the Son well, unless a special illumination is given to him by the Father Himself. This grace however is denied to the *wise* (Mt 11,25).

i. From all that has been said, one can conclude by affirming that the Synoptic Gospels consider Jesus the *Revealer par excellence,* for He is the only-begotten Son of the Father (Jn 1,18). Indeed "he who has seen Me has seen the Father" (Jn 14,9). This identity of nature explains very well the application made to Jesus Christ in the New Testament of the characteristics the Old Testament reserves only to Yahweh.[11]

Christ can reveal perfectly because He is the Son of God and

[10] Cf. A. Feuillet, in *Revue Biblique* 1955, 165–196; L. Cerfaux, in *Ephemerides Theologicae Lovanienses* 1955, 331 ss.

[11] Cf. S. Lyonnet, in *Ami du Clergé* 66, 1956, 33–48.

knows the secrets of the Father. The fundamental certainty of the apostolic Church is that Christ represents the supreme Revelation of God. His life-death-resurrection is the "salvific act" par excellence, the culminating manifestation of the love of the Father (Jn 3,16). Indeed Christ reproduces in Himself the divine salvific action, becoming thus the typical representation of the Holy God of the Old Testament. At the same time He summarizes in Himself the People of God, thus beginning the New Israel, the Church.

The essential theme of the Revelation of the New Testament is God's offering of salvation to all men, offered under the figure of the Kingdom of God, announced and established by Christ Himself. Jesus Christ becomes both the announcer of the Kingdom of God and its realizer. After Jesus's death the Apostles must continue preaching the Revelation which Christ entrusted to them. They must preach the Gospel of salvation to all men.

Faith is man's reply to the preaching of the Gospel. We are to be judged according to our attitude toward the word of God. Indeed, Christ announces the Revelation on which depends the salvation or the condemnation of men (Mk 16,15).

II. *The Acts of the Apostles*[12]

The Apostles have the obligation of preaching Revelation and of teaching it to the people. At the same time they must give testimony to the salvific mission of Christ (Acts 1,22; 4,2.18; 10,39.42).

a. In the first part the Author of the Acts of the Apostles often speaks of the testimony of the Apostles in favor of the Person of Christ and His Resurrection. The Apostles are *witnesses* of the entire mission of Christ, hence, they witness to what they have seen and believed (Acts 1,22). The announcing and the preaching done by these witnesses constitute Revelation.

The Apostles preach, teach, and witness to the word of Christ

---

[12] Cr. J. Dupont, *Etudes sur les Actes des Apôtres* (Paris 1967); IDEM, "La salut des Gentils et la signification théologique des Actes" in *New Testament Studies* 5 (1959 s) 132–155; H. Conzelmann, *Die Apostelgeschichte* (Tubinga, 1963).

(Acts 15,35). In other words, they proclaim the Good News of salvation preached by Christ ". . . there is no other name under heaven given to men by which we must be saved" (4,12; 10,36). They insist especially on the Resurrection of Christ (2,32; 3,15; 5,30; 10,41; 13,31) and on the idea that through His Resurrection He has been constituted the *judge* of the living and the dead (10,42), *Lord* (*Kyrios*) and *Christ* (2,36). Salvation is reached through faith and through Baptism (2,41; 18,8), which gives the remission of sins and confers the Holy Spirit (2,38; 5,31; 10,43; 13,38). The evangelical word preached by the Apostles is dynamic, efficacious, and coercive. The Apostles cannot do otherwise than preach the salvation brought by Christ. This Gospel is proclaimed with signs and wonders, which confirm the testimony given by the witnesses of the risen Christ (2,43; 3,6.16; 4,30). The miracles wrought *in the name of Jesus* (3,6) also show the glory which Christ received in the resurrection, as well as His divinity.

Hence the Acts of the Apostles describes the apostolic activity as a continuation of the activity of Christ. In fact the Apostles have received the word, the doctrine, and the Revelation of Christ. From the Lord Himself they have also the mission to testify to His resurrection and to preach and teach all that Jesus taught. The Apostles have fulfilled their mandate faithfully. Their task consists in this: to be witnesses, ministers, and delegates, messengers of Christ. Their testimony constitutes the object of our faith. The Revelation entrusted to the Church is contained in this apostolic testimony. Faith, which constitutes the reply of men to the preaching of the Apostles, is a divine work and the fruit of the interior action of the Holy Spirit, Who renders fruitful the word which is heard.[13]

b. According to J. Dupont, the theological scope of the Acts and its meaning would be to show how the message of salvation is manifested to the pagans. The unity between the intention of the Gospel of Luke and the Acts shows it to be thus. In fact, Luke wants to connect the conclusion of the Acts (28,25–28) with the

13 Cf. R. Latourelle, *Teologia de la Revelación*, p. 62.

text of Isaiah put at the beginning of His Gospel (Lk 3,3–6). With this it seems that Luke wants his writings to illustrate the salvation of God for all mankind and to insist on the universality of salvation. The conclusion of the Gospel of Luke (24,46–49) and the beginning of the Acts (1,8) illustrate the same idea. Jesus's discourse at Nazareth (Lk 4, 24–27) and the discourse of Pentecost (Acts 2,9–11) manifest horizons far wider than those of nationalistic Jews. These foresee the evangelization of the Gentiles. The episode of the conversion of Cornelius, which is of capital importance for the plan of the Acts (cc. 10–11), deals with the justification of the admission of the Gentiles into the Church. Peter will open the door of the Church to the Gentiles, but it will be Paul who will accomplish the annunciation of salvation to the ends of the earth, as far as the capitol of the Empire, Rome. In his discourses in the Acts, St. Paul, following Jesus Himself, insists on three Messianic signs: the sufferings of the Christ, His resurrection, and salvation being preached to the Gentiles.

Therefore, in composing the Acts, Luke wanted to show how salvation was being preached "to every flesh" and had reached "the ends of the earth," and how this universal orientation fulfilled the Messianic prophecies.[14]

III. Saint Paul[15]

In the thought of Paul, everything revolves around Christ Who

[14] J. Dupont, Etudes sur les Actes des Apotres, Paris 1967, 393ss.

[15] A. Deschamps, "Littérature et théologie pauliniennes" in Recherches Bibliques 5 (1960); L. Cerfaux, L'Itinéraire spirituel de Saint Paul (Paris 1961); IDEM, "Le Christ dans la théologie de saint Paul" Lectio Divina 6 (Paris 1954), also in English; IDEM, La théologie de L'Eglise suivant saint Paul (Paris 1965); F. Amiot, Les idées maîtresses de saint Paul (Paris 1959); J. M. Bover, Teologia de S. Pablo (Madrid 1946); L. Cerfaux, Jesucristo en S. Pablo (Bilbao, Desclée de Br., 1963); J. M. Gonzales Ruiz, "Función pleromática de la Iglesia según San Pablo" in XIII Sem. Bibl. Española, Madrid 1953, 73–109; O. Kuss, "Die Rolle des Apostles Paulus in der theologischen Entwicklung der Urkirche" in Münchener Theol. Zeits. 14 (1963) 1–59, 109–187; R. Schnackenburg, La Iglesia en el Nuevo Testamento (Barcelona, Estela, 1965); F. Spadafora, L'Escatologia in S. Paolo (Roma 1957); M. Denis, "L'apôtre Paul prophète messianique des Gentils" in Ephemerides Theologicae Lovanienses (1957) 245–318; F. Prat, Theologia di S. Paolo, I–II (Torino 1938 e 1953); L. Cerfaux,

died and rose. He is the converging point of every doctrinal explanation; He presides over all of history and human nature in the world and over the understanding of nature and of divine activity. Above all, Paul occupies himself with the glorified Christ, but this does not mean that within the Apostle there is a rupture between the Jesus of history and the Christ of faith. Before him, however, appears only the figure of the Lord and Christ (2 Cor 5,16), Who has completed the salvific plans of God, Who has become a fountain of life for us with His Spirit, through Whom we can have confident access to the Father.[16] Between Jesus and Paul there exists the same continuity as between Jesus and the Church. Therefore, all that Paul can say will be a homogeneous development, a growth of the faith lived by the Church.

The doctrine of St. Paul on Revelation insists in a special way on the ideas of the *mystery* and the *gospel* of Christ. Paul was made an apostle in order to preach the joyous message of the mystery revealed by God. The final doxology of the letter to the Romans (16,25–26) expresses the riches of the economy of Revelation extremely well. This occurs, almost in the same way, in the letter to the Colossians (1,25–27).[17]

L'Eglise des Corinthiens (Paris 1946); E. B. Allo, "Sagesse et Pneuma dans la premiére aux Corinthiens" in *Revue Biblique* 43 (1943) 321–346; P. Benoit, "Corps, tête, plérôme dans les épitres de la captivitë in *Revue Biblique* (1956) 5–44; M. E. Boismard, "L'Eucharistie selon saint Paul" in *Lumière et Vie* (1957) 93–106; A. Wikenhauser, *La mistica di San Paolo* (Brescia, 1958); S. Lyonnet, "Conception paulinienne de la Redemption" *Lumière et Vie* 7 (1958) 35–66; IDEM, La soteriologie paulinienne in *Introduction à la Bible*, II, p. 840891; IDEM, *Libertà cristiana e nuova legge* (Milano, 1963); R. G. Bandas, *La Redenzione, idea centrale in S. Paolo* (Roma 1961); C. Spicq, *La vita morale e la SS. Trinità secondo la dottrina di san Paolo* (Milano 1961); D. M. Stanley, *Christ's Resurrection in Pauline Soteriology Analecta Biblica*, 13 (Roma 1961; P. Benoit, "Le Legge e la Croce secondo S. Paolo" in *Esegesi e Teologia* (Roma, Ed. Paoline, 1964) p. 353–395; J. Cambier, "Justice de Dieu, salut de tous les hommes et foi" *Revue Biblique* 71 (1964) 537–383; H. M. Dion, La prédestination chez saint Paul" *Recherches de Science Religieusem* 53 (1965) 5–43; A. Feuillet, *Le Christ sagesse de Dieu* (Paris, EB, 1966).

[16] F. Prat, *La teologia di S. Paolo*, II (Torino 1927), p. 10.

[17] Cf. L. Cerfaux, *Le Christ dans la théologie de St. Paul*, Paris 1963; also English translation.

1. The Pauline "Mystery of Christ."

All Pauline theology is christocentric. Even when Paul speaks of God, he says that He is "the Father of Our Lord Jesus Christ" (2 Cor 1,3; Eph 1,3; Col 1,3). This paternity is placed on a metaphysical level, and in Jesus brings an equality of nature with God the Father. Indeed, Jesus is the "Son of God" in the strictest sense (1 Thes 1,10; Gal 4,4; Rom 8,29; Phil 2,7; Col 1,15ss), personal "Image" of Him (2 Cor 4,4; Col 1,15), "God" Himself (Rom 9,5; Ti 2,13). The theological reflection of Paul on the Person of Christ is founded on the christological faith of the whole primitive community. Without faith in the divinity of Jesus underlying eschatology, soteriology, and mysticism, the development of Pauline Christology would not be understood. Paul reflects especially on what Jesus has done, on how God has acted through Him, and on the condition of man before and after the intervention of Christ.

Pauline Christology is above all soteriological, i.e., it deals above all with the salvation of men and the reconciliation of the world through Christ. The center of Pauline thought is the redemption of all mankind through the cross of Christ. Christ is the realizer, the principle, and the mediator of salvation, to which man is called to participate. All this is summarized in the formula: *mystêrion tou Christou* = Mystery of Christ (Eph 3,4; Col 4,3).

This "mystery of Christ" considered in God is none other than His plan of salvation, proceeding from His love and from the free divine will (Col 2,2s). In Paul "the mystery of Christ" is conceived in a dynamic, rather than a static way. In fact, he treats of Christ dead and risen, Who dwells and works in our hearts (Eph 3,17), but Who demands our subjective, intellectual, and existential participation (Eph 3,18s; Col 3,3). Therefore "the mystery of Christ" signifies the mystery of the love of God for us, as well as the mystery of our union with Him in Christ, and the mystery of salvation procured for us by Jesus (Eph 3,12; Heb 9,15).

During the life of St. Paul the doctrine concerning the mystery

138

undergoes a certain evolution to a greater depth.[18]

In the older letters like 1 Corinthians and Romans, the *mystery* refers topically to the participation of the Gentiles in the advantages of salvation offered by Christ, and this through faith. At one time the pagans were considered pilgrims, and almost strangers as far as salvation was concerned. Indeed, this was reserved for the Jews. Now, instead, the divine plan for the salvation of all men is revealed; all are called to salvation through union with Christ (Col 1,25–28). Hence the *mystery* consists in the fact that the pagans are also "joint heirs and fellow members of the same body, and joint partakers of the promise in Christ Jesus through the gospel" (Eph 3,6).

On the contrary, in the letters of the imprisonment, the idea of the *mystery* is amplified; in fact *mystery* signifies the recapitulation of all things in Christ, and the submission of everything—the things of heaven as well as the things of earth—to Christ (Eph 1,10).

Therefore the mystery is Christ Himself and participation in Christ. Everything is established in Christ—in His manifestation, in the good that He offers us, in the way to God that He has shown us.

In the different texts of St. Paul, *the mystery is the divine plan of salvation,* hidden from eternity but now revealed through Christ, Whom God has established as the center of the new economy. At the same time God has established Him, through His death and resurrection, as the one principle of salvation for Jews and pagans alike, and as the head of all things. Indeed one is dealing with the total salvific plan (incarnation, redemption, election to glory). In a word, the *mystery is Christ Himself.*[19]

2. The Different Stages of the Revelation of the "Mystery of Christ."

The revelation of the mystery is made in different moments

[18] Cf. D. Deden, in *Ephemerides Theologicae Lovanienses* 1936, 403–442; B. Rigaux, in *New Testament Studies* 1958, 237–262.

[19] Cf. R. Latourelle, *Teologia de la Revelacion,* p. 64.

which correspond to the different features in the history of salvation.

a. First we have the mystery of the divine intention (= mystery of God). In this initial phase, the mystery is hidden in God. It constitutes the mystery hidden from the eternal ages (Rom 16,25; 1 Cor 2,7; Eph 3,5.9s; Col 1,26).

b. Later we have the realization of the mystery in Christ and through Christ (= mystery of Christ). What was once hidden, is *now* revealed (Rom 16,25; Col 1,26). With the life, death, and resurrection of Christ the phase of the realization of the mystery begins. Indeed in Christ, God's salvific plan is manifested and realized (Eph 1,7-9). This mystery is communicated first to the Apostles and prophets of the New Testament. They are the mediators and the ministers of this mystery (Eph 3,5); they are the foundation of the Church (Eph 1,22s; 2,20s). St. Paul is also an apostle and minister of this mystery (Col 1,25s). To Paul has been revealed in a special way that aspect of the mystery connected with the conversion of the pagans (Eph 3,8-9). And Paul, since he has been "chosen" and called for the conversion of the Gentiles (Rom 15,16; 1 Tim 2,7) has received a deeper understanding of this mystery (Eph 3,3-4).

c. After the revelation of the mystery by Christ Himself and by the Apostles, the mystery is presented to us as a *personal encounter* (= mystery of the Gospel, of the word, of faith). Once the mystery has been revealed to the forechosen, it is announced and preached to the faithful. The specific task of the Apostles is the proclamation of this mystery, i.e., of the gospel. For Paul *mystery* and *gospel* have the same value (Rom 16,25; Col 1,25s; Eph 1,9-13; 3,5s). Both deal with the same reality, i.e., with the divine plan of salvation, but in a different way. On one side, a revealed, manifested and communicated secret (1 Cor 15,1-2; Rom 2,16; 2 Cor 11,4; Gal 1,6) is dealt with; on the other side, one is dealing with announced and proclaimed good news (Eph 1,13; Col 1,5.23, etc.). The mystery and the gospel contain the same theme. They are concerned with the soteriological and eschatological aspects of Revelation (Eph 1,1–10.18; Col 1,28). Therefore this mystery (and this gospel) is preached to men as a plan of salvation under the form of *event* and *personal encounter.*

d. Finally, in its last phase, the mystery is considered in its relationship to all of mankind (= mystery of the Church). Since the mystery is the union or the recapitulation of all things in Christ, the Jews as well as the Gentiles must be united in one and the same organism of salvation. For this reason the Church appears as the final term of the mystery, its tangible and stable expression. Through the Gospel the salvific plan of Christ is revealed and proclaimed in the Church, and is effectively accomplished. The Church herself is the manifestation of the mystery of Christ (Eph 3,10; Col 1,16). Just as Christ is the mystery of God made visible, so the Church is the mystery of Christ made visible.[20]

3. The Knowledge and the Aim of the
   "Mystery of Christ."

The knowledge of the mystery or of the gospel is a dynamic knowledge, which can always become more perfect in the faithful. Hence there are different degrees of knowledge of the mystery. Those who are imperfect have an imperfect knowledge of the mystery; in fact they are incapable of understanding the wisdom of God (1 Cor 3,1–3). The perfect instead, i.e., those who are spiritually mature, have a deeper understanding of the mystery of salvation (1 Cor 2,6; 13,1; Eph 4,12s; Phil 3,15). Although in Paul this understanding is of a mystical order, all the faithful, nevertheless, are called to progress in the knowledge of the mystery of Christ.

The immediate aim of the revelation of the mystery and of the *Kerygma,* or preaching, is to bring all men to the obedience of faith (Rom 16,16), and to lead them to perfection in Christ (Col 1,18). In other words, the aim is to form the "body of Christ," which is the Church (Eph 1,22; 4,16; 5,23.30). Nevertheless the

20 Cf. R. Latourelle, *op. cit.,* p. 67s; C. Spicq, *Les Epîtres pastorales,* p. 120s.

141

final aim of the revelation of the mystery is "unto the praise of the glory of His grace" (Eph 1,6.12.14; Phil 2,11).

Describing the riches of the mystery of salvation (*Election, sonship, redemption*), Paul is profoundly shaken by the greatness of the salvific plan of God (Eph 1,14). Indeed, it is a work of the infinite wisdom of God and the extraordinary manifestation of His love for men (1 Cor 2,7; Rom 11,23; Col 2,2s). Paul speaks of this in the letter to the Ephesians 2,4–7.

The response of men to this infinite wisdom and love of God is total adhesion to this divine plan of salvation through *faith*. Faith however is possible only to those who want to listen to the word of truth and obey it. Indeed for Paul, faith consists in obeying the word (Rom 10,16.18; Gal 3,5) and the gospel (Rom 1,5; 16,26). The word therefore demands listening, acceptance, and custody.

However, adhesion to the evangelical preaching is not possible through simply natural forces. It requires the gift of the grace of God, the divine illumination, or the "unction" of God (2 cor 1,21s; 4,5s), which stirs up faith in the heart of him who listens to the gospel.[21] The preaching of the gospel constitutes the occasion for making a choice, and it will thus be the final prelude of separation. For some it will be a scandal and a reason for perdition (2 Thes 2,11; 1 Cor 1,18.21; Gal 5,11); for others, i.e., for those who believe, it will be the cause of final salvation (Rom 1,16s; Gal 3,11).

4.   The Historical and Eschatological Revelation of Paul.

Besides this understanding of faith and of love under the influence of the Holy Spirit (1 Cor 2,6; Col 2,2s), there exists another revelation—the eschatological revelation (1 Cor 13,12). The revelation that is announced by Paul is the historical revelation, i.e., the revelation made by the Historical Christ, in which the once hidden mystery is now revealed (Rom 16,25). This indeed is the revelation that constitutes the object of our faith,

[21] Cf. I. De La Potterie, in *Biblica* 1959, 24 s.

and is guided to its fulfillment in Christ and through Christ. Paul preaches this revelation, but he desires the escatological revelation even more. Then the Revelation of Our Lord Jesus Christ will be completed perfectly (1 Cor 1,7; 2 Thes 1,7), and all men will see the glory of the Son of God and the glory of the Christians (Rom 8,17ss).

This tension between historical and eschatological revelation, between the economy of the word and the vision is a noted characteristic of St. Paul (Phil 2,5–11).

Therefore revelation according to St. Paul is a free action of God, gratuitously made, through which God in Christ and through Christ manifests to the world His eternal plan of salvation to unite all things in Christ, the Savior and the Head of all creation. The communication of this plan comes about through the preaching of the gospel by the Apostles and the prophets of the New Testament. Under the motion and illumination of the Holy Spirit the response of man to the evangelical preaching is the obedience of faith. With the reception of faith begins the knowledge of the mystery of God; which increases until the vision of God in heaven is reached.

IV. Revelation in the Letter to the Hebrews.[22]

This letter tries to show the excellence of Christ as mediator and the superiority of the Priesthood of Christ over that of the Old Testament. In regard to the notion of Revelation, the novelty of this letter lies in its comparison between the Revelation of the New Covenant and that of the Old, and its exaltation of the demands of the divine word.

From the very first verses (Heb 1,1–2), the hagiographer speaks of the relationship between the two Covenants. Between

[22] Cf. C. Spicq, L'Epître aux Hébreux, I–II (Paris, EB, 1952–1953); IDEM, "El sacerdocio de Cristo en la Epistola a los Hebreos" Cultura Biblica 13 (1956) 232–38; T. Da Castel S. Pietro, "Il sacerdozio celeste di Cristo nella Lettera agli Ebrei" Gregorianum 29 (1958) 319–334; W. de Alfara, El cristocentrismo en Heb 1, 1–4: Estudios Franciscanos.60 (1959) 161–188.

the two there exists a relationship of *continuity* (God has spoken), but there also exists a difference (i.e., the superiority of the new Economy over the Old). The sacred writer also magnifies the pre-eminence and demands of the word of God, but always by means of the opposition between the Old and the New Testaments. Hence, he exhorts his readers to a greater docility toward the word of the Lord (Heb 2,1). Indeed, one owes more obedience to the Gospel than to the law of the Old Testament (Heb 2,2s). Christ is not like Moses, the servant. Instead, He is the *owner* of the house and the *Son* constituted by God as the head of the house (Heb 3, 1–6). Hence because of the origin and the superiority of the Mediator, the pre-eminence of the word of Christ demands from the faithful greater obedience and fidelity than in the Old Testament.

The word of God is *active, alive, efficacious, keener* than any two-edged sword, *extending* even to the division of soul and spirit, and *discerning* of the thoughts and intentions of the heart (Heb 4,12–13). The word of the Son, received and preached by the Apostles is confirmed by God through signs and charisms.

V. St. John[23]

John considers Christ as the Word (*Verbo*) of God. This

[23] Cf. O. Cullmann, *Les sacrements dans l'évangile johannique* (Paris, 1951); J. Dupont, *Essais sur la christologie de saint Jean* (Bruges, 1951); H. Van den Bussche, "L'attente de la grande Révélation dans le quatrième Evangile" Nouvelle *Revue théologique* 75 (1953) 1009–1019; F. M. Braun, Jean le Théologien, I–III (Paris 1964–1966); D. Mollat, "La divinité du Christ d'après saint Jean" *Lumière et Vie* 9 (1953 101–134; IDEM, "La foi dans le quatrième évangile" *Lumière et Vie* 22 (1955) 91–197; M. E. Boismard, "Jésus Sauveur d'après saint Jean," *Lumière et Vie* 15 (1954) 103–122; A. Feuillet, "L'incarnation rédemptrice dans les écrits johanniques," in *Introduction à la Bible* II (Tournai 1959) 890–914; IDEM, "Les 'ego eimi' christologiques du quatrième Evangile," *Recherches de Science Religieuse* 54 (1966) 5–22. 213–240; N. Lazure, *Les valeurs morales de la théologie johannique* (Paris 1965); J. Leal, "El simbolismo histórico del IV Evangelio" *Estudios Bíblicos* 19 (1960) 329–348; A. Feuillet, Le temps de l'Eglise selon saint Jean in *Etudes Johanniques* (Bruges 1962) 152–174; O. Cullmann, "L'évangile johannique et l'histoire du salut," in *New Testament Studies* 11 (1965) 111–122; I. De La Potterie-S. Lyonnet, *La vie selon l'Esprit, condition du chrétien* (Paris 1965).

concept influences the Johannine idea of Revelation. In fact, almost all the terms used in John's writings have a certain relation to the idea of word: "testimony," "light," "truth," "glory," "sign," "word," "to know," "to testify (witness)." In the Synoptics Christ teaches, preaches, announces the Good News of the Kingdom of God; in John He *speaks* and *bears witness.* He is certainly the Son Who speaks of His Father (Jn 1,18), the witness Who affirms what He has heard and seen in the bosom of His Father. In the Apocalypse, Christ is twice called the *faithful witness* (Rv 1,5; 3,14). Thus the Johannine notion of Revelation is intimately connected with the idea of testimony.[24]

1. Jesus Christ, Word (Logos) of God and Son of God.

Under the guidance and illumination of the Holy Spirit, St. John recognizes in the Person of Christ, the Wisdom and the Word of God, about which the sacred authors of the Old Testament had spoken (cf. Prv 8, 1–36; Sir 24,5–31; Wis 7–8; 9,10s). Jesus Christ therefore is the eternal Word of God, the *Creator* and the *Revealer,* but He is a Person. The Word of God has its perfect fulfillment in Christ, when it creates the world, when it imposes the law, when it announces salvation. For John, the *Logos* (= *Verbum*—Word) is a divine Person in intimate union and communication with the Father. He is a Person different from the Father, but at the same time He is God like the Father, Word of God, Logos of God (Jn 1,1). This Word, taking flesh among men (Jn 1,14), is the Son of the Father and the Firstborn of the Father. St. John attributes all revelation to this only-begotten Son (Jn 1,18).

Although it does not use our words of "revelation," "reveal," Johannine theology is in the highest degree a theology of Revelation. Applying the concept of *Logos* to Jesus, John gives Christianity its most comprehensive expression. The designation of Jesus as *Logos* tries to unite all creation in the revelation in Christ. The evangelist is thinking of the biblical "word" (cf Gn 1,3, etc.),

24 I. De La Potterie, in *Sacra Pagina,* II, p. 192–208.

more than of the Hellenistic meaning of "reason." In John the concept of *Logos* does have a marked cosmic reference (Jn 1,3), but different from Hellenism, it is understood as being rigorously personal, as a divine intermediary person. And with the unheard of expression, "and the Word was made flesh" (Jn 1,14), the dignity of being a cosmic, personal mediator is attributed to Jesus, historical mediator of salvation. This leads to the full universalism of revelation. With an incisive understanding the evangelist echoes the religious desires of his environment, the demands of the Judaic faith in the Messiah, as well as the demands of Gnosticism and Mysticism. He shows how they are fulfilled in the First-born of the Father (Jn 1,14). With the coming of Christ, God has shown us His love.

In John eschatology is not eliminated, but it no longer dominates the understanding of revelation. If in St. Paul the possession still depends on hope, in St. John the hope depends on possession. Hence the center of gravity of Christology is moved. The pre-existence of Christ and His post-existence are counterweighted (Jn 1,1s; 17,5). The Christian history of salvation refers only to the pre-existing Christ (Jn 8,58; 1,1–4). The earthly action of Jesus is no longer prevalently considered in the perspective of the hidden mystery, but in that of revelation (Jn 1,14; 1 Jn 1,1ss). In Jesus Christ, the reality of the living God shines in this world of sin and death (Jn 3,14ss). It is a discriminating reality which in this sense is presented as already in the act of judging and, above all, of bringing salvation and happiness. Faith in the *Logos* made flesh is the victory that has overcome the world (1 Jn 5,4).

In St. John, faith is essentially christological: Jesus is the Christ, the Son of God (Jn 14,1). For the fourth evangelist, faith is handing onself over to Jesus. It is giving one's self entirely to Him in a way that is not only intellectual, but also and above all vital (Jn 1,12; 3,21; 5,40; 6,35.37.44.56; 8,12.31; 9,5; 12,35.48; 15,4; 17,8). The fundamental object of faith is *Jesus,* the Christ and Son of God (Jn 20,31). His words, His testimony constitute a living reality, that vivifies (5,24; 8,51), that liberates (8,31), that purifies (15,3) and saves (12,47). The giving of one's self to Jesus is personal and total. Jesus must be received with the whole of one's being. Faith has a vital and existential sense that embraces the whole being and all of human life. Faith is an existential decision. Faith also has a dramatic character which consists in pronouncing oneself for or against life; he who believes has life (5,24); he who does not believe, has death (8,24).

According to St. John there are three stages of the manifestation and revelation of the *Word (Logos)* of *God:*

a. Creation is the first manifestation and revelation of God (cf Wis 9,1; Col 1, 15s). St. John clearly affirms: "All things were made through Him, and without Him was made nothing that has been made" (Jn 1,3). Since the world was created by God, the world must reveal the presence and the invisible perfections of God. Nevertheless, men refused to know and glorify the Creator of the world (Wis 13,1–9; Rom 1,18–23). Hence this first revelation of God did not fulfill its goal. For this St. John says: "He was in the world, and the world was made through Him and the world knew Him not" (Jn 1,10).[25]

b. Therefore God elected for Himself the people of Israel, and revealed Himself to them through the Law (Torah) and the Prophets. But not even this revelation reached its end: "He came unto His own, and His own received Him not" (Jn 1,11).

c. Finally, after God spoke to us by means of the Prophets, He *now* speaks to us by means of His Son: "And the Word was made flesh, and dwelt among us (pitched His tent among us: *posuit tabernaculum suum inter nos*)" (Jn 1,14). "No one has at any time seen God. The only-begotten Son, Who is in the bosom of the Father, He has revealed Him" (Jn 1,18). The Word-made-flesh manifests to us in a human way the divine salvific message, and reveals the love of God for men.

Since Christ is the divine person Who lives in the bosom of the

[25] Cf. M. E. Boismard, *Le prologue de S. Jean Paris,* 1953, p. 114.

Father, He is the only perfect and supreme revealer, surpassed by no one.

2. Christ the Witness of the Father;
   the Father Renders Witness to His Son.

Christ speaks as an authentic and genuine witness, for He is the Word of God and the Son of the Father (1, 1s.18). Only Jesus knows the Father, for He came from Him (6,46; 7,29; 16,27; 17,8), and He knows the Father just as the Father knows Christ Himself (7,29; 10,15). In fact, He is in the Father and the Father in Him (10,30; 17,21.23). Thus He can give authentic witness to the Father and to the salvific mission received from the Father ". . . we bear witness to what we have seen . . ." Jesus says (Jn 3,11). "I speak what I have seen with my Father . . ." (Jn 8,38).

The essential object of this testimony is that Christ is the Son of the Father and the Savior of the world sent by the Father, and that through faith in Him, men can reach eternal life (Jn 3,16; 17,3; 1 Jn 5,10s). The testimony, therefore, refers to Christ Himself and to His salvific mission.[26]

Not only does the Son bear witness to the Father and speak His words (Jn 3,34; 8,13s; 14,24; 17,8), the Father also bears witness to His Son and to the mission He has given Him (Jn 5,36; 8,18). The Father bears witness to the Son in two ways: first, through the *works,* second, through *attraction*. Indeed, the Father gives the Son the power to do the *works* the Father does, so that everyone may know that Jesus is sent by the Father (Jn 5,36; 10,15). Hence the works of Christ are like the works of the Father (7,21; 9,3s), since all that the Father possesses, the Son also possesses (17,10). Like the Father, the Son has power over life; He judges and raises the dead (5,25–30). Since the Father gives the Son His power and His works, this indicates the perfect union and identity of Will between the Father and the Son. The Father also bears witness to the Son through the attraction He

[26] Cf. R. Latourelle, *op. cit,* p. 81 x.

148

exerts on souls. For men to adhere to the word of the Son, it is necessary that the Father draw them to the Son. Indeed, Faith is a "gift" of the Father (6,65). It is for this reason that Christ can affirm that the Father gives Him the faithful who believe in His word (6,39; 10,29; 17,9–11). Without a doubt, the testimony of the Father and of the Son is essentially an invitation to believe. And this testimony is an act of the whole Trinity. The Son, sent by the Father, makes the Father and His love for men known (Jn 1,18; 1 Jn 4,8–10). Through the works performed by the Son, the Father bears witness that Jesus is the Son of God and the Messiah. Finally, the Holy Spirit not only gives an impulse towards the truth, but He also works in the hearts of the faithful for the purpose of preserving the word received through faith (1 Jn 2,20–27; 5,5–12).

3. Christ, God the Revealer and the God Revealed.

Since Christ is personally God and the Son of the Father, He is at the same time God the Revealer and the God Revealed. Christ reveals the word of God, and this word is Christ Himself sent by the Father (Jn 5,38; 17,3). Hence Christ is at the same time God Who speaks and the God Who is spoken of; He reveals the mystery of God and He Himself is this mystery (Jn 1,1; 14,5s). The words of Christ, like His Person, are the way, the truth, and the life (Jn 6,63; 17,17). To believe in Christ is to adhere to Christ and to His word. According to John, faith consists in this: in the knowledge of Christ's divine sonship and His salvific mission.[27]

The Revelation of Christ is also *light* and *life*. Christ is the light that leads to life (Jn 5,24; 3,16; 6,53; 10,10). But what is tragic in Revelation is that man can reject the testimony of Christ and go to perdition (Jn 1,11). The word of Christ is the word of salvation and life, but at the same time it obliges men to a definitive choice. For those who receive it, the word is salvation

---

[27] Cf. J. Alfaro, in *Gregorianum* 1961, 497–504.

and life (Jn 3,10–18; 1 Jn 3,1s); for those who do not receive
it, it is judgment and condemnation (Jn 12,47s).

4. The Apocalypse of John.

Here the picture is completely different from that of the fourth
Gospel. Agreement between the Apocalypse and other Johannine
writings is not lacking, as, for example, the designation of *Logos*
in Apoc. 19,13. But the Apocalypse does not center its theology
on the concept of *Logos* as do the Gospel and the letters. The
understanding of revelation is here directed entirely toward the
future. In the eschatological perspective and in the employment
of many visions, the Apocalypse shows a great affinity with the
Judaic apocalypse. Above all, the Apocalypse aims at strengthening
the Church, the depository of Revelation, in her first serious clash
with the power of the State, and at preparing her to be faithful
to Christ: "Be faithful unto death, and I will give you the crown
of life!" (Rv 2,10).

5. Conclusions.

St. John therefore considers Revelation as the Incarnate Word
(Logos) of God, Who, in the Person of Christ, addresses Himself or speaks immediately to the Apostles and by means of them
to all mankind, in order to testify to the love of the Father for
men. Indeed, the Father has sent His Son into the world, so that
everyone may believe in Him and have eternal life. Faith is the
response to the exterior witness of Christ, to the interior attraction
of the Father and to the witness of the Holy Spirit.[28]

VI. The Revelation of the New Testament as the Fulfillment of All Revelation.[29]

1. The Event and Its Interpretation.

The Prophets of the Old Testament are used to seeing in a deter-

[28] Cf. R. Latourelle, *op. cit.*, p. 77–86.

[29] Cf. H. De Lubac, "Le problème du dévéloppement du dogma," *Recherches
de Science Religieuse* 35 (130–160); E. Brunner, *Das Ewige als Zukunft und
Gegenwart* (Zürich 1953); J. Schmitt, *Jésus ressucité dans la prédication*

mined historical event the very special word of God, in which the divine salvific Will is revealed, and in which the prophets themselves are inserted. This divine word is placed in relation to the other preceding revelations, which are now re-interpreted in truth. The history of Revelation, in fact, and the history of its interpretation have an intimate and strict relation to the history of salvation, which dominates everything. This means that the prophecies of the prophets cannot be separated from the *events*.

Just as in the Old Testament, so too in the New Testament we find a continual and progressive evolution of the kerygma under the influence of new events; i.e., we find a progressive union of the actual events with a certain already-formed kerygma, which is always re-interpreted. There exists, however, an essential difference between the Old and the New Testament. In the New Testament, the actual event, which constituted the beginning of the re-interpretation, is considered the *decisive* event, i.e., *normative* for all salvation history. This means that all the things that precede are related to this decisive and definitive event. Thus, this event comprises in itself all past, present and future salvation history.[30]

The decisive and definitive event is that *God spoke by means of His Son* (Heb 1,2). From one point of view, this event includes all preceding and following salvation history; from another point of view this event is inserted into it. The New Testament

apostolique (Paris 1949); D. Grasso, "Il kerygma e la predicazione," *Gregorianum* 43 (1960) 424–450; O. Cullmann, *Christ et le temps* (Neuchâtel, 1957); versioni in italiano, spagnolo, inglese, tedesco; A. Nyssens, *La plénitude de vérité dans le Verbe incarné: Doctrine de S. Thomas d'Aquin* (Baudouinville, 1961); P. Althaus, *Il cosiddetto Kerigma e il Gesù della storia* (Quaderni di Divinitas, II, Roma 1962) pp. 55 ss; F. X. Durrwell, *La résurrection de Jésus, mystère de salut* (Le Puy, 1963); J. Dejaifve, "Révélation et Eglise," *Nouvelle Revue théologique* 85 (1963) 563–576; J. Jeremias, *The Central Message of the New Testament* (Londra 1965); H. Schlier, *Il tempo della Chiesa* (Bologna 1965); O. Cullmann, *Il mistero della Redenzione nella storia* (Bologna, Mulino, 1966); H. Fries, "La Rivelazione," in *Mysterium Salutis*, I (Brescia, Queriniana, 1967) p. 314 ss; L. Rubio Moran, *El misterio de Cristo en la Historia de la Salvación* (Salamanca, Sígueme, 1968) pp. 311–469.

[30] Cf. O. Cullmann, *Il Mistero della Redenzione nella storia*, Bologna, Il Mulino, 1966, p. 130.

not only changes the perspective, but it also constitutes the foundation of the interpretation of all of Revelation. In the New Testament one is dealing with the election of the One Person [Jesus] towards Whom the people of Israel tend, and from Whom the election of the "New Israel" draws its origin.

O. Cullman conceives the movement of the history of salvation in a linear sense which progressively grows more restrictive: from all of mankind to the people of Israel, from Israel to a "Remnant" of the people, from this "Remnant" to the One Person, i.e., Christ. From this *center* (= Christ), a new life-growth process begins from the group of the Apostles to the primitive community and to the Catholic Church. In this way the concept of the election of the people of God is conserved as a constant line of salvation history, and at the same time in the light of the Revelation of Christ this concept is given a new orientation. The verticality of the Christ-event does not abolish the horizontality of the historical process of the redemption, but it does give it a new meaning.[3] On this radically new orientation given by the event which recognizes faith as decisive, depends the more intense awareness of the New Testament witness as the "bearer of a revelation." This explains very well the pre-eminence of the *eye-witness testimony* to the Christ-event. Such testimony has no equal in the Old Testament. In this sense, the mediators of the revelation of the New Testament, the Apostles, have a greater importance than the prophets of the Old Testament. This difference is due to the fact that in Christ not only the redemption, but also the revelation of redemption, reach their culmination. From then on, all revealers are direct instruments of the One Revealer, Christ.

In the brief period of the primitive Church, i.e., from the death of Jesus to the death of the last Apostle, different re-interpretations of evangelical events are given. In fact, the Gospels, written and composed in this period, manifest the influence of their time and environment. The awareness which the authors of the Gospel

[31] O. Cullmann, *op. cit.* p. 131.

have of their revelatory work is clearly shown in the fourth Gospel, and also in the Synoptics, although less clearly. The authors of the New Testament already possessed the oral traditions, which had interpreted, at least in part, the kerygma coming from Christ Himself in the light of the new events (Easter and the sending of the Holy Spirit). Even the Apostles, witnesses of all the earthly (public) life of Jesus, understood the life of Christ perfectly only after His death and resurrection and with the help of the Holy Spirit. Since the primitive community had the full revelation of the events concerning the life of Christ only in the light of Easter, it was of great importance that some of the members of the Church be eye-witnesses of the events of the earthly life of Jesus. Indeed, the Apostles themselves had to connect the events of the life of Jesus with His Resurrection and interpret them in this light, while maintaining continuity between the new events and the kerygma they themselves were already preaching. After the events of Easter and of Pentecost, the Apostles understood clearly that all the things they had heard and seen in the life of Jesus constituted the *definitive revelation* of God.

The life, doctrine, redeeming death, and resurrection of Christ constitute at the same time only one central kerygma, in which the history of salvation reaches its peak. Jesus Himself is the author of the event of redemption and of its revelation. Hence the connection between the event of redemption and the revelation of this event is perfect. In fact in this appears the intimate link between redemption and revelation. In truth, Jesus reveals Himself as the culmination of the whole historical-salvific process: the Kingdom of God is manifested in His own person, and in Him is fulfilled the whole history of salvation (Mt 12,28). Nevertheless, it must be admitted that there is an evident progress between the interpretation of Jesus and the interpretation of the disciples after Easter. It must also be admitted that in reality there exists a continuity between the kerygma of the historical Jesus and the kerygma of the disciples.

On the other hand, the proclamation of Jesus as center and

fulfillment of the entire historical salvific process does not belong only to the primitive community and to the Apostles; it must also be attributed to Jesus Himself. Indeed, the primitive community affirms that Jesus of Nazareth—whose earthly life was known by the first witnesses—was the true executor of all of the salvation history of Israel and bearer of the definitive redemption. But in giving this interpretation, the primitive community and the Apostles themselves are not relying on the kerygma of the Old Testament, but on the kerygma of the historical Jesus, i.e., on His life and His preaching. Hence the process of connecting the new kerygma of the Apostles and the primitive community with the kerygma of Jesus begins immediately after Easter. The persons who brought this conjunction to an end were the eyewitnesses of the events of Christ. For this reason it is really very difficult to think that one is dealing with two different kerygmas.

We believe that everything can be easily explained if we admit that the new revelation received by the disciples, in the light of the paschal events, consists precisely in this: after the Resurrection of Christ all the things that the Apostles *had heard* and *seen* were fully illuminated for them and they knew and understood them with absolute certainty. The new faith, after the Paschal event, was faith in the revelation that Jesus had already given of Himself, i.e., of His Messianity, of His divine sonship and of His definitive salvific redemptive work. Without a doubt, the primitive community believed in the Messiahship of Jesus, for the same community had the full certainty that Jesus presented Himself as Messiah and had preached as such (contrary to what R. Bultmann thinks).

2. The Fulfillment of Revelation in Christ.

The New Testament is based on acceptance of the full and definitive Revelation by Christ. This Revelation is represented under a personal, historical, active form, which already appears in the Old Testament. In reality what Jesus reveals is the word of the love of the Father and His salvific will. We are not dealing with a system of ruth, but a way to follow. The *truth* that Jesus reveals is not an object of intellectual speculation, but the *way* and the *life* (Jn 14,6). It is *fidelity* and the duty of obeying God as in the Old Testament. Jesus speaks truly, but "He speaks" principally by means of His own Person, by means of His action rather than by work. Christ not only transmits the word; He Himself is the same substantial, living Word (*Verbum*).

a. According to the concept of the Old Testament, the Word of God is intimately connected with the *action of God:* it constitutes the *word-history,* the *word-action,* the *word-event.* This intimate interpenetration of word and action reaches its highest degree in Jesus Christ. Since Jesus Christ, is *the event,* the word and the action of God are identified as one in Him. In the life and action of Christ, in the deeds in which the divine power is manifested— especially in the cross, the resurrection, the exaltation and the sending of the Holy Spirit—the definitive action of God appears. It is manifested once for always, changing all and making all things new.

b. Also in Jesus the *name* "that is above every name" is present (Phil 2,9). As often happens in the New Testament, Jesus identifies "the name of God," "the name of the Lord" with Himself, with His own name, and attributes to His own name the same virtue, the same power. This substitution of the name of God with the name of Jesus shows in a decisive way the fulfillment of the self-manifestation and revelation of God in Christ. Indeed, in the name of Jesus is manifested clearly and finally what was, at the beginning, implicitly contained in the name of God but never brought to final perfection, i.e., to present God as a present and personal reality, as a revealed and manifested mystery. The *name of Jesus* is the name through which all are saved (Acts 4:12), the name through which everyone can invoke God, and through which the faithful are gathered together (Mt 18,20); the name through which God hears us (Jn 18,23). "For there is no other name under heaven given to men by which we must be saved" (Acts 4,12).

3. Jesus, Founder of the New Covenant.

Even in this, the fulfillment of Revelation is shown; in fact, Jesus founded a new and eternal Covenant, and thus fulfilled the ancient promise, which was certainly very important in the Old Testament. The multiplication of the covenants and their continual renewal indicated that the decisive and definitive reality had not yet arrived. Finally, with Jesus Christ, especially in the Last Supper and in the sacrifice of the cross, the new and eternal Covenant is realized, and a new and definitive community of salvation willed by God is founded (Mt 26, 26ss; Lk 22,19).

The definitive character of this new Covenant and the fulfillment of all the preceding ones are observed also in the fact that Jesus Christ, mediator of the new Covenant, is the Son of God and therefore transcends the Priesthood and the Liturgy of the Old Testament. Indeed He Himself is at the same time both priest and victim (Heb 4,14; 5,1–9; 7,24.28; 8–10).

All the promises of the Old Testament referred to the future Messiah. Jesus is truly the Messiah. All the evangelists try to show this. Matthew shows it explicitly. He considers all the events in Jesus's life as the fulfillment of the Messianic prophecies: "Now all this came to pass that what was spoken by the Lord through the prophet might be fulfilled" (Mt 1,22; 2,15.17, etc.). It seems that the Gospel of St. John originally finished with these words: "But these are written that you may believe that Jesus is the Christ, the Son of God, and that believing you may have life in His name" (Jn 20,31). Hence from the beginning the confession that Jesus was the Christ (= the Messiah) constituted the center of Christian faith, doctrine, preaching, actions of grace, etc.[32] In the early Church, preaching Jesus as the *Christ* or the *Messiah* was more appropriate for the Jews, while preaching Jesus as the *Kyrios* (= Lord) was more suitable for the pagans. Hence the confession and the compendium of the early Christian faith are

[32] H. Fries, in *Mysterium Salutis,* I, 303.

contained in the expressions: Jesus-Christ-Lord (Kyrios): Jesus is Christ, Jesus is Lord (Phil 2,11).

4. Jesus Christ, Executor of Revelation in Creation.

According to the doctrine of St. Paul, Jesus Christ is also the fulfillment of Revelation in creation. In fact, according to the Letter to the Colossians: Christ is "the firstborn of every creature" (Col 1,15). At the same time He is also the foundation and the end of creation. St. John and St. Paul speak clearly to us of this. Indeed, for John, Jesus is the Word Who was "in the beginning", through Whom all things were made (Jn 1,1.3). St. Paul, in the Letter to the Colossians, expresses this same idea even more clearly. "For in Him were created all things in the heavens and on the earth, things visible and things invisible. . . . All things have been created through and unto Him, and He is before all creatures, and in Him all things hold together" (Col 1,16–17). In the Letter to the Hebrews we read: "Who, being the brightness of His glory and the image of His substance, and upholding all things by the word of His power . . ." (Heb 1,3).

For this reason, Christ is the head of all the universe, and as such He can be called the first and the last, the beginning and the end, the alpha and the omega (Rv 1,17; 22,13). If, therefore, Christ is not only the foundation but also the end of creation, creation can be considered as always tending toward Christ. This same Christ constitutes the ultimate fulfillment of creation. Indeed, He is the fullness of all the work of creation, for He is the most perfect man and the new, authentic model or exemplar of man; He is the second and true Adam (1 Cor 15,21s.45s).

5. The Resurrection of Christ, the Greatest Sign of the Fulfillment of Revelation.

The greatest event of Revelation, fulfilled in history and in the Person of Christ, is the resurrection of Jesus from the dead. According to the New Testament this event is the clearest and most evident proof of the fulfillment of all Revelation. For this reason St. Peter says: "Therefore, let all the house of Israel know most assuredly that God has made both Lord and Christ, this Jesus Whom you crucified" (Acts 2,36). Thus the resurrection of Jesus Christ is the theme and the foundation of Christian preaching and faith. St. Paul says, ". . . if Christ has not risen, vain then is our preaching, vain too is your faith" (1 Cor 15,14).

The story of Easter and the Resurrection, on which all the evangelists and authors of the New Testament agree, cannot be considered something unreal. Concerning the modern question disputed by the critics: the answer to whether or not the Resurrection of Jesus is a historical reality depends upon the notion of historical reality held up by the aforesaid critics. If historical reality is considered such by the fact that its fulfillment can be explained in a natural way, either because the fact is an object of observation or because the Resurrection of Christ has internal analogies with ordinary history, then the Resurrection of Christ would not be a historical reality, for it does not comply with these conditions. As a fact and as a way of being, the Resurrection of Christ constitutes something new, entirely different from what is commonly found in empirical history. Indeed, the Resurrection is the irruption of a new and final eon, which in truth is characterized not by the fact that "the dead will rise to life," but by the fact that death will be definitively destroyed. According to W. Künneth, the Resurrection has only one significant parallel: the creation of the world.[33] Hence, as a reality the Resurrection surpasses all other historical realities. Without any analogies or empirical causality, the Resurrection of Jesus is verified in the world and in history, as a reality "not of this world, but in this world." If instead the denomination of "historical reality" refers to the realization of the Resurrection in the history of this world, then the Resurrection of Jesus is a historical reality in the eminent sense of the word.[34]

[33] *Theologie der Auferstehung*, München 1951.
[34] H. Fries, in *Mysterium Salutis*, I, p. 306s; R. Marlé-A. Kolping, Aufer-

The Resurrection of Christ shows that Jesus as *Lord* and *Christ* is the fulfillment of Revelation. This fulfillment of revelation must be understood in the sense of *today*, of *behold*, of the personal presence of God, in the sense of all the possibilities and of all the structures of revelation. St. Paul expresses these concepts in this way: "For the Son of God, Jesus Christ, Who was preached among you by us . . . was not now 'yes' and now 'no,' but only 'yes' was in Him. For all the promises of God find their 'yes' in Him, and therefore through Him also rises our 'Amen' to God unto our glory" (2 Cor 1,19s).

In the light of the Easter events, the early community was given the full revelation, even retrospectively, on the events in the life of Jesus. For the Apostles and the first Christians, it was clear that the life lived by Jesus and the teaching given by Him constituted the central *kerygma* in which the entire history of salvation culminated. At the same time, they had to hand on that already formed and reinterpreted *kerygma* of Jesus. In this *kerygma*, pre-existent to the Apostles and rediscovered by them after the death and resurrection of the Lord, Jesus Himself is the author of the redemptive event and its relative revelation. We know Jesus' *kerygma* only through the disciples. They are at one and the same time those who hand the *kerygma* on and those who reinterpret it in the light of the Paschal Happenings. Thus the great problem of the rapport between the "Kerygmatic Christ" and the "historical Jesus" is posed.

For the Apostles and the first disciples of Jesus there is undoubtedly a strict connection, because for them the risen Jesus is the same person Who completed His decisive work upon the earth; all their actual activity has its foundation in the life of the Incarnate Jesus. The conviction of this continuity grafts the process of reinterpretation onto the rapport between the Incarnate Christ and the glorified Christ. The consciousness of the disciples of being instruments of Jesus Christ, Who after His Resurrection create

stehung Jesu, in *Harvard Theological Review* I, p. 130–145; W. Pannenberg, *Grundzüge der Christologie*, p. 47–112.

the post-paschal tradition on His earthly work, is particularly evident in the Gospel of St. John (14,26; 16,12). The stronger this awareness is, the firmer the faith is that there can be no difference between the *kerygma* of the historical Jesus and that of the glorified or kerygmatic Jesus.

6. The Mission of the Holy Spirit as Fulfillment of Revelation

In the Old Testament the Holy Spirit is represented as the Spirit of God, as the operative power of God manifested in history and in creation. The Spirit of God speaks through the Prophets (Heb 1,1). The Prophets of the Old Testament affirm that the Messiah must possess this Spirit (Is 42,1ss; 61,1s). The effusion of this Spirit of God is promised for the Messianic time (Jl 3,1–5; Zec 12,10). The Holy Spirit also has part in the Incarnation of Jesus (Lk 1,35), in the life, preaching and apostolic activity of Christ (Mt 12,28; Lk 11,20). Jesus claimed the presence of the "Spirit of the Lord" in a special way (Lk 4,18), and it is manifested in Christ at the moment of His "Messianic consecration" (Mt 3,16; Mk 1,8).

This promise of the Holy Spirit (Acts 1,8) is fulfilled on the day of Pentecost (Acts 2). Without a doubt this event constitutes the last seal of the Revelation accomplished in Christ. Indeed, through the continual action of the Holy Spirit on the Apostles and on the Church new possibilities and new means of obtaining the salvation of Christ are incessantly offered.

According to St. Paul the mystery of Christ is known in the Holy Spirit (1 Cor 12,3). The faithful are aware, and through the Holy Spirit they know, that they are "sons of God," and can therefore call God: *Abba, Father* (Rom 8,15). The Church, as the Body of Christ, is vivified by the Holy Spirit and is brought to the unity of persons and of ministries (in the multiplicity of gifts) (1 Cor 12; Eph 4,4). In this sense the Church can be considered "the continuation of the union of Jesus with the Holy Spirit in the history of salvation, or as the mystery of the identity of the Holy Spirit in Christ and in Christians. In the Holy Spirit the

160

work of the salvation of Christ is offered and actualized. This happens through the apostolic preaching, which becomes the *kerygma* of Jesus, Kyrios, and Christ, thanks to the Holy Spirit Who introduces the faithful to the full truth in a way adapted to the new historically created situation.[35]

The Apostles receive the fullness of the Holy Spirit so that they can present Revelation and preach it to all the nations (Mt 28,18–20). This apostolic preaching about Jesus as "Lord and Christ" is extended to the same salvific event, i.e., to the work of Revelation accomplished in Christ. That is, as witnesses of the Resurrection chosen by God Himself, the Apostles belong to the Revelation of God in Jesus Christ crucified and glorified. This brings us to another consequence of maximum importance: the Revelation brought to fulfillment in Jesus Christ is "closed with the Apostles" (Denz. 3421). It is impossible to establish a year or a precise date for this closure; it deals rather with a certain objective determination. This objective determination is in the fundamental distinction between Revelation and Tradition, between origin and sequel, between normative constitution and continuation.

With this we express the absolutely unique and non-repeatable character of the Revelation accomplished in Christ and in His work. This means that it is impossible for there to be any other beginning of Revelation, in the sense of a personal self-manifestation of God. The only possibility is of a tradition through which the beginning is handed on and which has a certain evolution or development of Revelation inasmuch as it leads us—under the guidance of the Church—to a deeper and full understanding of the "original fullness."

7. Revelation and Its Fulfillment in the Church.

". . . God chose to reveal Himself and to make known to us the hidden purpose of His will" (*Dei Verbum,* n. 2). This form of Revelation through the *Son* in the Holy Spirit is definitive, ultimate

---

[35] H. Fries, *op. cit.* I, p. 308s.

and, in this sense, eschatological. Nevertheless the eternal salvation revealed through the Son in the Holy Spirit is salvation for all men, for all mankind. In a historical, concrete, and physical manner, the Church manifests to all men the universal salvific Will of God, and at the same time offers to all eternal salvation. Hence the mission of the Church is to offer salvation to all men, and thus constitute a sign of the merciful love of God for men.

The irrevocability of the definitive promise of God also pertains to the fulfillment of Revelation. This certainly presupposes that the Church, even though subject to human history and the deficiencies of men, cannot nevertheless deviate from her own origin and from her own intimate essence, thanks to the assistance of Christ in the Holy Spirit. Under the assistance and guidance of the Holy Spirit, she will always remain in the truth and in the salvation of Jesus Christ.

As a consequence of her universal mission, the Church is the Church of the world, of the people of God among the peoples of the earth. It is the mission of the Church to testify in a historical manner to salvation for all mankind. The Church does not exist, therefore, for her own glorification but for that of others: she is a sign of God's merciful love for all men.

8. Revelation as Future Fullness.

Under the aspect of fulfillment, Revelation still has a future. This future will be the fullness of what happened definitively in Christ . . . that future already inaugurated by this fulfillment, by this center, and wrought by Him. This fulfillment, already inaugurated, began with the revelation of Christ. The future consists precisely in "bringing to an end" what has already begun, and in showing how the "not yet" of Revelation is contained in the fulfillment of revelation.

On the other hand, the Kingdom of God has already been inaugurated by Jesus Christ. His words and His deeds, above all the resurrection from the dead and the sending of the Spirit, are evident signs of this reality of the Kingdom of God. But we must still pray for the coming of the Kingdom of God: "Thy Kingdom come," *Maranâthâ*. Even the parables of the kingdom presuppose this future. The Resurrection of Christ is the beginning of fullness: Indeed, in it is manifested what, at the end, will be without end, and it is the guarantee and pledge of all for which we hope. Christ is therefore "the hope of glory" (Col 1,27), but His resurrection is only the beginning of this future hope. Even faith looks to its fullness, and goes beyond itself to seeing "face to face," to knowing "even as I have been known" (1 Cor 13,12). The knowing or seeing "face to face" means the elimination of all the barriers that are part of faith, which is an indirect form of knowing. Therefore, the final fullness will be the complete, unlimited, unclouded revelation of divine glory, of the sovereignty and kingdom of God, to all who are saved. It will be the full sovereignty of God and hence full salvation. The Bible makes use of an image to signify this future state: it is the new creation, the new heavens and the new earth, the new Jerusalem, the holy city (Rv 21,22s).

The work of Jesus Himself is continued and realized through the Paraclete, and it must grow towards its fullness, towards the *total Christ;* hence the Church is the "pilgrim Church." These ideas are expressed by the Second Vatican Ecumenical Council in the Dogmatic Constitution on the Church, *Lumen Gentium,* ch 8, Nos 48–49. The march of all humanity is directed toward that supreme moment in which all will recognize the supreme authority of Christ and of God, and all differences will be eliminated so that there will be perfect unity in everything. Then the Son will hand the kingdom over to the Father, "that God may be all in all" (1 Cor 15,28).

9.   The Faith and Kerygma of the Primitive Community.

a. The term "kerygma" designates the official proclamation, the announcement of salvation to non-believers. In this annunciation the Apostles preached and taught two principal truths: Jesus Christ "died for our sins," and "He is truly risen" (Lk 24,34; 1 Cor

15,3). To the Apostles and first disciples, the death of Jesus appeared as a true defeat of the Messianic expectations placed in Him (Lk 24,21). It was the Resurrection that dissipated the misunderstandings and pointed the first community in the right direction. Nevertheless, the affirmation concerning the Risen Jesus is subordinate to the affirmation of Jesus Crucified. The death and the resurrection of Jesus the Messiah constitute the two fundamental truths of the announcement of Christ after Easter. Therefore the resurrection was not initially proclaimed for itself, but for its value as a hermeneutic criterion of Jesus's death on the cross. The Apostolic preaching was not satisfied with announcing the simple fact of Jesus's death, both because the death of Christ appeared to be in absolute contrast with the Messianic hopes of Judaism, and because it was necessary to explain to the pagans how this death could be according to the Will of God, or as the Jews put it, "according to the Scriptures." The resurrection made the primitive community understand how Jesus's death was acceptable to God (Eph 5,2; Ps 49,7). Thus it was understood in its redemptive and expiatory value. This idea led the Apostles to exhort men to repentance and to religion and moral conversion, another important element of the primitive Kerygma (Acts 3,10–26; 10,43).

b. With great strength the Apostles rendered testimony to the *resurrection* of Christ (Acts 4,33). The Easter christophanies conferred on the Apostles the certainty that the Crucified was living. And thus they began to preach Him. According to St. Paul, the body of the risen Jesus was a "spiritual" body (1 Cor 15,42–49), i.e., signed with the glory of God. Hence one is not dealing with a simple return to earthly life, but with its assumption into the divine sphere. The "witness" of the Apostles refers not so much to the fact of the resurrection, which in itself no one observed, but rather to their experience of the Risen Lord in Person. From this experience they go back to the fact. Today we find the echo of this event in some very old formulas and in the primitive confession of faith (1 Thes 1,10; 4,14; 1 Cor 15,1–7; Rom 4,24, 10,9; Phil 2,6–11; Col 1,13–20; 1 Pet 3,18.22).

The fact that the resurrection of the Messiah was an idea unknown to the Judaic apocalypse makes us presuppose that only the facts could have imposed this original announcement on the first Christians. Its justification "according to the Scriptures" (1 Cor 15,4) was conditioned by the anti-Judaic polemic, which obliged the first Christians to explain and justify the scandal of the cross (1 Cor 1,23). Undoubtedly it was the apologetic pre-occupation which brought the Apostles to a deeper understanding of the Old Testament and to a rereading of the entire Old Testament in a Christian light (Ps 16,10 = Acts 2,31; Ps 110,1 = Acts 2,34; Eph 1,20; Col 3,1).[36]

c. With the death and resurrection of Jesus, one part of history ends and a new part begins. The paschal mystery leads to a new element which integrates the kerygma from the very beginning: the persuasion that the final age of the world, the last days have finally come (1 Cor 10,11; Acts 2,17). The paschal experience of the Apostles did not simply manifest the salvific meaning of the life and death of Jesus, but also revealed that the future "eon" has erupted into the present time (Heb 9,26). Thus between the *kairós,* the time after the Resurrection of Christ in which we live now, and the final "day" of judgment there is no true qualitative jump, nothing substantially new, because our days are already "the last days" (Rom 13,11–14; Acts 2,17). The persuasion of the first Christians that ". . . the judge is standing at the door" (Jas 5,9), urges them to emphasize the urgency of the *metánoia* (Acts 3,19.26; 5,31; 13,38; 17,30), to put off the old man full of sins and to put on the "new man." This concept of the "new man" will be developed by St. Paul (Eph 4,24; Col 3,10).[37]

---

[36] Cf. J. Dupont, in *Ephemerides Theologicae Lovanienses* 1953 289–327.

[37] Cf. R. Penna, Saggio sulla teologia del N.T. in *Il Messaggio della Salvezza,* vol. 5, Torino, 1970, pagine 1156–1162.

d. Christology. The central point of the *kerygma* and of Christian preaching was faith in Christ. The greater part of the New Testament confessions are purely christological. The proclamation of Christ, indeed, is the point of departure of every Christian confession. We find this kerygma in the ancient formulations regarding the activity of Jesus and His own Person. They express the soteriological action of Christ. There are some that seem to attribute the primordial salvific act to God Himself: . . . "if you confess with your mouth that Jesus is the Lord, and believe in your heart that God has raised Him from the dead, you will be saved" (Rom 10,9b). Hence this act is salvific above all in Jesus's regard (Acts 2,24; Phil 2,9), but also in our regard, for He ". . . rose again for our justification" (Rom 4,25b; 1 Cor 15,45; Acts 2,33).

Nevertheless, God's resurrecting action presupposes a soteriological action of the Death of the Messiah, which is expressed in the ancient formula: "Christ died for our sins" (1 Cor 15,3; 1 Thes 5,10; Rom 4,25, etc.). Jesus's resurrection showed the power of His death, which was an expiatory sacrifice for the sins of all men. While the historic and salvific work accomplished by Jesus occupied the central place in the thought of the first Christians, the faith consequent to this work, i.e., the faith in the *Kyrios,* the "Lord," raised to the right hand of the Father and reigning over the Church and the world, acquired an even greater importance for the daily life of the Christians and the Church.[38] At the beginning of the Church the title *Kyrios, Lord,* represents the central point around which the most important expressions of faith are gathered. The text of 1 Cor 16,22 shows the antiquity of the designation. The Christian faith believed that Jesus as Lord-Kyrios, would continue to exercise His function as mediator of the Church and of the universe until the Parousia. The title Kyrios leads us to reflect upon the mystery of the Person of Jesus. The text of Phil. 2,9 affirms ". . . God has also exalted

[38] O. Cullmann, *Christologie du N.T.,* Neuchâtel 1958, p. 73.

Him and has bestowed upon Him the name that is above every name," i.e., the name of Kyrios = Lord, which is the equivalent of Adonai, the name of God Himself. To Him has been given "all power in heaven and on earth" (Mt 28,19), and thus no one is equal to Him. Consequently, faith in His divinity increasingly emerges and consolidates (Phil 2,6; Rom 1,4). It becomes clearer that what Jesus had become, He already was fundamentally from the very beginning. In this way faith is pushed to the stage of His pre-existence, which, according to Phil 2,6–11, is already a pre-Pauline fact. Conzelmann affirms that little by little, in the primitive Church the duty was felt of showing that Jesus's death was not just a past fact but could be announced today as the salvation of God. Hence, it was not enough to put death and resurrection together as two "acts"; instead the sense of their relationship had to emerge: together they form the totality of the salvific event, in which the resurrection remains the explicative factor (*ibid.*, p. 192). Hence, in the oldest strata of the apostolic teaching, we observe that the accent is placed on the intervention of God the Father, Who with His right hand exalted Jesus, His Servant (Acts 2,33; 5,31). Only "with a growing temporal and spatial distance from the early community" did they begin to obviously place the meaning of Jesus's death at the center.[40] Thus the process of clarifying the salvific facts in the consciousness and in the faith of the early Christians is completed.[41]

e. The title *Son of God* is characteristic of the Gospels. It is found only in a few places in the Acts (9,20; 13,33). In St. Paul *Kyrios* and also *Son* without any specification are more frequent. The title "Son of God" has its greatest employment by reason of its baptismal use.[42] There is another title that has great importance in John: the *Logos* (Jn 1,1–14; 1 Jn 1,1; Rv 19,13).

[39] H. Conzelmann, *Jesus von Nazareth und der Glaube an den Auferstandenen*, Berlino 1962, p. 194 s.

[40] H. Conzelmann, *Ibid.*, p. 192.

[41] Cf. R. Penna, Saggio sulla teologia del N.T. in *Il Messaggio della Salvezza*, vol. 5, p. 1170.

[42] O. Cullmann, *Le prime confessioni di fede cristiane*, Roma 1948, pp. 17–19.

However this does not seem to be a central christological concept in the New Testament faith, the way *Kyrios* does. Nevertheless, the title *Logos* "emphasizes particularly an important aspect of the Christology of the first Christians: the unity of the Word Incarnate with the Pre-existent Word throughout the history of revelation."[43]

f. As different New Testament texts show, there exists a very close connection between the risen Jesus and the *Holy Spirit,* so much so that it justifies the Pauline expression *Spirit of Christ* (Rom 8,9). In fact Jn 7,39 affirms ". . . the Spirit had not yet been given, since Jesus had not yet been glorified." Acts 2,33 says: "Therefore, exalted by the right hand of God, and receiving from the Father the promise of the Holy Spirit, He has poured forth this Spirit . . ." It seems that the Holy Spirit was impressed upon the faith of the primitive community through the vital and existential experience of the faithful. The most tangible sign of His presence in the primitive community was His intervention in the Resurrection of Jesus (Rom 1,4; 6,4; 8–11; 2 Cor 13,4; 1 Pt 3,18). His dynamic presence in the Church is manifested above all in the transformation of the primitive community. The community, living in the exalting atmosphere of the paschal experience is transformed by the Spirit of Christ, the determining factor of a life lived in faith long before He becomes an article of faith. In this way, the Holy Spirit is at the beginning of historical Christianity as the transforming agent of conscience and Christian faith. Everything in the Church starts from the experiential fact of the Spirit of Christ. Hence, just as the resurrection is the hermeneutical criterion of the cross, the Spirit is the hermeneutical criterion of the resurrection (1 Cor 12,3). To put one's self into personal contact with the risen Christ means to receive the Spirit.[44]

The divinity of the Holy Spirit is affirmed constantly in the

[43] O. Cullmann, *Christologie du N.T.* p. 224.

[44] Cf. Ingo Hermann, *Kyrios und Pneuma. Studien zur Christologie der paulinischen Hauptbriefe,* Monaco 1961; R. Penna, Atti 2, 1–11 e il valore storico-salvifico della Pentecoste in *Lo Spirito Santo nella liturgia della parola* Verba Vitae, 24 Treviso 1968, pp. 59–74.

pages of the New Testament. His personality, instead, is not so evident at the beginning of the apostolic preaching. However, starting from His actual effusion and experience and from their distinction from those of Christ, this personality is not long in crystalizing. The clearest reflection on this is found in St. Paul (2 Cor 13,13; Eph 2,18; 4,3–6; Ti 3,4–7) and in St. John (Jn 14–16). The expression used by Matthew 28,18s seems to go back to the epoch of the edition of the Greek Gospel of Matthew and is influenced by the preaching and rites of Baptism. The Holy Spirit is given as the realization of the ancient promises of salvation (Heb 11,13). The prophecies of Jeremias (31,31–34), Ezechiel (16,59–62; 11,7–20; 36,25–28) and Deutero-Isaiah (55,3; 61,8) find their consummation here. Hence Easter and Pentecost form an inseparable unity inasmuch as one would be unreachable without the other. It is the Spirit of Christ that saves us since He is salvific *Grace,* consisting in the fact that ". . . God has sent the Spirit of His Son into our hearts, crying 'Abba, Father' " (Gal 4,6).[45]

10. Conclusions.

a. The structure of Revelation in the New Testament is similar to that of Revelation in the Old Testament. Indeed Revelation is encounter, colloquy, "dialogue" with God, it is testimony, word, etc. of God.

b. The Kerygma of the Primitive Church presented these truths: Christ inaugurated the fullness of time predicted by the prophets: with His death and resurrection He obtained salvation for all men, according to the Scriptures; because of His resurrection He was exalted at the right hand of the Father as Christ and Kyrios (Lord). Furthermore, the actual existence of the Church constitutes the testimony of the Holy Spirit's assistance to her and hence everyone must do penance, receive Baptism and the Holy Spirit in order to participate in her life.

c. Revelation reaches its culmination in Christ and ends in

---

[45] Cf. R. Penna, *Saggio sulla teologia del N.T.,* p. 1164 s.

Him. Christ is the center and the fullness of all Revelation and of the entire history of salvation.

d. Revelation as an event constitutes the characteristic note of the revelation of the New Testament. Christ is presented as the new Adam, the new Moses, as a Davidic King according to the Will of God, as a priest according to the order of Melchisedech. His salvific work is liberation from the slavery of sin (Col 1,13s); the blood of Christ inaugurates the New Covenant (Synoptic Gospels); the miracles of Jesus renew the wonders of the Exodus (John). But in the New Testament Christ is the one event; everything is expressed to us in the word of Christ. God speaks through Christ once for always, but totally (Neb 1,1).

e. In the New Testament the doctrinal character of Revelation predominates, for the Son Himself speaks to us and shows us the divine word. In the Old Testament, instead, the historical character predominates. Nevertheless, even in the New Testament revelation happens through words, through deeds, through feats, etc.

f. In both the Old and the New Testaments Revelation is offered to us under the form of history, whose true religious sense is known only through the interpretive word of the same historical deed. Hence Revelation is given through history, but not only through history—indeed, on the contrary, also with the help of the word. And thus, the event of the cross, just like the event of the Exodus, is understood fully only through the word that interprets it and presents it to the faithful. Without the explanation of the word, revelation is not given in its full sense. Nevertheless, it cannot be affirmed that history and its interpretation exhausts the whole theme of Revelation.

g. Revelation is not given as a system of abstract truths about God or things related. It is given in history and through history. Indeed we know God and He attributes His salvific plan through the events of history. Hence the doctrine is presented in the form of significative events that make the salvific plan of God known. On the other hand the revelation of some mysteries or truths (e.g., the mystery of the Trinity) is given more through the word than through history. Nevertheless, it is licit to affirm that "historification" is an eminent characteristic of Christian Revelation. However, in the Old Testament the central problem for understanding Revelation well is the relationship between Revelation and history. In the New Testament, instead, it is the relationship between the Incarnation and Revelation, i.e., between Christ and Revelation.

h. Although Revelation is given to us with the help of and through history, it does not fall under historical relativism, and hence it is valid for all times. Indeed, Jesus Christ, Revealer *par excellence,* is God the Creator, Who governs man and the course of history. Furthermore, God protects the transmission of Revelation with the charism of inspiration, and He consigns it to the Church who has the charism of infallibility in order to preserve Revelation, defend it, present it, and interpret it authentically. In this way, Revelation, which takes place in history and through history, does not undergo the changes of history.

i. Finally, the Revelation of both the Old and the New Testaments is given to us in history and through history, for the word of God is essentially efficacious and always active: that which it says or promises, it does. God reveals His plan to mankind, and at the same time He puts it into practice.

CHAPTER 5

Revelation in the Church and in Contemporary Catholic Theology

INTRODUCTION

Catholic theology teaches clearly that Divine Revelation has a double aspect, *noetic* and *dynamic,* but it does not separate the noetic concept from the dynamic concept, as does Protestant theology. Indeed, Catholic theology intimately unites one to the other. Until modern times Catholic theology insisted more on the noetic or doctrinal aspect of Revelation, now instead Catholic theologians and the Church herself, through the Second Vatican Ecumenical Council, recognize the great importance of the Revelation of God in history and through history. In fact God reveals Himself through words, but also and above all through deeds and historical events. Before everyone else, the Hebrews consider history as the epiphany of God. For the Israelites time is linear: it has a beginning and an end. Salvation is realized in temporal history, it is related to different historical events that evolve according to the divine plan, and are ordered to a unique event, i.e., the death and resurrection of Christ. For the Greeks, instead, who consider history in a cyclic way, salvation cannot come from an event of history itself, but from outside of history. Israel dwells and lives in the material world, but its attention is centered in a special way on the religious meaning of historical events. In consequence, for Israel history is the place of the Revelation of God. The essence of Israel's faith is founded on the concept of the living God Who reveals Himself in history.

On the other hand, for Catholic theology Revelation also presupposes history and the interpretative word of this history, i.e., it presupposes the events and their interpretation. Thus today's Catholic theology also insists much on the colloquial aspect of Revelation. Indeed Revelation is a colloquy, a personal "dialogue" between God and man, a dialogue of love and friendship. Revelation is also considered as the encounter of God with the faithful soul through kerygma and faith, and as testimony which invites faith.

I. *Revelation as Word*

1. Following the research of philosophy and psychology on language (e.g. the studies of K. Bühler, H. Noack, M. Heidegger, M. Marleau-Ponty, M. Nédoncelle, L. Lavelle, G. Gusdorf, H. Delacroix, G. Parain, A. G. Robledo, J. Lacroix, etc.) contemporary theology insists with reason on the interpersonal, existential, dynamic character of the Divine Word.

K. Bühler distinguishes three aspects of the word:

a. The word possesses a certain theme. It means or represents something; it narrates some fact, etc.

b. The word is a call. Indeed it is directed to someone and it intends to provoke in him a reply or a reaction. Hence one is dealing with an appeal or a provocation with the scope of establishing a reply or a colloquy.

c. Finally, the word is the manifestation of the interior disposition of the subject who speaks.[1] Hence we can define the word in this way: it is the action through which a person speaks to another and expresses his thought in order to establish a communication.[2]

Thus the word is directed to another person, indeed it happens between *you* and *me*. Hence the word is above all and of itself an *interpersonal encounter*. But the word is principally a *call;*[3] in fact, it provokes a reaction, and thus tends to transform itself into

[1] Cf. K. Buehler, *Sprachtheorie* (Jena 1934) p. 2, 28–33.

[2] Cf. R. Latourelle, *Teologia de la Revelación,* p. 404.

[3] Cf. E. Dhanis, Révélation explicite et implicite" *Gregorianum* 34 (1953) 209s.

colloquy. The word certainly tends to communication, the end of which is multiple: at times it will be only utilitarian, as commonly happens today in propaganda, in newspapers, on the radio, on television, etc. In this case, the word is impersonal. At other times, instead, the word is an expression, an information, an instruction on the person; it is the witness and the revelation of the same person, principally when man in a certain way enters into his own word in order to discover the profound sense of himself.[4] Hence the word in this sense is the sign of intercommunication between two persons, the sign of friendship and of love; indeed, it presupposes mutual confidence and giving. When the word cannot express all the profundity of the love and donation, the gesture and the deed intervene: as in conjugal love, in the apostolate, in martyrdom.

2. In Revelation the living and omnipotent God speaks to man in an interpersonal and vital relationship in order to establish a communication and stir up a dialogue with him; in this colloquy God invites man to the obedience of faith and to intimate communion with Him. The word of God, however, is not just information and instruction; it is an active, efficacious, creative word; indeed, it does what it signifies and thus it transforms the life of mankind.

Through the word God puts Himself into interpersonal communication with man, and He does this not for a utilitarian motive, but for love and friendship. Indeed the Word of God is a word of love. This is shown principally in the fact that the transcendent and omnipotent God becomes the close God, near to us, God with us, *Emmanuel.* Certainly this fact, i.e., that God descends, condescends, and comes near to man, implies nothing other than His love and His desire for the salvation of man. In revealing Himself, God seeks to establish a bond of love and a communion of life with man, and calls him to a supernatural vocation. There is no doubt that God became incarnate for this

[4] Cf. G. Gusdorf, *La parole,* Paris 1956, p. 55; G. Auzou, *La palabra de Dios* Madrid, 1964, p. 463.

174

reason and condescends to speak to man in order to better elevate him. Thus God reveals Himself and manifests His salvific plan in His incarnate life, in His actions, in His deeds, in His way of acting and principally in His word.

The revelation and communication of God with man does imply the manifestation of the religious truths of the natural order, but it implies principally the manifestation of the secrets of God, such as the mystery of the Trinity, known only to the Son of God Himself (Mt 11,27; Jn 1,18; 1 Cor 2,11). The revelation of the mystery of the Trinity, with which God manifests to man His intimate life, is like the beginning in this world of a certain participation in the divine life, and constitutes the true self-giving of God to man. Indeed Revelation is a type of self-donation of God.[5]

Having completed His prophetic mission through the preaching of His message, Christ consummated His self-donation, already begun with preaching of the word of God, with the sacrifice of the cross. With His passion and death, Jesus manifests supreme love towards men (Jn 13, 1). In this way, the pronounced, preached word becomes the immolated word. Christ on the cross *reveals* (Jn 1,18) the supreme love of the Father[6] with His attitude and sufferings, even with his inarticulate voice.

II. *Revelation as Encounter*

1. The word becomes a reality when there is the encounter of this word with another *you*. This encounter can have different degrees of profundity, but in all of them the encounter tends to this: that the word and the reply are converted into an authentic colloquy, a dialogue, a mutual concentric communion, a reciprocal agreement. The mutual consent is certainly a condition necessary to make the encounter effective and impart a revelation and gift, since reciprocity is the fruit of revelation and donation.[7] This

[5] Cf. J. Alfaro, "Persona y gracia" *Gregorianum* 41, 1960, 11.

[6] Cf. R. Latourelle, *op. cit,* pp. 407–409.

[7] Cf. F. J. Buytendijk, *Phénoménologie de la rencontre* Paris 1953, p. 42.

colloquy, which can be a colloquy in mutual love, is given in the most excellent way in faith and in Divine Revelation.

In Revelation, God calls man and communicates to him the message of salvation. Only in faith, however, does the encounter of God with man take place truly and fully; and it is only in faith that the word of God is accepted and known by man. By means of His word, God invites man to the communion of friendship, and man responds to the divine invitation with faith. Hence, faith is the first encounter of man with God. On the other hand, when man listens to God Who speaks, the encounter between God and man occurs, developing through the communion of life.

Hence, Revelation and faith are essentially interpersonal.[8] Faith is the encounter with the personal God in His word. In truth, faith initiates in dialogue the encounter that will end only in the beatific vision. But already before that vision, a mysterious presence of God, a living relationship between God and man, between one Person and another is given.[9] The faith which operates through charity implies the availability and the donation of the whole person of the believer to God.

2. The characteristics of this encounter with God by means of faith are the following:

a. God always takes the initiative, and continually shows His divine condescension. "In this is the love, not that we have loved God, but that He has first loved us, and sent His Son as propitiation for our sins" (1 Jn 4,10).

In fact God impresses upon our intelligence the tendency, the supernatural impulse, which inclines us toward God, the First Truth and Supreme Goodness.

b. Another characteristic of this encounter is the free choice or decision that it demands. This is most important, indeed it can change our entire personal existence. Since He is *Verbo,* the Word of God, the word of Christ constitutes the foundation, norm and

---

[8] Cf. S. Tommaso, *Summa theologica* 202, q. 11, a. 1 c.

[9] Cf. J. Alfaro, Persona y gracia *Gregorianum* 1060, 11 s; R. Aubert, *Le problème de l'acte de foi,* Lovanio 1958, p. 696–703.

criterion of all things. One is dealing with the free choice to make for God or for the world, for the word of God or for the word of man. Faith is a decision through which man chooses God and thus changes the direction of his entire life. In a certain sense faith is death to one's self and complete giving to God. But in order to do this it is necessary that love intervene and entice us. This love is stirred up by the word of God, which is the sign of the love of God (1 Jn 4,8.16) and which was revealed in the supreme sacrifice of the cross. In this way Revelation as encounter is changed into acceptance, colloquy, and mutual consent, through the allurement of the love of Christ and the manifestation of the Holy Spirit Who intimately transforms men.

c. The last characteristic of the encounter with God is the profundity of communion, which is established between man and God. Whoever receives the word of Christ and remains in Him, passes from the condition of servant to the condition of son and friend of God (Gal 4,4–6; Rom 8,15; Jn 15,15), and becomes a participant in the knowledge and love of the Father and of the Holy Spirit. Then in the heart of man there dwells the love with which the Father loves the Son and the Son loves the Father (Jn 17,21–26). Through union with Christ, and through the union of the Son with the Father, the faithful are joined to each other and to the Father, just as the Father is joined to the Son. And the Holy Spirit vivifies them with the divine life of the three Divine Persons. Thus St. John can say that we are in communion with the Father and with His Son Jesus Christ (1 Jn 1,3.6); that we are in Christ and we remain in Him (1 Jn 2,5s.24; 3,24; 4.13.16; 5,20).

Hence no human encounter can reach that intimate communion which is given in faith if the love of the Trinity does not intervene. And thus Revelation as a word, encounter, a testimony, is the work of love (1 Jn 4,8–10). Even faith is the work of love. Indeed, faith is gratitude for God's plan of love and its (faith's) insertion into God's salvific plan.[10]

10 Cf. R. Latourelle, *op. cit.* p. 417 s.

III. *Revelation as Testimony*

Revelation is also *testimony,* and it invites us to a decision, i.e., to faith.

Sacred Scripture describes Revelation as the testimony of God. In the Old Testament the prophets render testimony to the truth; in fact they say: "Thus says the Lord. . . ." They also testify to God by their works, their life, their patience in persecutions, and at times even by their martyrdom. In the New Testament Christ is the witness of Revelation *par excellence,* for He shows us what He saw in the bosom of the Father and invites us to the obedience of faith. The Apostles and the first disciples also give witness to the life and doctrine of Christ, and exhort all men to embrace the faith of Christ. Therefore, as witnesses of the life of Christ, the Apostles transmit to the Church a direct testimony. On the other hand, the Church receives this testimony reverently, preserves it and protects it religiously; she presents it, explains it and interprets it more deeply and clearly.

The New Testament describes the revealing action of the Most Holy Trinity under the form of mutual testimonies. The Son witnesses to His Father, and the Father witnesses to the Son through His works, through the attraction of souls, and principally through the Resurrection. The Son also witnesses to the Holy Spirit; in fact He promises Him as educator, consoler and sanctifier. After His coming on the day of Pentecost, the Holy Spirit witnesses to the Son, by the Son to the minds of the faithful. He makes Christ known and explains the profound sense and the fullness of His words. This exchange of testimonies of the Most Holy Trinity with men has as its aim the presentation of Revelation and the nourishment of faith. This trinitarian witness constitutes the connection of union between eternity and time, between heaven and earth.[11]

The documents of the Magisterium of the Church also describe Revelation as a testimony. Most of the times, however, they do

[11] Cf. R. Latourelle, *op. cit.* p. 410.

so in an implicit way, e.g.; when they speak of Revelation as a word which has authority, as the word of uncreated Truth, as the infallible and truthful word, to which man replies with faith (Denz. 1637, 1639, 1789). The Anti-modernistic Oath is the only document that speaks explicitly of Revelation as a word testified to, attested to (Denz. 2145). On the other hand, theologians define Revelation as an expression of God Who attests. Indeed, the mystery of God can be known only from the testimony of God Himself. For this reason Christianity is a religion of testimony, for it is a manifestation of the Divine Persons, and this manifestation came about only through witness. When Christ speaks or teaches, He manifests the mystery of His Person. All of the Gospels are a colloquy of love in which Christ progressively reveals the mystery of Himself, the mystery of the three Divine Persons, and the mystery of our divine filiation. The Apostles are the witnesses of the life of Jesus, but they are principally witnesses of His Person.

The witness of God is infallible, for when He testifies, God is at the same time the absolute and ultimate foundation of the infallible truth of His testimony. In Christian Revelation the signs and miracles prove the authenticity of the testimony of Christ and the Apostles. The divine invitation to believe can be either exterior or interior. By means of the prophets, Christ Himself, and the Apostles, God announces to men His salvific plan and invites them to accept the faith: "Repent and believe in the Gospel" (Mk 1,15; 16,15). But God can work even in the interior of man. Sacred Scripture calls this action interior revelation (Mt 11,25; 16,17), illumination (2 Cor 4,4–6; Acts 16,14), unction (2 Cor 1,2s), attraction (Jn 6,44), internal testimony (Jn 5,37; 1 Jn 5,6). By means of this interior action, God can invite man to assent to the truth and thus acknowledge the divine testimony. Under this divine light man adheres totally to the divine testimony in itself and of itself.[12]

[12] Cf. R. Latourelle, *op. cit.*, p. 414.

These are the principal ideas that today's Catholic theology studies and extols especially after the encyclical of Paul VI, *Ecclesiam Suam* and the Second Vatican Council.

IV. *Revelation According to the Documents of the Church*

1. Revelation According to the First Vatican Council.

The First Vatican Council distinguished two modes of divine manifestation or two ways that bring us to the knowledge of God. In a pre-synodal outline prepared by Franzelin the *natural manifestation* of God through creatures and the manifestation of God *through the light of human reason* are acknowledged.[13] In a note of the outline the *"objective manifestation of God through creatures"* is opposed to *Revelation* properly so-called.[14] While the first outline thus opposes the *natural manifestation* and *Revelation* the final text approved by the Council distinguishes the knowledge of God *through a natural way* and the revelation of God *through a supernatural way*. The Council affirms, "Holy Mother Church teaches that God, beginning and end of all things, can certainly be known from created things through the natural light of reason. Indeed the invisible things of God are seen and understood by the creatures of this world through the things that have been made (Rom 1,20) but nevertheless it pleased God's wisdom and goodness to reveal to mankind Himself and the eternal decrees of His Will through another way, and that is the supernatural way" (Denz 1785).

From this it follows that the knowledge of God through creatures and reason constitutes a certain revelation and manifestation of God through a natural way. But Vatican I affirms the possibility, not the fact, of knowing God through the light of reason. This possibility is founded on man's nature itself, and is not extinguished by sin. Nevertheless, it deals with a divine knowl-

---

[13] Cf. *Tractatus de divina Traditione et Scripture,* 1870, p. 415, nn. 1, 2.
[14] Cf. Mansi, 50.

edge different from the personal revelation of God made to men through interior illumination, through the word, and through exterior historical deeds.[15]

Speaking of this latter revelation, Vatican I affirms the fact and the existence of the positive, supernatural revelation of the Old and New Testaments. God is the author and cause of this revelation, and He has given it to us because of His goodness and wisdom. The material object of Revelation is God Himself and the decrees of His Will; i.e., the decrees of salvation. This Revelation has been given to all mankind. That which unites the Old Covenant with the New is the word of God; indeed, the word of the Son is the continuation and consummation of the revelation of the Old Testament. The revelation of the Old Testament was successive, fragmentary, multiform; the revelation of the New Testament instead is one, total, and definitive. Vatican I insists on revelation chiefly as the spoken word. It is God Who speaks to men. From this we deduce that for Vatican I Revelation is of a *theocentric* character.

Vatican I teaches that "Revelation must be considered absolutely necessary . . . for out of His infinite goodness God ordered man to a supernatural end, to participate in the divine goods, which far surpass the understanding of the human mind" (Denz 1786). Nevertheless, it recognizes that Revelation is not absolutely necessary for knowing truths of a natural order: "To this divine revelation must be attributed the possibility that those things which belong to the divine sphere and are not of themselves inaccessible to human reason even in mankind's present condition can easily be known by all with firm certainty and without errors" (Denz 1786). Pius XII's encyclical, *Humani generis* speaks explicitly of "moral necessity": "Divine revelation must be considered *morally necessary* so that those things of religion and morals which are not of themselves inaccessible to reason even in mankind's present

[15] Cf. R. Aubert, Le concile du Vatican et la connaissance naturelle de Dieu" *Lumière et Vie*, marzo 1954, p. 41ss.

condition, can easily be known by all with firm certainty and without error" (Denz 2305).[16]

2. Revelation in the Documents of Pius XI and Pius XII.

In his encyclical *Mortalium Animos* (June, 1928), Pius XI considers Revelation an historical fact, an intervention of God in history, under the form of words directed to mankind. "This revelation, effective immediately and continued under the Old Law, was perfected by Jesus Christ Himself under the New Law."[17] Pius XI speaks of Revelation in the objective sense of some doctrine or abstract truth; in fact, he uses the terms "revelation," "sacred doctrine," "summary of truths," "deposit of revelation" almost in the same sense.

Pius XII describes Revelation in an objective sense with the expressions "revealed truth," "doctrine of the faith," "deposit of faith," "revealed deposit" (Denz 2307, 2315, 2325). According to *Humani generis*, "Christ the Lord entrusted to the Church the entire deposit of faith—Sacred Scripture and divine Tradition—that she would guard it, defend it, and interpret it. . . . God also gave to the Church her living Magisterium to illustrate and explain those things which in the deposit of faith are contained obscurely and almost implicitly."[18]

3. Revelation in the Doctrine of Paul VI.

Paul VI is the first who, in an official document of the Church, i.e., the encyclical *Ecclesiam Suam* (August 8, 1964), insists very much on the colloquial, "dialogic" character of Revelation: "Revelation, i.e., the supernatural relationship which God Himself, on His own initiative, has established with the human race, can be represented as a dialogue in which the Word of God is expressed in the Incarnation and therefore in the Gospel.

[16] Cf. S. Tommaso, *Summa teol.* 1, q. 1, a. 1; *Contra Gentes,* 1, c. 4.
[17] *Cf. AAS* 20, 1928, p. 8.
[18] Enciclica *Humani generis,* 12–8–1950; Dz 2313 s; Munificentissimus Deus, 1–11–1950; *AAS* 42, 1950 p. 756–757.

The fatherly and holy conversation between God and man, interrupted by original sin, has been marvelously resumed in the course of history. The history of salvation narrates exactly this long and changing dialogue which begins with God and brings man a many-splendored conversation. It is in this conversation of Christ among men (cf Bar 3,38) that God allows something of Himself to be understood, the mystery of His life, unique in its essence, trinitarian in its Persons. He tells us finally how He wishes to be known: He is love. He tells us how He wishes to be honored and served by us: love is our supreme commandment. The dialogue thus takes on full meaning and offers grounds for confidence. The child is initiated to it, the mystic finds a full outlet in it.

We need to keep ever present this ineffable, yet real relationship of the dialogue, which God the Father, through Christ in the Holy Spirit, has offered to us and established with us if we are to understand the relationship which we, i.e., the Church, should strive to establish and to foster with the human race.[19]

The preceding documents of the Church conceived Revelation as an *exchange of word* between God and man (Denz 1638, 1785, 2145),[20] but did not add anything more. Instead, Paul VI, describing Revelation as a colloquy, a "dialogue," and a conversation, emphasizes the interpersonal and dynamic character of Revelation. Indeed, the living God, full of love, begins a colloquy with men in order to establish with them a communion of thought and life.

This colloquial structure is that which precisely distinguishes Revelation. In truth, Revelation assumes the form of a long and moving colloquy between God and the creature, which was interrupted by the sin of Adam, but which was resumed again through the sheer love of God and was marvelously continued in spite of Israel's infidelities.

The encyclical *Ecclesiam Suam* notes the trinitarian character of this colloquy: the Father begins the colloquy; the Word, through

[19] *AAS* 56, 1964, pp. 641–642.
[20] Cf. *AAS* 20, 1928, p. 8; 29, 1937, p. 156.

His Incarnation, is its mediator; the Holy Spirit leads the faithful to understand and welcome the word of Christ. The principal *object* of this colloquy is the mystery of divine life in one single essence and in the trinity of persons. God reveals Himself as the God of love (1 Jn 4,8), showing us how He wants to be honored and served by us, since love is our supreme commandment. Furthermore Revelation itself constitutes the manifestation of love and follows the work of love.

The unspeakable colloquy that God the Father, through Jesus Christ, opened in the Holy Spirit and began with us, shows us in what the colloquy of the Church with all men, and what the colloquy of each individual with others ought to consist. The colloquy is a means of knowing one's self and others; indeed, in it two realities, two persons mutually manifest the secrets of their minds.[21] Furthermore, the colloquy presupposes an acceptance and a mutual donation. There is no true colloquy if it is not founded on respect for the other and on full openness to what the other says. In this sense Paul VI affirms: "This type of relationship indicates a proposal of courteous esteem, of understanding and goodness on the part of the one who inaugurates the dialogue; it excludes the *a priori* condemnation, the offensive and time-worn polemic and emptiness of useless conversation."[22] For a true and authentic dialogue, trust is needed between the two who speak. It is also necessary that neither of the two intend to impose his own opinion. Trust weaves the spirits into a mutual adhesion to a Good, which excludes every egoistic aim. This becomes possible through charity in the same colloquy. All of these things are very well expressed in the encyclical *Ecclesiam Suam:* ". . . the dialogue supposes and demands comprehensibility. It is an outpouring of thought . . . a second characteristic of the dialogue is its meekness, the virtue which Christ sets before us to be learned from Him: 'Learn from me, for I am meek and humble of heart' (Mt 11,29). The dialogue is not proud, it is not bitter, it

[21] Cf. J. Lacroix, La filosofia del dialogo in *Studi Cattolici* 8, 1964, p. 57.
[22] *AAS* 56, 1964, p. 644.

is not offensive. Its authority is intrinsic to the truth it explains, to the charity it communicates, to the example it proposes; it is not a command, it is not an imposition. It is peaceful; it avoids violent methods, it is patient; it is generous.[23]

Nevertheless, between the colloquy of God with men and the colloquy of men with other men there exists an *analogy*, certainly not an identity. In fact in the divine colloquy God Himself calls man with His infallible word and invites him to accept the faith.

The encyclical *Ecclesiam Suam* assigns these different properties of colloquy to Revelation:

a. "The dialogue of salvation was opened spontaneously on the initiative of God: 'He (God) has first loved us' (1 Jn 4,10), it will be up to us to take the initiative in extending to men this same dialogue, without waiting to be summoned to it."[24]

b. "The dialogue of salvation began with charity, with the divine goodness: 'God so loved the world that He gave His only-begotten Son' (Jn 3,16). Nothing but fervent and unselfish love should motivate our dialogue."[25]

c. "The dialogue of salvation was not proportioned to the merits of those toward whom it was directed, nor to the results which it would achieve or fail to achieve: 'It is not the healthy who need a physician' (Lk 5,31). So also our own dialogue ought to be without limits or ulterior motives."

d. It is the most extraordinary colloquy of all for the salvation it brings, and yet it never obliges men to accept it. The Encyclical says: "The dialogue of salvation did not physically force anyone to accept it, it was a tremendous appeal of love which, although placing a vast responsibility on those toward whom it was directed (cf Mt 11,21), nevertheless left them free to respond to it or to reject it."[26] Furthermore, the Encyclical teaches that the signs of Revelation do not constrict man's liberty, but on the contrary, help

---

[23] *AAS* 56, 1964, p. 645.
[24] *AAS* 56, 1964, p. 642.
[25] *Ibid,* p. 642.
[26] *Ibid,* p. 642.

him to better give assent: "Even the number of miracles and their demonstrative power were adapted to the spiritual needs and dispositions of the recipients, in order that their free consent to the divine revelation might be facilitated without, however, their losing the merit involved in such a consent."[27]

e. No one is excluded from this colloquy of salvation: "The dialogue of salvation was made accessible to all; it was destined for all without distinction. In like manner, our own dialogue should be potentially universal, i.e., all-embracing and capable of including all."[28]

f. Finally, this colloquy is the work of the wise and patient divine pedagogy; indeed, it has followed the slow psychological and historical maturation of mankind: "The dialogue of salvation normally experienced gradual development, successive advances, humble beginnings before complete success (cf Mt 13,31). Ours, too, will take cognizance of the slowness of psychological and historical maturation and of the need to wait for the hour when God may make our dialogue effective."[29]

Finally the Encyclical speaks of the obligations of the Church concerning Revelation. In the first place, " . . . if . . . the Church has a true realization of what the Lord wishes it to be, then within the Church there arises a unique sense of fullness and a need for outpouring, together with the clear awareness of a mission which transcends the Church, of a message to be spread. It is the duty of evangelization. It is the missionary mandate. It is the apostolic commission.

An attitude of preservation of the Faith is insufficient. Certainly, we must preserve and also defend the treasure of truth and of grace which has come to us by way of inheritance from the Christian tradition. 'Guard the trust and keep free from profane novelties in speech and the contradictions of so-called knowledge' (1 Tim 6,20). But neither the preservation nor the defense of

[27] Ibid. p. 642 s.
[28] Ibid, p. 643.
[29] Ibid., p. 643.

186

the Faith exhausts the duty of the Church in regard to the gift which it possesses.

The duty consonant with the patrimony received from Christ is that of spreading, offering, announcing it to others . . . did not John XXIII . . . place even sharper emphasis on its teaching in the sense of approaching as closely as possible to the experience and understanding of the contemporary world?"[30]

Hence fidelity and adaptation are two functions of the Church in regard to Revelation. The Church must use these two ways of proceeding in perfect harmony. Nevertheless, fidelity does not signify a static and sterile preservation of Revelation. On the other hand, "to what extent should the Church adapt itself to the historic and local circumstances in which its mission is exercised? How should it guard against the danger of a relativism which would falsify its moral and dogmatic truth?"[31] "The desire to come together as brothers must not lead to a watering down or subtracting from the truth. Our dialogue must not weaken our faith. An immoderate desire to make peace and sink differences at all costs is, fundamentally, a kind of skepticism about the power and content of the Word of God which we desire to preach."[32]

4. Revelation According to the Second Vatican Council.

a. The *Promulgation of the Constitution on Divine Revelation.* On November 14, 1962; the Second Vatican Council began the examination of the draft *De fontibus Revelationis.* The parts of this first draft were the following:

(1) The two fonts of Revelation; (2) Inspiration, inerrancy, and literary composition of Scripture; (3) The Old Testament; (4) The New Testament; (5) Sacred Scripture in the Church. The questions directly regarding Revelation spoke of the fact of Revelation, its transmission, the function of Christ and the Apostles in the economy of Revelation, the two sources of Revelation, and

[30] Ibid., p. 639–640.
[31] Ibid., p. 646.
[32] Ibid., p. 647.

the function of the Magisterium of the Church in relation to the deposit of faith. But this first draft was rejected by the greater number of the Fathers of the Council.

For this reason on November 20, 1962, John XXIII ordered the revision of the draft and set up a mixed commission for this purpose. This commission finished the revision of the draft in March, 1963. But the Conciliar Fathers expressed the desire that the draft treat more broadly the question of Tradition and Revelation. Thus on March 7, 1964 the doctrinal commission set up a subcommission to correct the draft once again. This subcommission divided the first chapter, "On the Word of God," into two (1) *Revelation Itself;* (2) *The Transmission of Divine Revelation.* This new draft was discussed in the third session of the Council (September 30—October 6, 1964) and in general it pleased everyone. However, some corrections were still proposed on chapters I and II, which are without a doubt the best of the whole draft. Once these corrections were made, the document was presented in the Council session and obtained favorable votes from almost all of the Council Fathers on the days of September 20, 21, 22, 1965. It was finally promulgated officially by Paul VI on November 18, 1965 under the title *Dogmatic Constitution on Divine Revelation—Dei Verbum.*

b. *The Doctrine of the Constitution Dei Verbum.* The final document approved by the Council constitutes the fifth official edition. Without a doubt the *Constitution on Divine Revelation* together with the *Constitution on the Church—Lumen Gentium* is the best document of Vatican II. Concerning the doctrine of Revelation the following things are worthy of mention:

aa. The expression "Dei Verbum" expresses in a certain sense the entire theme of the conciliar document, the *Dogmatic Constitution on Divine Revelation.* The living God spoke to mankind. The expression *Dei Verbum* is applied above all to Revelation. The "Word of God," through which God reveals the mystery of His Will, although proclaimed once for always ($\epsilon\phi\acute{a}\pi a\epsilon$) still remains and is prolonged in Scripture and in Tradition.

188

bb. *Chapter I.   Revelation*

Chapter I begins affirming *the fact* of Revelation. "In His goodness and wisdom, God chose to reveal Himself and to make known to us the hidden purpose of His will." There it speaks of the object of Revelation: the hidden Mystery is Jesus Christ Himself, "through Christ, the Word made flesh, man has access to the Father in the Holy Spirit and comes to share in the divine nature." (Chapter I, n. 2).

A little later the Council further determines the *nature* of Revelation. The invisible God comes out of the silence of His mystery and "out of the abundance of His love speaks to men as friends and lives among them, so that He may invite and take them into fellowship with Himself." Hence, in order to define the nature of Revelation, the Council has recourse to the analogy of the *word,* which after all is used in Scripture itself, in the documents of the Church, and in the theological tradition. The Word of God with which God Himself communicates with men is a word of love and friendship. ". . . God out of the abundance of His love speaks to men as friends."

Just as man can communicate his thought in many different ways (with acts, deeds, words, gestures, images, symbols, etc.), so too can God. With men, however, God chooses chiefly two ways of communication: the way of history and the way of the Incarnation. Revelation was brought to an end through the intimate connection of *deeds and words:* "This plan of revelation is realized by deeds and words having an inner unity: the deeds wrought by God in the history of salvation manifest and confirm the teaching and the realities signified by the words, while the words proclaim the deeds and clarify the mystery contained in them" (N. 2). The term *gesta* [deeds] (more personalistic than *facta* [acts]) designates the salvific actions of God, i.e., all the works which God has brought to fulfillment and which constitute the history of salvation. When the Council speaks of deeds and words as constituent elements of Revelation, it is insisting on the historical and sacramental character of Revelation: indeed, in history God works through events, and through words explains and interprets their historical and almost sacramental meaning.

This is the first official document of the Church in which Revelation is thus described. Hence, it is of extraordinary importance. Previously, the documents of the Church insisted on Revelation by means of the word; now instead it speaks of *deeds and words* (*gestes verbisque*) intimately connected among themselves.

Through this Revelation concerning God and the salvation of man the intimate truth in Christ shines on us; indeed, in Christ, the Father, the Son, and the Holy Spirit are revealed to us. It is also shown that man was chosen by God and was called from the beginning of the world to be an adopted son in Christ. At the same time Christ is the *mediator* and the *fullness* of all Revelation (No. 2). Jesus is also the *way* which leads us to God (Jn 1,18; 14,6; Mt 11,27); He is also, as we have already said, the *fullness* of Revelation,[33] i.e., it is God Who reveals and Who is revealed, the author and object of Revelation; it is God Who reveals the mystery and is the same mystery personally expressed.[34]

Vatican II then describes the different stages of Revelation before Christ. "God, Who through the Word creates all things (cf Jn 1,3) and keeps them in existence, gives men an enduring witness to Himself in created realities (cf Rom 1,19–20). Planning to make known the way of heavenly salvation, He went further and from the start manifested Himself to our first parents. Then after their fall His promise of redemption aroused in them the hope of being saved (Gn 3,15), and from that time on He ceaselessly kept the human race in His care, in order to give eternal life to those who perseveringly do good in search of salvation. Then, at the time He had appointed, He called Abraham in order to make of him a great nation (Gn 12,2). Through the patriarchs, and after them through Moses and the prophets, He taught this nation to acknowledge Himself as the one living and true God, provident Father and just Judge, and to wait for the

[33] Cf. *AAS* 29, 1937, p. 150.

[34] Cost. dogmatica *Dei Verbum* sulla divina Rivelazione, c. 1, n. 2.

Savior promised by Him. In this manner He prepared the way for the gospel down through the centuries" (No. 3).

"Then, after speaking in many places and varied ways through the prophets, God . . . sent His Son, the eternal Word, Who enlightens all men, so that He might dwell among men and tell them the innermost realities about God (Jn 1,1–18). Jesus Christ therefore . . . completes the work of salvation which His Father gave Him to do (Jn 5,36; 17,4) (No. 4). In this way, Christ, Who is the culmination and the fullness of all Revelation, established the superiority of the new Revelation over the old, and the relationship existing between both phases of salvation history. The element of continuity between these two phases is *God* and His *Word*. Furthermore, Christ is the fulfillment and the perfection of Revelation because ". . . Jesus perfected revelation by fulfilling it through His whole work of making Himself present and manifesting Himself: through His words and deeds, His signs and wonders, but especially through His death and glorious resurrection from the dead, and finally through sending the Spirit of truth. Moreover, He confirmed with divine testimony what revelation proclaimed: that God is with us . . ." (*Ibid.,* No. 4).

Since Christ is the eternal Word of God and the only begotten Son sent into this world to reveal the divine secrets fully, the Revelation given by Him cannot be transitory. "The Christian dispensation, therefore, as the new and definitive covenant, will never pass away, and we now await no further new public revelation before the glorious manifestation of our Lord Jesus Christ" (*Ibid.* No. 4). Jesus Christ therefore is the last word and the end of Revelation. All things are completed in Him.

The Council continues: " 'The obedience of faith' must be given to God Who reveals, an obedience by which man entrusts his whole self freely to God, offering 'the full submission of intellect and will to God Who reveals; and freely assenting to the truth revealed by Him' " (*Ibid.,* No. 5). Indeed, the Council considers faith as a link between God and man which establishes a living and *personal* relationship which embraces understanding and love. In this way, through Revelation, God *comes, condescends* to man and opens to him the secrets of His intimate life in order to stir him to love. Man, in turn, through faith, is converted to God and adheres fully to Him in the life of friendship. Hence *faith* is man's reply to God's *gift*.

The Council then considers the revealed truths necessary to man in his actual condition, and affirms: "Through divine revelation, God chose to show forth and communicate Himself and the eternal decisions of His Will regarding the salvation of men" (*Ibid.,* No. 6). Hence God not only announces salvation, he also offers it. Indeed, revelation presupposes the manifestation and the communication of life. God does not reveal Himself to satisfy the curiosity of men, but to save them. Finally, the Council teaches that man can certainly know God from created things with the natural light of human reason: ". . . it is through His revelation, that those religious truths which are by their nature accessible to human reason can be known with ease, with solid certitude, and with no trace of error, even in the present state of the human race" (*Ibid.,* No. 6).[35]

cc. *Chapter II: The Transmission of Divine Revelation.*

In this Chapter II, the Council deals with the transmission of Revelation. On this theme it affirms: "In His gracious goodness, God has seen to it that what He had revealed for the salvation of all nations would abide perpetually in its full integrity and be handed on to all generations. Therefore, Christ the Lord, in Whom the full revelation of the supreme God is brought to completion, commissioned the Apostles to preach to all men that gospel which is the source of all saving truth and moral teachings. . . ." In this text, the Council insists on saying again that Christ is the *fulfiller* of all Revelation, and He Who brings it to its fullness.

It then teaches that the Apostles have faithfully completed the mandate of Christ to preach the Gospel with examples, with oral preaching and with laws. The Apostles themselves, together with

[35] Cf. R. Latourelle, *Teologia de la Revelación* pp. 354–372.

some disciples, have committed the message of salvation to writing. For this reason, from that moment on, Revelation is handed down under two forms: the form of Tradition and the form of Sacred Scripture. "This sacred Tradition, therefore, and Sacred Scripture of both the Old and the New Testament are like a mirror in which the pilgrim Church on earth looks at God, from Whom she has received everything. . . ." The Council continues: "And so the apostolic preaching, which is expressed in a special way in the inspired books, was to be preserved by a continuous succession of preachers until the end of time. . . . What was handed on by the Apostles includes everything which contributes to the holiness of life and, the increase of faith of the People of God . . ." (*Ibid.,* No. 8). Considering the dynamic aspect of Tradition, the Council teaches this: "This tradition which comes from the Apostles develops in the Church with the help of the Holy Spirit. For there is a growth in the understanding of the realities and the words which have been handed down. This happens through the contemplation and study made by believers, who treasure these things in their hearts, through the intimate understanding of spiritual things they experience, and through the preaching of those who have received through episcopal succession the sure gift of truth. For, as the centuries succeed one another, the Church constantly moves forward toward the fullness of divine truth until the words of God reach their complete fulfillment in her" (*Ibid.,* No. 8).

The truths handed on in Tradition are known through the writings of the Fathers of the Church, through the Liturgy, through the praxis of the Church, and through theological reflection. Tradition also has a great importance in that through it the Church knows the full canon of the sacred books. The sacred writings themselves are more profoundly understood and unceasingly made active in her; and thus God . . . "uninterruptedly converses with the Bride of His beloved Son . . ." (*Ibid.,* No. 8). Hence Sacred Scripture and Tradition are not two parallel and independent ways. Instead, "there exists a close connection and communication between Sacred Tradition and Sacred Scripture. For both of them, flowing from the same divine wellspring, in a certain way merge into a unity and tend toward the same end" (*Ibid.,* No. 9). The reason for this strict union is that both make up *the word of God.* "For Sacred Scripture is the word of God inasmuch as it is consigned to writing under the inspiration of the divine Spirit. To the successors of the Apostles, Sacred Tradition hands on in its full purity God's word, which was entrusted to the Apostles by Christ the Lord and the Holy Spirit. Thus, led by the light of the Spirit of truth, these successors can in their preaching preserve this word of God faithfully, explain it, and make it more widely known. Consequently, it is not from Sacred Scripture alone that the Church draws her certainty about everything which has been revealed" (*Ibid.,* No. 9). Hence Sacred Scripture and Tradition complete and illumine each other mutually.

"Sacred Tradition and Sacred Scripture form one sacred deposit of the word of God, which is committed to the Church," so that the entire holy people may draw life from this deposit. "The task of authentically interpreting the word of God, whether written or handed on, has been entrusted exclusively to the living teaching office of the Church, where authority is exercised in the name of Jesus Christ. This teaching office is not above the word of God, but serves it, teaching only what has been handed on . . ." (*Ibid.,* No. 10). The Magisterium of the Church therefore defines itself as minister of the word of God. In bearing the word of God, the Church is not mistress, but servant. This affirmation can contribute much to the ecumenical dialogue. No conciliar document before this one ever spoke in this way.

Finally, the Council describes the work of the Magisterium in detail. In truth the Magisterium of the Church teaches only what has been handed on, "listening to it devoutly, guarding it scrupulously, and explaining it faithfully by divine commission and with the help of the Holy Spirit. It draws from this one deposit of faith everything which it presents for belief as divinely revealed.

"It is clear, therefore, that Sacred Tradition, Sacred Scripture, and the teaching authority of the Church, in accord with God's most wise design, are so linked and joined together that one cannot stand without the others, and that all together and each in its own way under the action of the one Holy Spirit contribute effectively to the salvation of souls" (*Ibid.*, No. 10).[36]

c. *Conclusions.*

1. Therefore in the dogmatic Constitution *Dei Verbum* all the essential questions related to Revelation are treated: the nature, the object, the end and the economy of Revelation (Nos 1–2); the progress and the pedagogy of Revelation (No. 3); the central role of Christ as God Who reveals and God revealed (No. 4); the response to Revelation through faith (No. 5); the transmission of Revelation and the different forms of this transmission (Nos 6–8); the relations between Scripture and Tradition and of both of them with the Church and her Magisterium.

2. Revelation is a divine action, a divine intervention into history, an interpersonal communication belonging to the category of the word, encounter with the living God, Who determines the homage of the whole person and the consent of the mind to the announcement of salvation. It also exalts the divine condescension, for in order to reveal Himself, God chose the way of history and of the Incarnation.

3. The text of the Constitution *Dei Verbum* is perfect in the light of the *trinitarian perspective* and this confers on the whole document that *personalistic* aspect which the Conciliar Fathers wanted. For this reason, the terms *word, colloquy, society, communication, participation, friendship* and *love* also manifest the personalistic character. Revelation is considered as an initiative of God and a manifestation of the personal mystery of God. God Himself places Himself in a personal relationship with man and reveals to him the intimate mystery of His life. Man responds to God's request through faith.

[36] Cf. R. Latourelle, *op. cit.*, pp. 374–385.

4. Another characteristic note of the Constitution *Dei Verbum* is Christocentrism. Christ constitutes the unity of the entire economy of salvation and the object of Revelation. The object of Revelation is God Himself Who intervenes in human history and Who manifests Himself to men in Christ and through Christ. The revealed Mystery is the same Christ, author and consummator of our faith, revealer and sign of Revelation. This Christocentrism is shown in Nos 2,4,7. Christ is the author, object, center, culmination, fullness of all Revelation. The Old Testament prepares the revelation of Christ; the New Testament completes it and realizes it.

5. The importance given to the Church in the Constitution *Dei Verbum* constitutes another noted characteristic. In the Church, the Gospel is preserved live and whole (No. 7) : The Church actualizes and hands on the Revelation, received from the Apostles, through the Church, spouse of Christ, and by means of her possesses the fullness of the truth of the word of God through contemplation, study, and life (No. 8). God speaks uninterruptedly with the Church, spouse of Christ, and by means of her, the word of God re-echoes throughout the world (No. 8). By means of her own Magisterium, the Church interprets the word of God, conserves it religiously and presents it faithfully and infallibly. Christ entrusted to the Church, His spouse, the double ministry of the word and of the sacrament, for the Word of God, in Christ, has been given to us under the form of Word and of Sacrament.[37]

6. The Second Vatican Council is the only council which describes Revelation in its activity and actuality. It teaches that Revelation reached its perfection through the intimate conjunction of deeds with words. Indeed, the works manifest and confirm the doctrine and the meaning of the words, while the words proclaim and illumine the meaning of the works and deeds. This same structure is used in both the Old and the New Testaments.

[37] Cf. R. Latourelle, *op. cit,* pp. 386–389.

Index

Abel, F. M., 102
Albright, W. F., 39, 68
Alfaro, J., 149, 175–176
Alliance, 35, 46, 47, 70, 113
Allo, E. B., 137
Althaus, P., 151
Amiot, F., 136
Ammorite epoch, 34
Amon, 10
amphora, 125
anawim, 85–86, 90, 101
Ancient of Days, 106
anthropomorphisms, 100
anthropopathisms, 100
Anti-modernist Oath, 179
Antiochus Epiphanes, 102–103, 108
Apocalypse of Baruch, 114
Apostles, 120–121, 128, 134–135, 140,
    143, 152–154, 164, 178–179, 187,
    192, 194, 196
Apostolic tradition, 2, 20, 121
Ark of the Covenant, 42, 53, 56, 84
Arnaldich, L., 21
Ascension, 35, 121
Assumption of Moses, 103, 114
Assyro-Babylonians, 32
Aubert, R., 176, 181
Auzou, G., 39, 174

Babylonians, 9, 11, 72
Babylonian exile, 45–46, 66, 73–74, 76,
    79, 84, 86, 109, 114
Baptism, 46, 54, 58, 131, 135, 160,
    169
Bandas, R. G., 137

Bartina, S., 21
Baruch, 103
Bea, A., 117
Benoit, 20, 137
Bethel, 37
Blessed Virgin, 34, 97–98, 122, 126
Blessings, 50–51, 65
body of Christ, 141, 160
Boismard, M. E., 137, 144, 147
Book of Esdras (IV), 103
Book of Henoch, 103
Book of the Law, 97
Bourke, J., 87
Bover, J. M., 136
Braun, F. M., 144
Brownlee, W. H., 102
Brunet, A. M., 64, 86–87
Brunner, E., 150
Buehler, K., 173
Butler, B. C., 118
Buytendijk, F. J., 175

Cambier, J., 137
Campbell, E. F., 64
Cantinat, J., 67
Castellano, G., 92
catechesis, 119, 121
Catholic theology, 172 ff
Cazelles, H., 31, 39, 87, 93, 102
Cerfaux, 136–137
Chaine, J., 67
Chaldees, 34
Charlier, 12
charisms, 144, 171
Chary, T., 87

Chosen People, 1, 6, 13, 21–22, 40–41, 45, 57, 66, 69, 74, 81, 85, 96, 103, 107, 110–112

Christ, 1, 4–5, 15, 31, 33, 38, 45–46, 54, 57–58, 62, 67, 97, 99, 101, 113, 115–117, 120–121, 128, 130, 134–140, 143, 146, 148–150, 152, 154–166, 168–171, 175–179, 182–184, 187, 190–196

Christians, 131, 165

Christocentrism, 196

Christology, 138, 146, 166, 168

Church, 6–7, 20, 30, 42, 58, 101, 123, 126, 128, 134, 150, 152, 160–162, 169, 180, 183, 195–196

colloquy, 3–4, 173–177

Colombo, D., 102

Colunga, A., 92

Commandments, (See Decalogue)

community, 154, 156, 159, 163, 168

Congar, Y. M., 64

Conzales, A., 64

Conzelmann, H., 134, 167

Coppens, J., 76, 102

Counter-reformation, 8

covenant, 30, 32, 35, 40–41, 46, 48–52, 54, 62–63, 65–66, 73, 75, 77, 80–81, 87–88, 94, 97, 107, 112, 131, 143, 156, 191

creation, 21–23, 27–28

Creator, 38, 79–81, 97–98, 100, 107, 145

Creed, 43, 55

Croatto, J. S., 12, 64

cross, 38, 54, 138, 155–156, 168, 170, 175

Cross, F. M., 31

Cullmann, 12, 16, 144, 151–152, 166–168

curses, 50–51

dabar, 12, 75, 79, 83, 94

Danielou, J., 21

Da Castel S. Pietro, T., 143

DacLaurin, E. C. B., 39

Darlap, A., 16

Da Spinetoli, O., 118, 123, 125

Daube, D., 39

de Alfara, W., 143

debarim, 48, 75, 98

Decalogue, 40, 48–50, 53, 75, 98

Deden, D., 139

De fontibus Revelationis, 187

De Fraine, J., 21, 64

Dejaifve, J., 151

Delacroix, H., 173

De La Potterie, I., 142, 144–145

Delcor, M., 87

De Lubac, H., 150

Denis, M., 136

Dennefeld, L., 87

deposit, 20, 194

depository (of revelation), 150

Deschamps, 136

de Surgy, 12

Deuteronomic tradition (D), 27, 55, 59–60

de Vaux, R., 31, 39, 64

De Wit, C., 39

Dhanis, E., 173

dibbar, 114

didaché, 121

Diez Macho, A., 21

Dion, H. M., 137

Dogmatic Constitution on Divine Revelation (Dei Verbum), 119, 124, 187ff

Dubarle, A. M., 21, 39, 76, 102

Duesberg, H., 93

Dupont, J., 134–136, 144, 165

Durrwell, F. X., 151

Easter, 122, 153–154, 158–159, 164, 169

Ecclesiam Suam, 180 ff.

Egypt, 57–58, 95

Egyptians, 10, 40, 43, 45

Eissfeldt, O., 67

election, 34, 75, 142

El Khalil, 36

Elohistic tradition (E), 27, 37, 84

Emmanuel, 71, 174

encounter, 13–14, 140–141, 173, 175 ff., 195

etiology, 26, 28

Eucharist, 58, 122, 131

Eucharistic banquet, 125

Eucharistic sacrifice, 91

eyewitness, 152–154

Fathers of the Church, 18, 193
Fernandez, A., 87
Festorazzi, D. F., 93, 95
fidelity, 50, 155, 187,
filiation, 132, 179
Filone, 115
finger of God, 44
First Cause, 23, 24
Forman, C. C., 93
formulations, 121
Franken, H. J., 92, 144
Freedman, D. N., 64
friend of God, 36, 177
Fries, H., 25, 29, 32, 151, 156, 158, 161
Feuillet, A., 25, 31, 92–93, 102, 106, 133, 137, 144
fullness of time, 44
future life, 51, 108

Gadd, C. J., 76
Gallucci, D., 93
Garafalo, S., 67
Gaubert, H., 31
Gelin, A., 67, 76, 93, 102
Gilbert, J., 67
Ginsberg, H. L., 93
gnostic influences, 101
Gnosticism, 146
Goettmann, J., 102
Good News, 135, 145
Gonzalez, A., 31
Gonzales Nunez, A., 68, 93
Gonzales Ruiz, J. M., 21, 67, 136
Gospels, 119, 126, 129, 135, 140, 142, 144, 150, 152, 167, 169, 179, 182, 192, 196
grace, 58, 169
Granild, S., 68
Grasso, D., 151
Greeks, 172
Grelot, 12, 21, 67, 76, 102
Gusdorf, G., 173–174

Hades, 110
Haran, 34
Heidegger, M., 173
Hellenism, 146
Henning, J., 102
Hermann, I., 168

hermeneutic, 118
hesed, 99
Hexateuch, 56
High Priest, 116
Historical Jesus, 159
historification, 171
historical relativism, 171
historiographers, 118
history of revelation, 151, 168
History of Salvation, 15–17, 20–21, 32–34, 37–38, 41, 45, 49, 62–63, 65–66, 70, 80, 96, 98, 102, 109, 140, 146, 151–153, 160, 170, 183
Hittite pacts, 50
hokamin, 94
hokmah, 94
Holy Spirit, 4, 20, 46, 142, 149–150, 153, 155, 160–162, 168–169, 177–178, 183–184, 193–194
Humani generis, 30, 181–182
Hyksos, 40

idolatry, 49, 69, 72, 77, 109
Incarnation, 5, 16, 116, 160, 171, 182
individual responsibility, 78
individual retribution, 85, 19
inerrancy, 187
infidelity, 51, 54, 56–57, 63, 77–78, 100
inspiration, 187
Instruction on the Historical Truth of the Gospels (April 21, 1964), 119ff

Jacob, E., 39, 111
Javierre, A., 5
Jeremias, J., 151
Jesus, 54, 57, 67, 119, 124, 126, 128–131, 133, 136–138, 146–148, 156–168
John XXIII, 187–188
John the Baptist, 127
Judge, 103, 135, 165, 190
justification, 36

kairós, 165
kerygma, 121, 141, 151, 153–154, 159–161, 163–166, 169
kingdom of God, 120, 124, 128–129, 132–134, 145, 153, 162–163

Kolping, A., 158
Künneth, W., 158
Kuss, O., 136
Kyrios, 135, 156–157, 161, 166–167, 169

Laconi, M., 102
Lacroix, J., 173, 184
Lagrange, M. J., 118
Lamarche, P., 87
Lambert, G., 39
Lamb of God, 132
Last Judgment, 92, 132
Last Supper, 123, 156
Latourelle, R., 135, 139, 141, 148, 150, 173, 175, 177–179, 192, 195–196
Laurentin, D., 118
Lavelle, L., 173
Law, 48, 53, 88, 94, 97–98, 100, 103, 107, 110, 114, 130
Lazure, N., 144
Leal, J., 144
Le Deaut, R., 39
Lefèvre, A., 87, 102
Leon-Dufour, X., 118
liberation, 43, 55, 63
Lindblom, J., 68
literary genre, 26
liturgy, 119, 125, 156, 193
Logos, 11, 31, 95, 115–117, 145–146, 150, 167
Lohfink, A., 39
Lord of History, 74, 77
Lumen Gentium, 163, 188
Lyonnet, S., 133, 137, 144

Madonna, (See Blessed Virgin)
Magisterium, 8, 178, 182
Malevez, 12
Mansi, 180
Maranâthâ, 163
Marlé, R., 158
Marleau-Ponty, M., 173
Mary, (See Blessed Virgin)
Mass, 38, 123
Massaux, E., 67
Mediator, 53, 60, 65, 81, 84, 116, 138, 140, 143–144, 146, 152, 156, 184, 190
memrâ, 114–115

Mendenhall, G., 39
Mesopotamia, 95
message of salvation, 1, 31, 135, 176, 193
Messiah, 17, 65–67, 71, 81, 89, 92, 95, 99, 101, 103, 106, 116–117, 128–131, 146, 149, 154, 156, 160
Messianism, 66–68, 71, 74, 81–83, 89–90, 95, 100–101, 106, 130–131
metánoia, 165
midrashim, 103, 124
Milik, 104
Miller, A., 93
miracles, 120, 125, 130, 132, 170, 179
Mollat, D., 144
monogenism, 30
monotheism, 28, 49, 69, 86, 95
Mortalium animos, 182
Munoz Iglesias, S., 118
Murphy, R., 93
Mystery of Christ, 45, 117, 128–129, 138–141, 160
myths, 27

nabì, 60
name of Jesus, 155
name of Yahweh, 41–42, 91, 99
nationalist movement, 90
natural law, 23
Nédoncelle, M., 173
Neher, A., 67
New Adam, 125, 170
New Covenant, 52, 54, 78, 86, 156, 170, 181
New Israel, 125
New Law, 54
New Moses, 170
Noack, H., 173
Noah, M., 76
Noth, M., 39, 59
Nyssens, A., 151

obedience of faith, 174, 178, 191
Olavarri, E., 87
original sin, 31

Pannenberg, W., 159
Parain, G., 173
Parrot, A., 31
Pasch, 39

paschal events, 154
paschal lamb, 45–46, 57
paschal mystery, 165
Paul VI, 182
paleontology, 30
panim, 56
Parousia, 17, 35
Passion, 121, 128, 175
Passover, 44–45, 61, 125
Patriarchs, 32–33, 36–38, 41
Penna, A., 102, 165, 167–169
Pentateuch, 40, 56
Pentecost, 136, 153, 160, 169
People of God, 35, 45, 52, 54, 91, 93, 107, 134, 152, 162
Persian Empire, 87, 102
Persian period, 92, 105
Philistines, 64
Philo, 115–116
philosophy, 173
Pisanello, V., 118
Pius XI, 182
Pius XII, 182
polygenism, 30
polytheistic religion, 23
Porporato, S., 64
post-existence (of Christ), 146
Prat, F., 136–137
preaching, 142–143
Preamble, 47
pre-existence (of Christ), 146, 167
pre-Mosaic period, 41
Priesthood, 143, 156
Priestly tradition (P), 38, 42, 53, 54, 99, 107, 110, 159
Pritchard, J. B., 76
promise, 16, 34, 38, 41, 48, 59, 64, 100, 107, 156, 162, 169
prophetism, 67
Prophets, 46, 53, 55–56, 66, 75, 82, 110–114, 128–129, 143, 160, 178–179
Protestants, 3
Protestant theology, 172
Proto-evangelium, 30
Providence, 77, 96, 100, 104

Qumran, 83, 103

Rabbi, 128, 130

Ramses II, 40
Rasco, E., 118
redemption, 44, 57, 138, 142, 153–154
remission of sin, 129, 135
remnant, 67, 69, 70–72, 78, 81–82, 90, 152
Renckens, H., 21
repentance, 62–63
Resurrection, 38–39, 92, 108–109 119–122, 128–129, 131, 134, 136, 139–140, 153–155, 157–159, 162–166, 168–169, 172, 178
retribution, 51, 96, 99, 100, 108–110
Revealor, 145, 149, 171
Revelation, 2–5, 13–18, 20, 25, 30–33, 35, 37, 39, 41, 46, 48, 64, 68, 73, 82, 92, 98, 105, 110 ff, 128–130, 132–134, 137, 139, 141–143, 145–147, 149–150, 152–154, 156–163, 169–193, 195–196
Ricciotti, G., 64, 67, 93
Rinaldi, G., 67, 102
Robert, A., 31, 93, 98
Robledo, A. G., 173
Rolla, A., 31, 39, 73, 93
Rowley, H. H., 39, 67, 76, 93
ruah, 63
Rubio Moran, L., 31, 67, 131, 132, 151

sacraments, 58, 196
sacrifice, 38, 131, 156, 166
St. Thomas, 38, 176, 182
Salguero, J., 21, 30, 50, 59, 76, 86, 116
salvation history (See History of Salvation)
Sanhedrin, 131
Savior, 47, 65, 81, 103, 105, 107, 113, 148
Schlier, H., 151
Schmid, J., 118
Schmitt, J., 150
Schnackenburg, R., 136
Schoekel, L. Alonso, 92
Seleucids, 9, 104
Servant of Yahweh, 81 ff., 92, 122, 131–132
Seti I, 40

201

Sheol, 108
Siebeneck, R. T., 87
Simon, M., 64
Sinaitic Covenant, 46–48, 50–54, 74, 78, 84, 97
Sitz im Leben, 118
Son of God, 57, 121, 128, 133, 138, 143, 145–146, 156, 167, 175
Son of man, 131–132
Sons of the prophets, 68
Spadafora, F., 76, 136
Spicq, C., 137, 143
Stamm, J. J., 39
Stanley, D. M., 137
Steinmann, J., 76
Stuhlmueller, C., 76
Sumerians, 32
Sumeric Age, 9
Synoptic Gospels, 117, 119, 128, 133, 170

Talmon, S., 102
Targum Onkelos, 114
Temple, 42, 76–77, 88 ff., 100, 107, 110, 126, 115, 132
Testa, P. E., 102
testimony, 148, 178 ff.
thaumaturge, 59, 61
theocracy, 89
theophany, 37, 41
Torah, 12, 75, 94, 98, 114
Tournay, R., 92
tradition (also, Tradition), 6–8, 19–21, 119–121, 153, 161, 186, 193 ff.
transcendence, 89, 95, 111, 114–115
Tresmontant, C., 67
Trinity, 149, 175 ff.
Tsevat, M., 64

Ugaritic, 32
universalism, 91, 146

universalist movement, 90
Ur, 34

Vaccari, A., 102
Vaganay, L., 118
Van der Bussche, H., 64, 144
Van Imschoot, P., 102
Vatican Council I (First Vatican Council), 24, 180, 187 ff.
Vatican Council II (Second Vatican Council), 3, 5, 8, 18–20, 119, 126, 163, 172, 180
Vattioni, F., 64, 76, 93
Vawter, B., 67
Verbum, 97, 145
Verbo, 144, 155, 176
vocation, 34, 40, 41, 59, 81, 174
Von Rad, G., 61, 64, 68

Wikenhauser, A., 137
Will of God, 14, 22–24, 52, 56, 68–69, 75, 80, 83, 98, 100, 110, 112, 162, 164, 170
wisdom, 19, 23, 92–94, 97, 114, 116, 141, 145
Wiseman, D. J., 76
witness, 134, 148, 153–154, 164, 178–179
Word Incarnate, 54, 97, 116, 125, 150, 168
Word of God, 2, 7, 8, 37, 48, 51, 69, 70, 75, 94, 98, 100, 112, 115, 128–129, 144–145, 148–149, 155, 174, 176, 182, 187 ff.

Yahwism, 88
Yahwistic tradition (J), 27, 37, 40, 41, 59, 84
Yerushalmi I, 115

Zachary, 122

3, 5-8 ✓

118-119
123
170-171, 174
181

195-196